DRESSING THE QUEEN

BY THE SAME AUTHOR

Inside the Royal Wardrobe:
A Dress History of Queen Alexandra

The Dress Diary of Mrs Anne Sykes:
Secrets from a Victorian Woman's Wardrobe

Dressing the Queen

Two Hundred Years of Makers and Monarchy

KATE STRASDIN

Chatto & Windus

LONDON

1 3 5 7 9 10 8 6 4 2

Chatto & Windus, an imprint of Vintage, is part of the Penguin Random House group of companies

Vintage, Penguin Random House UK, One Embassy Gardens,
8 Viaduct Gardens, London SW11 7BW

penguin.co.uk/vintage
global.penguinrandomhouse.com

First published by Chatto & Windus in 2026

Copyright © Kate Strasdin 2026

The moral right of the author has been asserted

Penguin Random House values and supports copyright. Copyright fuels creativity, encourages diverse voices, promotes freedom of expression and supports a vibrant culture. Thank you for purchasing an authorised edition of this book and for respecting intellectual property laws by not reproducing, scanning or distributing any part of it by any means without permission. You are supporting authors and enabling Penguin Random House to continue to publish books for everyone. No part of this book may be used or reproduced in any manner for the purpose of training artificial intelligence technologies or systems. In accordance with Article 4(3) of the DSM Directive 2019/790, Penguin Random House expressly reserves this work from the text and data mining exception.

Set in 11.8/14.75 pt Dante MT Pro
Typeset by Six Red Marbles UK, Thetford, Norfolk
Printed and bound in Great Britain by Clays Ltd, Elcograf S.p.A.

The authorised representative in the EEA is Penguin Random House Ireland,
Morrison Chambers, 32 Nassau Street, Dublin D02 YH68

A CIP catalogue record for this book is available from the British Library

ISBN 9781784745332

Penguin Random House is committed to a sustainable future
for our business, our readers and our planet. This book is made
from Forest Stewardship Council® certified paper.

For Sarah Hosking at the Hosking Houses Trust,
and for the makers, known and unknown

Contents

	Introduction: Many Hands . . .	1
	The Makers	
1	Ceremonial Splendour	13
	The Velvet Robe and the Silk Weavers of Braintree	
2	Little Hands	29
	Ruby Essam and the Embroiderers	
3	Presented at Court	45
	Clara Mobbs and Her White Feathers	
4	All That Glisters . . .	59
	Harold Goodship and the Diamonds	
5	Coats of Many Colours	73
	Of Norwich Shawls and Hardy Amies's Tailor-mades	
6	If You Want to Get Ahead . . .	89
	From Straw Plaiters to Palace Milliners	
7	Best Foot Forward	105
	The Shoes of Gundry and of Rayne	
8	Fashioning a Silhouette	121
	The Art of the Dressmaker	
9	Fits Like a Glove	137
	Dents of Worcester and Cornelia James	

Contents

10 **Queens of Couture** — 149
    The Modern Designer from Hartnell to Parvin

11 **A Travelling Wardrobe** — 165
    The Trunks of Harriet Cave and the Cases of Pendragon

12 **Sharp Suits** — 179
    Tailor-mades by Redfern and the Elusive Madame Vernon

13 **Off-duty Tweed** — 195
    The Scottish Kilts and Pringle Knits

14 **The Secrets of Stockings** — 211
    The Lost Arts of Ann Birkin and John Meakin

15 **Silk and Structure** — 225
    Corset Making from Madame Roxey Caplin to Rigby & Peller

16 **What Lies Beneath** — 237
    Of Linen Maids and Laundrywomen

17 **Hidden Women** — 251
    The Dressers and Their Domain

18 **Public Grief** — 267
    Whitby Jet and Courtaulds Crape

Epilogue: New Beginnings — 283

Acknowledgements — 289
List of Illustrations — 291
Notes on Sources — 297
Select Bibliography — 311
Index — 313

INTRODUCTION

Many Hands . . .
The Makers

In July 2017 I was halfway through a month-long lecture circuit of the east coast of Australia, a tour that took me from Sydney to Cairns. I spoke in large libraries and small town halls; school assembly rooms and local cinemas. I had reached the small town of Tewantin, which sits on the Noosa river, a broad inlet of water running westwards on the coast of Queensland. It is a leafy coastline 135 kilometres north of Brisbane where young families holiday and kids learn to surf. It is about as far away from the trappings of British monarchy as you can imagine. There I found myself in the Anglican church of St Mary's delivering my lecture on the history of underwear from the lectern.

Among the joys of the job as a dress historian are the conversations that take place afterwards: fleeting encounters with members of the audience, none of whom I will ever meet again but who leave small mementos of their lives with me as I pass through. On this occasion a slim elderly woman flanked by her two daughters had waited to speak to me of her travels across Europe in the early 1950s. Many Australian teenagers took advantage of relatively cheap air tickets in a post-war migration to see the world. The woman told a remarkable story. In 1952 she found herself in London and somehow came to the attention of Norman Hartnell, the British fashion designer favoured by the royal family. Her proportions matched those of the new young Queen Elizabeth II and she was hired as a fit model. Standing in for the royal body when Hartnell needed to cut and drape new designs, she recalled standing in her knickers whilst he judged the gowns that would later clothe the Queen. She described in great detail the long tables in the embroidery room upon which were draped the various pieces of the coronation gown. Each embroiderer, dressed in a grey uniform with a white coverall, worked the beads, sequins and metallic threads into the symbols of commonwealth that encrusted the gown. As the old lady recounted her story, both of her daughters stood, mouths open, looking at their mother. It was clearly the first time they had ever heard of this chapter in her life. She had never thought it interesting enough to tell and so it might have remained untold.

On the morning of 2 June 1953, all of those detailed preparations would come together in the ceremony of a lifetime when the young Queen Elizabeth II left Buckingham Palace in the Gold State Coach on her way to Westminster Abbey. It had been nine months since she had first approached designer Norman Hartnell to ask him to make the coronation dress. On that October afternoon, five years after Elizabeth had worn the wedding dress he had designed, he was handed the commission of his career. He recalled: 'I can scarcely remember what I murmured in reply. In simple conversational tones the Queen went on to express her wishes.' She desired that the gown be of white satin and similar in form to her wedding dress. Following their meeting, Hartnell went away to study the complex histories of coronation protocols, spending his days in the London Museum and the London Library. He read about the drama of Queen Elizabeth I's coronation and her love of splendour but ultimately decided this was 'too gaudy'. He read about Queen Anne's bejewelled gold tissue dress and the more restrained version chosen by Queen Victoria. He wrote in his memoir: 'After gathering all the factual material I could, I then retired to the seclusion of Windsor Forest and

Many Hands . . .

there spent many days making trial sketches.' The weight of tradition sat with him during these days as he developed his ideas. 'I thought of lilies, roses, marguerites and golden corn; I thought of altar cloths and sacred vestments; I thought of the sky, the earth, the sun, the moon, the stars and everything heavenly that might be embroidered upon a dress destined to be historic.' The result was eight drawings which he took to the Queen. They ranged from the simplest of white gowns edged with a frost of embellishment to a gown laden in symbolic motifs. He recalled: 'I liked the last one best but naturally did not express my opinion when I submitted these paintings to Her Majesty.'

The Queen's active participation in the design was to be a feature of their working relationship. Having studied the eight sketches, she informed Hartnell that she liked the final design the most for its lavish embellishment but preferred that the emblems should be stitched in colour rather than the silver that the designer had drawn – too like her wedding dress, she decided. She was also keen that the design should reflect not only the nations of Great Britain but the various dominions of which she would now be Queen. And so Norman Hartnell set to creating his ninth and final sketch, an undertaking he described as 'more complicated than I had expected' as he repositioned the various floral symbols in order to accommodate more. He was almost thwarted by the news that rather than the aesthetically pleasing daffodil as representative of the Welsh nation, he had instead to include a leek. It was this design, gracing the embroiderers' tables at his Bruton Street premises in the months leading up to the coronation, which the young Australian model had watched take shape as she stood in the studio to be fitted for a Queen.

Norman Hartnell was not the only maker charged with outfitting the Queen for this worldwide spectacle. Tucked beneath the hem of the white satin gown were the shoes made by French designer Roger Vivier, known as the Fabergé of footwear, in collaboration with British brand Delman Ltd. Having made the shoes worn by the Queen Mother to the coronation of her husband in 1937, he brought all of his experience to bear on the pair he created for her daughter, Queen Elizabeth II. The coronation service was to last three hours and so, sparkle aside, they had to be comfortable. The Queen asked for an invisible internal platform to be incorporated into the design to ensure ease of wear. The result was an ornate, soft gold leather sandal, whose heel was studded with real rubies. Inspired by the rose windows of Chartres Cathedral, Vivier included the fleur-de-lis motif, echoing the Imperial State Crown.

Suspended over the shoulders of Norman Hartnell's white satin by thick golden cords was the purple velvet Robe of Estate. Extending over twenty feet in length, the coronation robes represented a tradition stretching back centuries. Royal portraiture captures many a monarch on canvas, surrounded by the plush flow of velvet pooling around the royal foot, garments that harked back to a period where to be monarch was to rule, and sartorial symbolism meant power. Queen Elizabeth's robe was made by the famous royal robe maker Ede & Ravenscroft, an object of eye-watering labour intensity. A new robe such as this was traditionally made for the new monarch for part of the ceremony, whilst existing robes might be reused at other points in the coronation. To embellish the velvet took a team of twelve embroiderers, working by hand the motifs of wheat ears and olive branches to represent prosperity and peace. Eighteen types of gold thread were used with names that form a gilded poetry: smooth purl; rough purl; large gold bullion; gold passing; spangles; crinkled plate; gold twist. Each filament contributed to the complexity of the robe and the motifs that took 3,500 hours to stitch.

It is the ceremonial robes that are the least familiar to contemporary audiences. The semi-ecclesiastical garments that form a central part of the service date back to the days when to be crowned by the Archbishop of Canterbury amounted to being literally anointed by God. These vestments – the Dalmatica, a long loose robe with wide sleeves, and the Supertunica, a sleeved coat of gold silk – were imbued with this spiritual significance and as such were objects not governed by the styles of the day but which rather reverted to long-held, centuries-old traditions. As was the cloth of gold Robe Royal that the Queen wore on that June day in 1953 as she was invested with the regalia of state, handed each piece in careful order before the three-hundred-year-old St Edward's Crown, weighing over four pounds, was placed on her head.

Eight grey geldings drew the Gold State Coach that day. The sovereign's procession consisted of 250 church leaders, prime ministers, military officers, civic leaders and Yeomen of the Guard. There were over 8,000 guests, and 129 nations were represented. The Queen wore three crowns and changed her clothes twice, the anointing taking place in the simple white cotton gown known as the Colobium Sindonis, which had also been designed by Norman Hartnell. There were 2,000 journalists and 500 photographers with a television audience in the UK alone of 27 million. The planning was overseen by the Earl Marshal, the 16th Duke of Norfolk, who had scheduled that the Queen and Duke of Edinburgh would arrive at Westminster Abbey at 11.15 with the crowning of the new monarch taking place at precisely 12.34. Queen Elizabeth II was crowned at 12.33 and 30 seconds. It was a spectacle that had been months in the planning and rehearsing, and that followed generations of tradition, so much of which relied upon dress. The Queen's clothes were constructed around her, each garment a symbol of her new status and each conveying an aspect of ceremony, communicating not only the institution of monarchy but this young woman's own intentions as a modern monarch.

I wonder if the young woman on her travels from Australia found somewhere to watch the coronation ceremony, perhaps as one of a group crowding around a newly purchased television set? Maybe she was amongst the crowds that thronged the streets on the day of the coronation, waving as the gold fairy-tale coach rolled past, its grey horses nodding ahead. I don't know if she was even in the UK when the young

Queen was crowned. I wish I had asked her. I wish I knew her name and regret now that I was not able to spend longer with her, to learn more of her unique time in Hartnell's employ. Countless hands contributed to the dressing of the regal body that day: goldwork embroiderers and Hartnell's own in-house stitchers, weavers and leather workers. At the palace, the Queen's dressers would have carefully helped her into her white satin gown, buckled her ruby-encrusted sandals and fastened the cord of her robe. Faceless, nameless to most, but absolutely indispensable.

∼

There is one element that unites all of the makers and workers here: the Office of Robes. Prior to the nineteenth century, meeting the cost of personal adornment was something that the monarch and their family were responsible for out of their own private funds. By the later years of the eighteenth century, however, the structure of financing the monarchy was beginning to shift and the creation and contents of the monarch's wardrobe came under the jurisdiction of the Treasury. The royal household had become an unwieldy beast by then; a plethora of different departments all working to different agendas meant that conflicts and miscommunications frequently arose. Almost 1,000 royal servants worked under the jurisdiction of different branches of the royal household but within the walls of the royal residence they were divided broadly into two. The Lord Steward's Department was tasked with the provisioning of the palace, responsible for the payment of suppliers and all of the myriad requirements 'below stairs'. Meanwhile, the Lord Chamberlain's Department controlled the 'above stairs' appointments and the ceremonial world of the monarchy. Tensions arose when boundaries became blurred and the two worlds collided.

Baron Stockmar, friend and adviser to Prince Albert from 1837 to

Many Hands . . .

1847, wrote incredulously of the state of affairs when Victoria came to the throne: 'The Lord Steward finds the fuel and lays the fire: the Lord Chamberlain lights it. The Lord Chamberlain provides the lamps; the Lord Steward must clean, trim and light them. The inside cleaning of windows belongs to the Lord Chamberlain's department but the outer parts must be attended to by the Office of Woods and Forests so that windows remain dirty unless the two departments can come to an understanding.' It was within this tumultuous state of affairs that the Office of Robes had to operate, straddling the two departments with its links to suppliers and cleaners on the one side and its close connection with the royal body on the other. Determined to streamline the practices, Prince Albert set about a radical overhaul of the household, eradicating outdated extravagances and bringing order to the running of the departments. The Master of the Household was made responsible for coordinating the daily duties of each area, ensuring that for the first time communication might actually result in efficiency.

The Great Wardrobe of the monarch was of ancient origin, rooted in centuries of tradition. Emerging from the administrative complexities of medieval kingship, the term originally described the physical space where the monarch's clothing, armour and valuables were stored, but grew to encompass the various roles and mechanisms required of it, distinct from other factions within the household. For a time it did relate to a specific building in the City of London, a house in Blackfriars acquired by King Edward III and used as a storage facility to house the trappings of royalty. As an administrative structure it was vast, overseeing not only the monarch's clothing, furs and jewels but also tapestries, furniture, saddlery and valuable commodities such as spices brought from overseas. Officials employed within the wardrobe ranged from the Embroiderer and the Armourer to the Confectioner, skilled artisans whose work revolved around the comfort and daily whims of God's anointed King. The meticulous accounting required for this flow of goods all took place within the Blackfriars building, a steady stream of clerks keeping the books that would record the names of those men and women who supplied the household.

Over centuries of royal record keeping, these volumes have retained a constancy alongside the drama of monarchy. Through family conflict, overseas campaigns, civil war and public unrest, the clerks continued to keep their meticulous notes in the large leather-bound tomes, linking the privilege of royalty to businesses tasked with the appearance of the institution. The Blackfriars building was destroyed in the Great Fire of London in 1666 and later relocated to Buckingham Street before it was eventually subsumed into the operations of royal residences and was no longer to be a separate entity. But thanks to the early establishment of accounting rigour, the archives are full of tantalising glimpses into the workings of that world. Almost all histories of royal dress have focused their attention on the gilded royal swan gliding across the waters of society with very little written about the furious activity taking place beneath the surface. Yet whenever I visit the Royal Archive in Windsor or the National Archives in Kew, it is the notes written by the dressers, the payments received by wardrobe maids and the invoices of tailors that I find most interesting.

Competition to clothe the monarch has always been fierce and by the fifteenth century a formal solution was found to reward those tradespeople whose goods were deemed to be of the best quality. As head of the royal household, the Lord Chamberlain conferred a Royal Warrant of Appointment on those suppliers who contributed regularly to the daily life of the monarch, a practice that has survived into the twenty-first century. It was often of significant benefit to the businesses themselves. From the 1700s, these tradespeople would frequently capitalise on their Royal Warrant through the display of the royal arms above their premises or placed prominently at the top of their letterheads. In 1840, the Warrant Holders Association was formed as an administrative body to support the warrant holders, a function it continues to serve to this day.

Royal patronage was keenly sought by makers, being beneficial to both reputation and income. In 1888, the Somerset firm Egerton Burnett made an application to Queen Victoria's Office of the Robes for a warrant in recognition of fabric the company had supplied to the royal household. They received a terse reply: 'Occasional purchase of goods from a tradesman does not entitle him to a Royal Warrant, which distinction is reserved for those only who habitually and continually service Her Majesty with goods.' Undeterred, Egerton Burnett advertised instead their 'Royal Serge' along with a large coat of arms of indeterminate origin and the words 'Under the Direct Patronage of the Royal Families of Europe'. If they couldn't obtain the actual Royal Warrant, they could at least create the illusion of one in a bid to boost sales.

Behind the single name attached to the Royal Warrant of Appointment are countless others, those who filled workshops and factories or undertook work in their own homes. Many thousands of them were women, juggling the demands of running a household with a job in the needle trades which was often poorly remunerated. It is these women in particular, neglected by more traditional histories, who fascinate me the most. An old English rhyming couplet, part of which has entered the popular vernacular, runs thus: 'A man may work till set of sun. A woman's work is never done.' How many of these women felt that their work was never done? As their fingers darted over buttonholes or plaited straw destined for fine bonnets, did they think too of the laundering yet to be done at home or the meal to be cooked?

For centuries, royal women have sallied forth from their royal residences, splendidly attired, to meet the demands of any given event. Be it the opening of a hospital, the planting of a tree or a night at the opera, their appearances have been made under the watchful eye of an eager public and an often critical press. Scrutiny has been their constant companion and their clothing, at once both familiar and unattainable, has offered a focus for collective debate. But once the palace door closed and the carriages departed, who was left behind? There is a great machine that underpins the appropriate appearance of these public women, one whose many cogs turn in different places, at different speeds and different times in order to smooth the path of royal dress.

To be considered a success, the men and women working in and for the great Office of Robes must remain invisible. Take, for example, a young German woman named Frieda Arnold. In the 1850s, Frieda was employed in the royal household as a dresser to Queen Victoria, recording her experiences in letters to her family. In 1856 she wrote a description of her life in London. It was a round of balls and gowns and music; of silk slippers and lace-trimmed bonnets. She travelled on yachts and in cushioned carriages. She lived at the centre of one of the most glittering social circles at that time and yet who amongst us has ever heard her name? Frieda Arnold's life was lived in the shadow of the most famous woman in the world; as Queen Victoria's dresser she was always present but never seen. She wrote home: 'From early in the morning until late at night there are endless preparations to make and adornments for parties to help with, and my poor brain has to know weeks ahead on which day this or that ball, or this or that concert takes place, without my own feet ever dancing a step, or my own ears ever discerning a note of the beautiful music they play!'

Those persons whose responsibility it has been to make, maintain, clean, pack, transport and fit the garments and accessories that adorn a royal body have traditionally worked in the shadows. Their roles are many and varied. Hatters, tailors, shoemakers, corset makers, dressmakers, furriers, fan makers, lacemakers and embroiderers appear in the records. There are dressers, wardrobe maids, launderers, messengers, clerks and transporters. These were all people whose labour went largely unnoticed but the fruits of whose efforts were appreciated by millions. Their stories

Many Hands . . .

have remained untold. They exist still in the meticulous records of the royal household, in countless memos, accounting ledgers, invoices and pensions documents. They appear in letters or advertisements but there is little substance to these often fleeting references. Names and dates do not reveal much about the lives they are accounting for. So who were they? What did life look like for those people working in or supplying to the royal wardrobe? Chapter by chapter, this book metaphorically dresses a number of queens and queen consorts – Queens Victoria, Alexandra, Mary, Elizabeth the Queen Mother and Queen Elizabeth II. From the most regal of royal appearances cloaked in history and the robes of state to the linen next to their skin, this is a book not about royal dress as experienced by royal women – there are plenty of those – but instead it is the story of Frieda Arnold the dresser; of Amelia Blazeby, court dressmaker; of Clara Mobbs, feather curler. It seeks out shoemakers and milliners; tailors and embroiderers. It turns the spotlight away from the wearers and on to the artisans who, garment by garment, brought all of their skills to the creation of objects that would become a part of the iconography of royalty, whilst themselves remaining almost entirely hidden. This is for them. These are their stories.

CHAPTER I

Ceremonial Splendour
The Velvet Robe and the Silk Weavers of Braintree

Number 29 Woodfield Road in Braintree, Essex, is a red-brick terraced house like millions of other red-brick terraced houses. It has bow-fronted windows, sash frames painted white, and a shallow-pitched, grey slate roof. It is unremarkable. In 1939 it was the home of one John Beard, then in his middle fifties. Every day John would perhaps take breakfast with his wife Gertrude; his son, another John, might already have left for his job as a young grocery assistant. His daughter, Jean, would be readying herself for school as John shouldered his bag and bid his family farewell. Each morning he would walk half a mile through the streets of Braintree, maybe with a friend, maybe alone, until he reached the white-painted wooden weaving sheds of the New Mills factory, the same walk he had taken every day of his working life for forty years. The mill belonged to Warner & Sons. Like his grandfather and father before him, John was a silk weaver.

The vision of a king or queen in their ceremonial robes is like a fantasy. These are garments that bear no relation to ordinary life, to the everyday. The robes, tunics and surcoats of state seem almost mythical, versions of them dating back centuries and featuring in countless portraits. Long, extravagant robes swoop around the royal subjects on canvases depicting the sheen of fur and silk velvet, but these paintings reveal nothing about the skilled labour required to create them. In keeping with the long-held traditions bound up within these robes, some of those businesses whose job it was to produce them are amongst the oldest manufacturers in the UK, if not the world. Warner & Sons and Ede & Ravenscroft between them were responsible for the weaving and stitching of the ceremonial garb that is so central to these glittering occasions of state. But whilst the objects themselves have featured prominently as part of public spectacles, those makers of robes, those weavers and stitchers, have received scant attention. Seeking them out in the mills of Braintree and the workshops of London became one of my first goals.

And so I find that John Beard, from the age of seventeen, had taken his place at his wooden treadle loom each day. Unlike the huge mills that housed the power looms of the cotton industry in the North of England, this was a much smaller affair, the window-lined wooden sheds allowing in as much daylight as possible for the silk workers to weave their magic, each hand loom operated by a single person. Every weaver had served their time and learned their trade, often from their fathers. They acquired the mystical-sounding skills of warping, quill winding and twisting in order to reach the rank of master weaver, an apprenticeship that started in childhood. When, in 1949, Queen Elizabeth the Queen Consort requested a tour of the Warner's factory, it was John Beard who was tasked with a demonstration of his craft: 'Mr Beard . . . who had been 53 years with the firm, showed the Queen how he twisted a new warp to one just finished – sometimes as many as 20,000 threads having to be joined.' The twisting by hand of 20,000 silken threads is an almost unimaginable undertaking from a twenty-first-century viewpoint, but for more than half a century this was exactly the skill that John Beard and many of his peers had honed.

The Warner family were descended from a long line of textile workers. At the beginning of the eighteenth century, William Warner specialised as a scarlet dyer, the first of five generations in his family to follow the trade that was so central to the British economy. In 1870 Benjamin Warner established a small silk-weaving factory, bringing all of the inherited knowledge of his forebears with him into this new venture which, by 1887, had won him royal commissions. By 1894 the business had expanded, its reputation and royal patronage serving to boost orders, and so the company moved to the New Mills factory in Braintree, most of the weavers following their looms to this unfamiliar town fifty miles north-east of London. When John Beard started working for Warner & Sons in 1896, he would have been acquainted with older weavers, men such as Sam Watson who would go on to be responsible for weaving the purple velvet used to make the Robe of Estate worn in 1911 by King George V. The mill dominated the life of the Watson family, as it did for so many others. Of Sam and Catherine Watson's nine children, five worked with silk, following in their father's footsteps to the sheds. Each day they would enter to the clatter and rattle of the old looms, knowing that their father was working on one of the most important pieces of cloth the factory would produce.

Not all of their prized fabrics were made in the modern factory setting, however. Some of the older weavers chose to continue working from their homes in the East End of London, their looms a part of the furniture alongside chairs and tables and beds. George Doré was one such weaver who preferred to remain in the city of his birth, still weaving from his house in Bethnal Green. It was here that he would work on the specially chosen petunia-coloured velvet that would become the coronation robe in 1902 of the Queen Consort Alexandra. When George was only six years old the 1851 census included him in the household of his father, Isaac, and his mother, Ann, on Park Street, a road on which every occupant including Isaac was listed as a hand-loom weaver. George's family were one of many to have originated from Spitalfields and the Huguenot refugees. The migrant population of Huguenots were welcomed to Britain in the years after 1685, the then government voting to contribute £200,000 to their aid. One year alone saw fifteen thousand refugees settle in London and, of these, many were artisans in the silk industries. So here they remained, men like George carrying the inherited knowledge of their ancestors from their small homes in London's East End into some of the grandest spaces in the land.

The same year that the census had recorded George and his family and countless others at their looms in Bethnal Green, Charles Dickens wound his way up a narrow wooden staircase and into the workshop of a Spitalfields silk weaver, a space that would have been familiar to the Dorés. Interviewing workers for his journal *Household Words* he spoke to a thin, hollow-cheeked man working on a length of black velvet. Dickens complimented the man on the quality of the velvet that was visible on the loom and asked how it was produced:

> 'Every time I throw the shuttle, I cut this wire, as you see, and put it in again – so!' Jarring and clashing at the loom, and glancing at us with his eager eyes.
> 'Is it slow work?'
> 'Very slow.' With a hard dry cough, and the glance.
> 'And hard work?'
> 'Very hard.' With the cough again.
> After a while he stops, perceiving that we really are interested, and says, laying his hand upon his hollow breast and speaking in an unusually loud voice, being used to speaking through the clash of the loom:
> 'It tries the chest, you see, leaning for'ard like this for fifteen or sixteen hours at a stretch.'

The weaver could earn three shillings a day for those fifteen or sixteen hours, but only if he had enough work to occupy them which, he explained, was not necessarily a given. There were four looms in the room, one operated by his wife and another that he let to a young weaver for a shilling a week, contributing to their rent of the space which was both home and workshop. The children slept beneath the quiet looms at night and ran and played amongst their crash and clatter during the day until they were old enough themselves to start learning. At the age of only six, George Doré was still described as a 'scholar' in 1851, but it would not have been long before his schooling was over and he would be drawn to the relentless back and forth of the loom.

Dickens remarked on the beauty of the fabric in the Spitalfields home, so at odds with the room in which it was made. The weaver briefly described the complexity of producing silk velvet: 'Every time I throw the shuttle I cut out this wire, as you see, and put it in again – so!' Such a sparse description, offered between the rattle of his loom and the background crash of the two others, could barely convey the skill required for producing velvet. Whether in houses or factories like Warner's, it was the very process that both Sam Watson and George Doré had perfected when they were charged with the creation of coronation velvet. On their creaking wooden treadle looms, they had to handle six times as many threads as a plain silk, the extra required to create the fine loops that would be cut to produce the soft pile of the cloth. In a plain weave, the warp is lifted to create the 'shed' through which the shuttle with the warp passes back and forth. For velvet, narrow metal rods (the equivalent of 2 millimetres wide) are inserted periodically – the wires which the weaver described to Dickens – creating the loops which would then have to be so carefully cut by hand. This is how the unique surface of velvet is created and why it was so desirable as a luxury fabric beloved of kings and queens.

Age and experience were much sought after when it came to the royal commissions. George was approaching his sixties when he undertook the coronation robe and Sam Watson was fifty-one. In 1953, Lily Lee was sixty-six and already retired when she was asked to contribute to the velvet robe of Queen Elizabeth II. Lily was the sixth of seven children born to Walter, a bricklayer, and Hannah, described as a 'crape weaver'. Here then were the textiles that were spun into the fabric of family life so that by the age of fourteen Lily was already a factory hand, living at home, a large family housed in a small brick house on Mount Pleasant Road near Braintree. Her brothers all worked in a local iron foundry and so Lily was the only one of her siblings to work for Warner & Sons, influenced perhaps by her mother's former occupation. By 1911 at the age of twenty-four she had progressed to become a silk weaver, a position she was to hold for more than three decades. When she and fellow veteran weaver Hilda Carver were tempted out of retirement for this commission of a lifetime, they found themselves at the heart of a public storm of speculation around the coronation garments. This was not unexpected for Warner's. When they were weaving the mantles for the coronation of King George VI in 1937, they decided to arrange open days for local people. The response was overwhelming: 'Visitors arrived not only from the town of Braintree, but by car from all over East Anglia and the Automobile Association had to be called in to help with car-parking.' In 1953 they opened their doors once again, photographs capturing the queues of visitors snaking along the factory pavement, waiting for a glimpse of the silks within. There are photographs, too, of Lily Lee. In one black-and-white portrait, she is shown at her loom, the elderly wooden contraption arcing away from her as she makes some adjustment, a width of shining velvet visible at her fingertips. Hilda and Lily were each required to make eighteen yards of the twenty-one-inch-wide silk velvet. They were able to complete between six and nine inches a day, slowly working the thousands of fine purple threads into the soft knapped cloth destined to sweep across the historic flagged floor of Westminster Abbey. There is a second photograph of Lily and Hilda holding up a length of their royal velvet. Even without colour, the sleek sheen of the cloth is discernible. Lily wears a button-down overall, the collar

Ceremonial Splendour

Lily Lee, silk velvet weaver, 1952.

of her floral frock just visible beneath. Round spectacles attest to the decades of close work and her once keen eyes scanning for imperfections as the shuttle passed back and forth.

Once the velvet was carefully removed from the loom by Lily Lee or Sam Watson or George Doré, it was carefully parcelled up and sent on to the next group of remarkable makers. To Ede & Ravenscroft, robe makers par excellence who have been supplying the British monarchy with ceremonial robes for centuries. It was their job to take the specially woven velvet and add the component parts that would turn fabric into robe. Glimpses of the robe makers themselves are few and far between, however. The gorgeous fruits of their labour have become iconic, viewed by millions in paintings, in photographs, on television screens and in exhibitions but the makers themselves remain elusive. They were tailors by trade, part of a workforce that numbered in the thousands in London alone until well into the twentieth century when more and more suits were acquired off the peg. There was a sharp division in the quality of life and work for a tailor, depending on location. The East End of London with its growing rag trade and ready-to-wear market saw journeymen tailors experience far lower pay and poorer working conditions. In the 1880s over a quarter of a million Jewish immigrants settled in London, many of whom sought work in the sweated industries and lower-end tailoring workshops. A report commissioned by the House of Lords in 1888 stated that 'the average number of hours of labour was 14 per diem, but that 16 and even 18 hours were by no means uncommon'. Conditions were considerably better in the West End amongst the establishments catering to the more affluent. In 1892 the *London Art Fashion Journal* described the workrooms of Savile Row tailor Henry Poole: 'The King Street workrooms were spread over three floors of which the topmost was considered the healthiest . . . it had no coke burning stove and there were ventilators in the roof.'

One of the other innovations at Poole's was introduced at their Clifford Street workshop. Here, a series of mirrors were installed in the workrooms to allow customers to view the tailors at work. What they would have witnessed had changed little since the eighteenth century and were these customers to describe what they saw, it would bear comparison with countless tailoring workrooms across the capital, including the more unusual output of Ede & Ravenscroft. Those fourteen hours of labour described in the House of Lords report would have seen the tailors undertaking a variety of different tasks required for the creation of their garments. The cutting would take place on large tables strewn with measuring tapes and chalk slivers whose abstract marks made at speed on the cloth acted as a kind of second language to the tailor. Once cut, the pieces would be stitched, the tailors sitting on the broad tables in a pose familiar to practitioners of yoga: one knee crossed over the other, the raised knee acting as a steadying support for the cloth as the tailor's needle flew back and forth. The *Harmsworth Encyclopaedia of Retail Trading* described the interior requirements of a tailor's shop, equipment that would have been universal: 'There should be a broad bench provided . . .

for the men to sit on, a sewing machine with wide table, a stove for heating the irons . . . a selection of irons from 10 to 20 lb, sleeve boards, duplex press boards, iron stands, bowl and other sundries.' The workshops at Ede had to contend with the scale of garment that far exceeded that of a normal suit. Yards of precious velvet, lengths of snowy ermine and rolls of plain-weave silk must be carefully handled at the same time as being evenly worked. Before the middle of the nineteenth century all of the making was undertaken by hand but whilst the invention of the sewing machine, which was widely available by the 1850s, certainly eased some of the processes, much of the more intricate work would still have been stitched by hand.

A 1952 British Pathé newsreel offers the merest peek into the workrooms of Ede & Ravenscroft when it recorded preparations of robes for the impending coronation. Shelf after shelf is filled with long trunks, labelled with the names of the peers whose robes are traditionally stored and maintained at the royal robe maker. For a matter of seconds only, the camera pans across the workroom, catching in grainy black-and-white the men and women working at the robes, their knees draped in the furs and velvets soon to cloak the attendees of the coronation ceremony. The focus moves to three unnamed women, stitching at speed with needles flying through the luxury fabrics in front of them, slightly incongruous against their woollen cardigans and crape dresses. Their techniques and the structure of the room itself in 1952 could just as easily have been transplanted to the coronation of 1937, or 1911 or 1902. The workers might have changed from the waistcoated men of the nineteenth and early twentieth centuries to include more women but almost every other element of the place would have been unchanged, such is nature of the trade.

But who were these robe makers? Simply put, I cannot find them. Census records pick up tailors a-plenty. The owners of robe-making establishments appear in London city trade directories, men like John

Palmer of Chancery Lane or Andrew Schabner of Tavistock Street, but these are the briefest of sightings. Census records also include men like Frank Gadney whose robe-making workshop was situated in Oxford, servicing the academic robe industry of university life. The Ede & Ravenscroft company records are rich in many respects, ledgers spilling with details of orders, materials, payments, advertisements. Customers and suppliers feature plentifully but somewhere in the middle, tucked away in the basement, are the makers themselves, out of sight. One of the few publications to write about the trade features a small colour photograph of Mrs Rose Batteson, described as a robe maker at Ede & Ravenscroft in the 1980s. She is standing, head bowed, as she looks intently at the cuff of the Lord Chancellor's robes, trimmed in gold braid. Rose appears again in the merest of mentions, thanks given to herself and her husband in a minuted report for their assistance in setting up an exhibition of robes at St George's Chapel, Windsor, in 1985. I can find her nowhere else. Such is the nature of their work, visible in every sense of the word and yet almost impossible to trace in the act of creation.

If the makers are conspicuous by their absence, the proprietors are not. The company's history is a well-documented affair and it reveals the most remarkable story. In an industry traditionally dominated entirely by men, the path to Ede & Ravenscroft's success was paved by three women, separated by time but connected in their endeavours on behalf of this unique firm. These three women would make an immeasurable contribution to the founding and expansion of the business that has been trading since 1689. This was the year that the Shudall family began to make robes from their premises in Holywell Street, now the bustle of Aldwych in London. Whilst fulfilling orders for individual clients, they began also to make a name for themselves as excellent makers of both clerical and state robes. They stitched the raven-like cassocks of the clergy, the golden mantles of bishops and the rich blue robes of the

Knights of the Garter, commissions which finally brought them to the attention of the monarch.

By the mid-eighteenth century the business was being undertaken by William Shudall and his wife, Martha. William would make visits to the royal residences to agree the terms of his work, and the flow of ceremonial robes continued to pour from their workshop. Their spousal partnership was not destined to last, however, and in 1757 William died. It would have been reasonable to expect this to prompt a change of ownership, that Martha might have handed the reins of the business to a male relative or sold to a rival robe maker, but she made the decision to continue to run the business herself. The customer's ledger dating from 1741 to 1763 indicates just what this amounted to, when in 1760 George II died and Martha Shudall found herself responsible for the creation of dozens of robes for the coronation of King George III. They included those for the King himself, the Dukes of York and Cumberland, the Barons of the Cinque Ports, bishops and judges. On 22 September 1761, the new King was crowned in a ceremony lasting over six hours and prompting huge celebrations in the city. Horace Walpole recorded: 'Oh! The buzz, the prattle, the crowds, the noise, the hurry.' The artist Allan Ramsay captured in paint the work of Martha Shudall's robe makers, his portrait of the King a riot of velvet, gold and ermine, celebrating a garment that no longer survives and stitches worked by fingers long forgotten.

The firm would continue its run of royal patronage until, by the accession of Queen Victoria, it was managed by a former apprentice, Joseph Ede, and his wife, Anne. They lived at 193 Fleet Street with their two children above the shop that bore their name. Residing to the west of the Royal Courts of Justice, they had remained within ordering distance of their legal clientele but the patronage of royalty still loomed large in the accounts ledgers. As Queen Victoria's coronation approached in 1838, Joseph Ede, as appointed robe maker to Her Majesty, began to take the orders required for another change of monarch. As well as making new garments, the company was also able to undertake the repair and refurbishment of existing ceremonial robes, as members of the aristocracy reached into their clothes presses and shook out the mothballed velvet for a much-needed revamp.

In 1862 Joseph died at the age of sixty-one. Like Martha before her, a century earlier, Anne chose to take control of the robe-making business and coordinated the order books for the next six years until her own death in May 1868. The neat columns of accounts charting orders, supplies, goods paid for and customers tell us nothing about what those six years were like for Anne. Did she relish the opportunity to head up so prestigious an establishment? Did she simply continue running the firm as she had already been doing, proud now of her own name on the Royal Warrant awarded by Queen Victoria on 7 April 1862? Following Anne's death, her son Joseph, aged twenty-three and as yet unmarried, took up the threads of the business.

Joseph moved the firm from its existing premises on Fleet Street, his own former home, to a new residence at 93 and 94 Chancery Lane where it has remained to this day. It was here that he brought his new wife, Rosanna Ellen Ravenscroft, in April 1871. Rosa Ravenscroft had been born and brought up only a few hundred yards away on Serle Street where she lived with her father, Burton, a prominent wig maker, her mother, Rosanna, and her nine siblings, the youngest of whom was only four when Rosa left the family home to marry Joseph Ede. Given the similarity of their occupations, clothing the legal profession from top to toe, wig to gown, it seems likely that the families were acquainted. Certainly Rosa did not have to move far following her marriage. But like the women before her, fate had its own plans. On 7 September 1871, when they had been married a mere six months, Joseph died. And so for the third time in the history of the royal robe maker, a woman was appointed as warrant holder. She was only twenty-four and could easily have handed responsibility over to her father or one of her two older brothers, and yet she chose to manage the firm herself, a role she would occupy for the next sixty years.

For thirty of those years she created her own opportunities wherever possible. Surviving correspondence records her lobbying for patronage, writing to heads of state around Europe to request the honour of their custom. When Queen Victoria died in 1901, Rosa was quick to act, writing to both Buckingham Palace and every one of the country's peers. She signed off each letter with the hopeful note: 'Trusting to be favoured with your commands, which shall have our personal attention.' Yet Rosa did not remain a steadfast widow tied only to the demands of her work. On 30 March 1878 she married London banker Henry Nightingale in a union that would last more than thirty-five years. By 1911, the year of the coronation of King George V, Rosa had moved from the bustle of her former life – the workrooms and offices of the robe maker – to a suburban villa on Wimbledon Common. What is noticeably absent from the public records accounting for Rosa's life, however, is any mention of her role as proprietor of one of the oldest robe makers in Britain. She is always Henry's wife, but each of the three census counts during her marriage fails to mention her own occupation. Presumably she chose not to share this information, playing, on paper at least, the role of respectable, domesticated woman but the reality was one of relentless hard work. All the while she was overseeing the busy workrooms of the Ede tailors.

Rosa Ede spent her whole career familiarising herself with the robe-making world and, being hugely knowledgeable about the robes that filled their premises, regularly fielded a whole host of different enquiries. Following an exhibition of King George V and Queen Mary's coronation regalia in the Museum of London in 1915, the curator contacted Rosa for advice following an infestation of moth. She wrote back: 'In reply to your esteemed favour with reference to the Coronation Robes which we are freeing from moth and hope to return within three weeks. We cannot tell what damage has been done to the fur until taken off and baked.' She goes on to give detailed instructions as to the future care of the complex garments and the treatments they should receive. Rosa advises further: 'We would suggest as a preventative in the future the liberal use of naphthalene, the manufacturers of this tell us that as far as their knowledge goes they do not think it would harm the Embroidery.' And what embroidery it was. The liberal embellishment of gold across the glowing velvet was a quite separate marvel, the work of an entirely different establishment.

Fast-forward to the digital age, however, and there is one more woman who is making her presence felt in the workrooms of the royal tailor. Ji Hae An is a Korean British tailor who works at Ede & Ravenscroft and through her social media content shares her work chalking, cutting and stitching the fine fabrics that pass through her fingers. *W* magazine

Ede & Ravenscroft tailor Ji Hae An Sykes.

George Doré, silk weaver, at his loom, late nineteenth century.

describe her as a 'young maker at the forefront of evolving what being British and working on Savile Row looks like'. She follows in the footsteps of the Ede & Ravenscroft women before her, Martha Shudall, Anne Ede and Rosa Ede, all pioneering in their own right.

There is a photograph of George Doré. He is seated at his loom in his house on Globe Road in Bethnal Green, staring intently at the cloth before him through small round steel-rimmed spectacles. He has a neat pointed beard. His white shirtsleeves are rolled uniformly to the elbow and his dark waistcoat is buttoned. At the end of each day he must have stretched and creaked in tune with the wooden joints of his loom as he eased his limbs into movement again. I wonder what he felt in that last moment of creation, as the final thread of bright petunia was woven into the cloth of Queen Alexandra's velvet robe. Did he purchase souvenir editions of the newspapers recording details of the coronation ceremony that took place on 9 August 1902? Did he raise a toast to the new King, or did he simply return to his loom and begin its preparations for the next commission?

The weaving sheds of Warner & Sons and the robe-making workshops on Chancery Lane still stand. Robes are still stitched and pressed, conserved and repaired. When the various coronation mantles were re-worn by King Charles III and Queen Camilla in 2023, as well as following the tradition of one new robe, they were subsequently displayed amongst the crimson splendour of Buckingham Palace, a testament to the hands and skills of George Doré, of Sam Watson, Lily Lee, the indomitable Rosa Ede and others whose names have gone unrecorded – but who spun into being these fantastical ceremonial robes.

CHAPTER 2

Little Hands
Ruby Essam and the Embroiderers

Encased in yellowed, crispy cellophane in a box in my wardrobe is the first piece of stitching I ever completed. Designed as a bookmark, the long piece of pink fabric with helpfully placed holes in regular squares was the canvas for my occasionally wonky primary-coloured stitches running the length of the cloth. It was an activity beloved of British primary schools in the early 1980s and I suspect countless similar bookmarks found their way into cupboards and tins (and bins). For me, this was to be the first of a lifetime of fascination with hand embroidery. I would stitch my way through evenings, weekends and school holidays churning out samplers, canvas-work cushions, innumerable pictures. It was a pastime I hid in the shadows, aware as I was that I knew nobody else who was interested in embroidery. I stitched intermittently through isolated periods of my life, through two pregnancies and through early motherhood. As my confidence grew, I embroidered on trains, in airport departure lounges, in hotels and tents. During the pandemic I finished a huge wool-work panel of meadow flowers, the project providing an anchor in uncertain times. Embroidery has been my solace through life's trials.

Alongside the pleasure I have found in the act of stitching, so grew my interest in the work of embroiderers past, the legacy of their skill left behind in the glow of their textiles even if their names were absent.

For centuries the art of the embroiderer was an important one in the wardrobe of the monarch, the King's (or Queen's) Embroiderer a vital post in the royal household. It was a lifetime appointment, the successor only chosen as the incumbent neared the end of their life. They were responsible not just for the embroidery of clothing but for all manner of accoutrements from saddles to banners, at a time when conspicuous hand embroidery was a sign of high status. In couture embroidery, the workers in the Parisian ateliers are called the 'petites mains', the little hands. Those creators of high-value textiles are known simply by the anonymity of their hands, and so it has been for centuries, be it the King's embroidery atelier or that of French high fashion. Putting names or faces to those hands is another matter altogether.

On 11 November 2008 as a young doctoral student, I stepped across the threshold of Kensington Palace and into the room that had been the birthplace of Queen Victoria. Closed to the public, it had been set up for the day in such a way that I might study some of the most spectacular ceremonial garments that had been made for Queen Alexandra, whose clothing was the subject of my research. I had read all of the published literature about the former Princess of Wales, long-suffering wife of Edward VII and patient daughter-in-law to Queen Victoria. I felt I knew much about her life in the abstract but there is something quite magical about suddenly finding yourself examining the objects themselves in three-dimensional glorious technicolour. Long tables were covered in whispery layers of acid-free tissue paper and a team of conservators had made the journey from Hampton Court in a van, bringing with them the unwieldy boxes containing these treasured garments. As the violet velvet robe was unfurled from its box like a many-petalled iris, the uniqueness of such a piece struck me. I still have my pencil notes complete with inexpert sketches and my slightly breathless observation: 'Very gorgeous vibrant purple . . .' The weight of the velvet, the depth of the gold braid trim, the richness of fur and the vast scale of the whole, were quite remarkable. Even then I pictured not just the Queen who had worn the robe but the countless persons who had contributed to its creation. The new Queen's wardrobe accounts recorded the amount paid to each of the contributors to her coronation gown. Ede & Ravenscroft were paid £410, Warner's received £37 for the gold braid whilst the Ladies' Work Society received £860 for the staggering amount of gold embroidery that covered almost the entirety of the petunia velvet robe.

The Ladies' Work Society had been founded in 1871 by a Miss Boulton whose aims were verbosely recorded in a 1900 column in *The Times*: 'It was founded to provide employment for gentlewomen whose circumstances rendered it necessary that they should occupy their time remuneratively.' In other words, it helped women of the middle classes who had fallen on hard times make some money by applying one of the skills that they were likely to have acquired in their possibly quite limited education – embroidery. They would hold regular sales of work and their pieces could be purchased by members of the public or the aristocratic sponsors who contributed as an act of popular philanthropy. By the 1902 coronation the society had been established for over thirty years, with Queen Victoria's daughter, Princess Louise, in post as president. It was thanks to her influence that the Ladies' Work Society received the commission for the Queen's coronation robe. The velvet woven by George Doré and constructed by the tailors at Ede & Ravenscroft was now to be covered in embroidered golden crowns. Little was known of the women whose needles passed through the glossy velvet to build the regal motifs ordered by Queen Alexandra. A long description of the gown in *The Times* took up almost two columns of the broadsheet newspaper. Tucked away in the last eight lines were the all-important names: 'Those who were part of the work were the Misses Jessie Robinson, E. Briant, D. Lang, L. Bennett, A. Giles, Thurston-Thompson, E. R. Harriss, J. Cossins, R. Smith, M. Martyn, A. H. Lock, A. Butt, O'Meara and Murray-Daly with Miss Slandon as manager.' It seems important to account for all of their names here since they are almost impossible to find elsewhere. R. Smith is probably Rosina Smith who kept tiny scraps of cloth and thread from her work on the royal robes along with a small piece of paper that recorded her contribution, saving them in a small screw-topped jar which now survives in the archives of the Royal School of Needlework. I had thought that Rosina Smith might be an unusual name on the census records and searched in hope of locating her but it appears to have been a particularly popular name in London at the turn of the century. There were 6,770 pages of Rosina Smiths. I found a factory labeller, a boot machinist, a factory hand, a weaver, a domestic servant, a patient in a hospital, a dressmaker, a boot cleaner, an office cleaner, a biscuit maker, a commercial clerk, a laundress, a boarding-house keeper, a brush drawer, a nurse. No Rosina Smiths who were embroiderers.

Life for these women, whose fortunes had changed requiring them to work for a living probably for the first time in their lives, was often uncertain. Their situations were precarious. The migration of single women from different regions around the UK to London looking for respectable accommodation had likewise grown during this period, and so workers like Rosina Smith or Jessie Robinson might have found themselves in one of the new working women's lodging houses that were springing up all over London. The largest of these, the Ada Lewis Women's Lodging House, had opened in 1913 and was able to accommodate 214 women in single cubicle spaces with an additional 46 in special double rooms for those who could afford it. There was a shared dining area and sitting room to try and alleviate the isolation that many of these women may have felt and there were often sewing rooms and libraries. By day their fingers might be busy stitching the gowns of a queen and by night they would lie in a narrow bed under a roof with hundreds of other single women all trying to fashion a life for themselves.

The Ladies' Work Society was only one of many organisations with similar aims. The most famous of these and the one with the longest association of embroidering for the monarchy is the Royal School of Needlework. The School of Art Needlework, as it was, had been founded in 1872 by Lady Victoria Welby Gregory, whose ambitions were to revive the dying art of ornamental embroidery and to provide work for 'gentlewomen' who found themselves in straitened circumstances. Lady Welby immediately hired the services of Mrs Anastasia Dolby who herself had royal connections as a former embroiderer to Queen Victoria. Anastasia lived in Camden with her husband, Edward, a lithographic artist and watercolourist. It was perhaps the artistic, unconventional nature of their household that meant Anastasia, a married woman, was able to take on the role of superintendent at the new institution, managing the tuition of the women who had applied for a place. From the outset, the ambition of the school was for them to be economically viable, taking on commissions that would pay their way. The women who undertook the lessons were supposed to have some working knowledge of embroidery which would be honed by the programme of teaching offered by the school. This consistency of process was vital since it would form one of the key tenets of the organisation. Once a student's work was considered skilful enough, she might progress to the workrooms where large commissions were fulfilled. There would be a number of individual embroiderers working on a single piece at any one time, but it was essential that it looked like the work of just one hand. This was of especial significance for the work on royal orders, and remains the case to this day.

'Never a seat shall go cold' is a phrase at the heart of the school. If one stitcher left the workroom her space would immediately be filled by somebody else. No single person should ever receive more credit for an embroidered piece than another, and yet thanks to the detailed records of the RSN, the names of some of those known to have contributed to royal commissions have survived. When Queen Victoria died in 1901, the order for an embroidered funeral pall was rejected by larger firms on account of the short notice. Princess Helena, daughter of Queen Victoria and patron of the School of Art Needlework, assured the royal household that her organisation could fulfil the requirements. 'From the moment the order was given to when the finished pall left Exhibition Road, the job had been with the RSN for 48 hours. As repeated commentary would confirm, the embroidery was undertaken in just 21 continuous hours of stitching.'

The woman who oversaw the relentless stitching of the funeral pall was Louisa Wade, manager of the workroom from 1875. She would hold the position for a half-century, the first of many women for whom the school would become a lifelong commitment. Louisa's place in the world mirrored that of many of her colleagues. In 1881, she was living at home with her parents, Nugent and Louisa, on 28 Soho Square. At the age of thirty-seven she was unmarried but so were all of her siblings who also lived at home. All nine children from Susanna aged forty-one to Beatrice aged twenty-one still inhabited the Georgian town house facing the square of gardens. Whilst it was hardly the cubicled space in a lodging house inhabited by so many other single working women, it must still have had the air of a boarding space filled with the comings and goings of many adults under one roof.

Alongside Louisa for most of her career was the school's designer, Nellie Whichelo. She spent her days working in the paint room on Exhibition Road, the school's headquarters, devising the designs that would eventually come to life through stitching. It was Nellie who worked on the patterns for King Edward VII's coronation mantle, Nellie who would discuss her ideas and the practicality of turning those visions into embellished cloth. Like Louisa, Nellie was not on the breadline but nor was she independently wealthy. In the 1880s, Nellie lived at 11 Warwick Road with her mother, a widow in her forties, and siblings. Her mother ran a private boarding house, the three-storeyed building offering a variety of rooms for rent. In later years Nellie would live with her sister on Werter Road in Putney, just south of the river from the South Kensington workrooms where her artistic talents were given free rein. Like so many of their colleagues at the School of Art Needlework, these were women who never married and for whom their own income was essential.

Where I, the hobbyist, have had the luxury of treating embroidery as a peaceful pastime to unwind from the everyday, the women working at the School of Art Needlework were stitching in a very different space. Surviving photographs give a sense of the activity in the school's workroom. Large tables and myriad rectangular embroidery frames are positioned around the many-windowed room. The women sit with heads bowed, one hand on the top of the work and the other beneath to pull the needle through from the hand above. The cover of *Black and White* magazine for 19 April 1902 featured an illustration of the embroiderers at work on the coronation mantle, each woman surrounded by the tools of her trade. Scissors rest on the frames alongside tins, spools of thread and a piece of cloth pooled deep with the singular beads and embellishments being stitched to the robe. The frames have changed little over the years. The wooden bars of the frame would be adjusted according to the size of the work, slotting into each other with worn regularity, and then the cloth stretched and stitched to the bars, ensuring even tension. Was there a buzz of chat in the room as they worked? Were they able to talk of their lives whilst stitching or did Miss Wade oversee a room of quiet and concentrated hush? The longevity of so many of the women's employment would suggest that it was a pleasant place to work, offering them security and a work environment that might have been difficult to find elsewhere.

Such continuous service, whilst indicating the generally stable nature of their employment, did sometimes come at a cost for the school. Since there was no state pension and many of these women had no disposable income if they finished work, many of them continued beyond the point of efficiency. Susan Kay-Williams, chief executive of the RSN from

2007 until 2024 and author of a detailed history of the school, found evidence of these difficulties: 'The oldest retired at 82, and this led to other issues, as the older staff worked more slowly than was accounted for when the work had been costed.' When Nellie Whichelo had retired from the school, she was granted a pension owing to the length of her service. This was a discretionary decision, by no means universal to all former employees. However, Nellie had found it difficult to live out her retirement on the funds allocated to her and approached the RSN. The executive committee met and discussed her plight: 'It was agreed that Miss Whichelo's money should be increased to £2 per week in the light of her 60 years of service.'

This uncertainty of later life as an unmarried or widowed woman was an ever-present anxiety before more comprehensive social welfare and housing were available. For Ruby Essam, another long-time embroiderer at the RSN, the wage that she earned from stitching in the workrooms was a vital contribution to her family income. Ruby's mother, Martha, had been widowed by the time that Ruby was three years old and so, like Nellie's mother, she had embarked on a life punctuated by the transient flow of lodgers. By 1939 and at the age of eighty-one, Martha Essam was living with her daughter Ruby at the Wimbledon Endowed Almshouses. For centuries, almshouses had offered one means of alleviating poverty for the few inhabitants lucky enough to be awarded accommodation. Wealthy philanthropist Charlotte Marryat held fairs in the grounds of her home to raise money for the Wimbledon Almshouses which were first endowed as a charitable organisation in 1839. Additional properties were approved in 1912 and it was here that Martha Essam and embroiderer Ruby lived, able to support themselves with the subsidised accommodation and Ruby's salary for her work at the Royal School of Needlework.

Ruby Essam joined the school in 1913 aged fifteen to complete her diploma. Three years later, she was awarded her certificate, a beautiful floral bordered sheet that attested to the completion of her studies and subsequent move to the workrooms to begin a career that would span more than six decades. A photograph that appeared in the *Sphere* on 21 February 1953 showed Miss Essam at her frame stitching the imperial crown that would feature at the bottom of the new Queen's purple Robe of Estate. The raised surface of the crown is flanked by the snips of gold, coils of thread, a small quilted pincushion and scissors, whilst Ruby's right hand holds the needle poised above the glittering motif. It was not her first contribution to royal robes as she had undertaken some of the stitching for King George VI's coronation in 1937, one of thirty-five women to work on the various regalia required for the day. By 1953 Ruby was one of twelve other embroiderers whose hands crafted the decorated robe of Queen Elizabeth II. A far cry from the modest arrangements of the Wimbledon Almshouses, Ruby spent her days that February in the workroom that was by then under police guard as the media speculation mounted. After sixty-three years, Ruby retired from the workroom at the age of seventy-nine, awarded a pension of £36 per week by the school. She had not only contributed so much of her life to the school as a stitcher but had come to act as a mentor to new training school students, teaching where once all those years ago she had herself been taught.

If the Royal School of Needlework had acquired a reputation as embroiderers for the most formal of royal occasions, there were women elsewhere in the city who were stitching and beading in other workrooms, the couture embroiderers working in high fashion and for household names, designing and making garments for a host of royal women. Norman Hartnell's continuing influence over royal style was in no small part due to the embellishment practices that remained at the heart of his designs. Unlike his peers, Hartnell kept his embroidery in-house, employing women in his workroom in Bruton Mews near to his Bruton Street headquarters. Jane Hattrick enjoyed the unique experience of interviewing some of these embroiderers for her doctoral research, preserving stories that had not been recorded anywhere else. Situated above the tailoring room, photographs of the embroidery space show a well-lit room of long windows and roof lights to maximise the natural light flooding into the room. The embroiderers are shown grouped around pieces of work, large rectangular tables allowing women to sit up to four together, a close and communal workspace facing your colleague as you plied your needle. The head of the workroom for many years was Miss Edie Duley who oversaw the lavish work on both the Queen's 1947 wedding dress and her coronation gown in 1953. Norman Hartnell himself in fact acknowledged her contribution, albeit briefly, in his 1955 autobiography *Silver and Gold*. Describing the preparations for the coronation, he recalled, 'The spring of 1953 was the busiest season we had ever known, and the excitement of preparation ran high as the final days arrived.' As well as the Queen and her attendants, Hartnell had been commissioned to clothe dozens of other attendees and the workrooms were swamped with orders. Hartnell noted, however, that 'throughout this period Miss Edie Duley and her wonderful young women were in control of all the great embroideries'. In 1955, one of these wonderful young women was Maureen Markham. Maureen came to Hartnell's directly from her training at the Barrett Street Trade School, one of the needle-trade schools that would go on to form the London College of Fashion. Early in the twentieth century, trade schools such as Barrett Street had been formed to offer girls a specialised education that would open the door to workplaces requiring a skilled workforce. The curriculum consisted of one third general education and two thirds on the more specific skill set around the needle arts. Barrett Street also offered a day-release programme and evening classes for young women already in work but keen to formalise their working knowledge, employed as they might be in the top fashion houses of the West End.

Little Hands

Norman Hartnell's embroidery workshop, 1944.

Maureen must have been one of the last few to complete her training, as the trade school initiative did not survive long past the end of the Second World War and few would remember the role of these establishments today. Jane Hattrick interviewed Maureen about her decade spent at Hartnell's, the period during which so many of the Queen's gowns were ordered and embellished within the fashion house: 'According to Markham the embroidery was carried out first onto the pieces of the garment after they had been cut out and these pieces would be stretched onto a frame.' For the most complicated of patterns, Miss Edie would draw the design on paper in black and white. 'The embroidery design was then sketched out onto tracing paper and the "goods" chosen. The design would be "pounced" or pricked through paper onto the fabric for

Dressing the Queen

Embroidery sample for Queen Elizabeth's coronation dress.

the embroideresses to work in beads or other "goods".' Maureen had been one of the embroiderers to work on the now famous 'Flowers of the Fields of France' gown, worn by the Queen on the first night of her state visit to France in 1957, decorated with embroidered bees, grasses, grains and flowers. Maureen recalled how the work had been stitched behind blacked-out windows to avoid the increasingly intrusive lenses of the newspaper cameras. Her greatest anxiety remained with the dress itself and how the embroidery might be affected. After so many hours of tiny stitches and the painstaking application of so many thousands of coloured beads, Maureen hoped there would be 'nice plush cushions to sit on so as not to crush the embroidery'.

Whilst so many of these women are silent and voiceless, Maureen was able to recount her own experiences for a short television interview when Buckingham Palace opened its doors on a major exhibition of the Queen's wardrobe to mark her ninetieth birthday. Standing in front of a

1957 white duchesse satin gown, beaded with broad circles and worn in America in 1957, she recalls: 'I remember sitting under the window doing this one with four girls, we sat four a-side on this one . . . it's very intricate, very close work. It took hours and hours, I think we were on it for weeks.' This was presumably the first time that Maureen had seen the gown since she had fixed her final bead, before it was carefully bagged and whisked away from Bruton Mews to the Queen for its final fitting. Perhaps she saw the photograph of young Queen Elizabeth descending a staircase in Virginia for the state dinner and felt pride in her work, on display for all the world to see.

Embroidery for the royal family was undertaken not only by charitable enterprises and high-end fashion houses, however. There were individuals, professional stitchers, whose work brought them into the orbit of the palaces to leave their mark on an abundance of textiles. In the collections of the Museum of Jewish Heritage, there is a beautiful trade card in scrolling calligraphy that came from the firm of Victor Abraham. The early-nineteenth-century card assures customers: 'Orders for Exportation executed with neatness and dispatch.' The Abrahams specialised in military embroidery and metallic lace for uniforms and it was this knowledge of goldwork that won them the commission to embroider the cover for the throne at the 1837 coronation of Queen Victoria. Victor's son, Samuel, joined the family business as a young man, and aged seventy-three was still describing himself on the 1901 census as a 'military and royal embroiderer'. The contribution of London's Jewish population to the needle trades in the nineteenth century was huge. Countless tailors, dressmakers, designers and stitchers contributed to the style of the city. Samuel became a prominent figure within his community and created embroideries for synagogues around the country, but following the death of his wife, Sarah, he left London and spent his last years close to the sea, living with his daughter Ada in Eastbourne. Behind him were decades of golden embroideries decorating sacred spaces, thrones and the shoulders of military men.

In more recent years, it has been the firm of Hand & Lock that has displayed the Royal Warrant as embroiderer to the royal family. It too has a long history, one that began in 1767 when Monsieur Hand arrived in London, one of thousands of Huguenots fleeing religious persecution on the continent. Like Victor and Samuel Abraham, he became a commercial embroiderer, selling his wares to Savile Row tailors and military makers, the firm continuing in his name for two hundred years. In the 1950s, a young couture embroidery designer named Stanley Lock had built an impressive clientele around London and beyond, earning him his first Royal Warrant in 1972. It was only in 2001 that the military expertise of Monsieur Hand and the couture stitching of Stanley Lock were combined. Today, the sum of those two parts operates from a relatively modest three-storey brick building on London's Margaret Street. It is only a few yards from the bustle of Oxford Circus but it feels like another world – at least that was my impression when I visited for some research in 2017. I walked past the embroiderers on the ground floor working at their frames, a scene that would have been familiar to Ruby Essam or Maureen Markham. The tools of their trade remain unchanged from the reels of glowing silks to the humble pincushion, the fine pointed scissors and of course the needle. Ruby or Maureen or Edie Duley or Nellie Whichelo might have walked into this workroom and felt immediately at home. They would have been able to set up a frame, thread the needle and follow the design in front of them as these women were doing a century or more later.

I climbed the stairs to the third floor and found myself in an archivist's dream, the combined material of the two companies amounting to drawers of military goldwork sketches, letters from Hardy Amies and Cecil Beaton, swatches of beadwork attached to drawings of Diana, Princess of Wales. Embedded in this archive and threaded through each and every letter, sketch, sample and design are the imprint of the hands that worked on them. The owners of those hands remain nameless and faceless but their work survives, housed in wood-panelled splendour or hanging in environmentally monitored museum spaces. Different hands contribute still to embroidering the royal wardrobe. Sixty different embroiderers from the RSN worked on the hand-cut lace motifs applied to the ivory silk tulle of the Duchess of Cambridge's wedding dress in 2010, each signing a pledge to secrecy in the months leading up to the ceremony. Hand & Lock were awarded a Royal Warrant in 2019 and contributed to both the funeral of Queen Elizabeth II and the coronation of King Charles III. The practices of Hartnell's embroidery workroom are just about within living memory. These form a thread stretching back and connecting embroiderer to embroiderer, stitch to stitch, hand to hand. Their individual names might sometimes be lost, but their work remains intact.

CHAPTER 3

Presented at Court
Clara Mobbs and Her White Feathers

On a breezy, chill day in the middle of March 1958, an open-topped vintage Rolls-Royce bowled along the Mall in London, one of the occupants holding aloft a placard across which was written 'Goodbye Dear Debs'. The route was thronged with onlookers, enjoying the spectacle of well-heeled young women and their parents lining the railings around Buckingham Palace whilst they waited for the very last formal presentation at court. Amongst them was Fiona MacCarthy, dressed in the Season's most fashionable pale blue silk, awaiting her entrance to the palace alongside her mother. As they climbed the Grand Staircase, flanked with Beefeaters and other uniform-clad dignitaries, she felt the otherworldliness of the experience. She wrote that as they stepped along the red-carpeted galleries 'the debutantes were entering an *Alice in Wonderland* world of stagey pomp and comic fancy dress'. The experience was soon to take on a more competitive edge, however. 'The debs were now denuded of their tweed or camel overcoats, thronging through the palace, eyeing one another as if entering heat one of an old-time beauty contest, which in a sense it was.' In a centuries-old tradition, these were the young women 'coming out' into Society. They had spent months being measured and fitted for their presentation gowns in preparation for their moment in front of the monarch.

The spectacle of court presentation is now two generations in its passing. It was already anachronistic by the late 1950s – the landscape of post-war Britain was not prepared to accommodate the lining up of hundreds of privileged and monied young women to curtsey in front of the Queen. The roots of court presentation stretch back centuries and represented the nuances of influence at court, the jockeying for position and aspirations of those surrounding the monarch. Gatherings of courtiers in formal spaces around the king and queen had been taking place for generations, witnessing the favour and fortunes of influential members of society in the orbit of the monarch. It was King George III's consort, Queen Charlotte, who, in the latter years of the eighteenth century, took to regularly inviting young women of note to her 'Drawing Rooms' and by the turn of the nineteenth century these had expanded to such an extent that the artist and caricaturist Thomas Rowlandson captured the crush of proceedings in one of his detailed cartoons as proud mamas and portly papas thronged the palace and entered the scrum of presentation.

But what to wear for such a rarefied occasion? The reign of Queen Victoria would witness the preserving in aspic of the routines and etiquettes surrounding the appearance of young women and royalty themselves at these events. Strict guidelines governed the clothing choices of the women being presented at court, and were published for anxious parents to pore over, keen to ensure that not a satin slipper-clad foot should be put wrong. The names of these young women are easy to find, representing as they did the most prominent members of 'Good Society'. Even this was prescribed carefully in instructional guides. The volume *Rules and Manners of Good Society* emphasised that, although presentation was being opened up to a wider sector of society by the later years of the nineteenth century, those working in the retail trade were over the line that could not be crossed. Yet it was precisely those tradespeople whose labour produced the fans, the feathers, the trains and the gowns that formed the centrepiece of each young woman's court presentation.

For decades these ensembles remained largely unchanged. The court gown must be of a pale or white fabric. A train must be worn, suspended either from the waist or shoulders. Two or three white feathers must be attached to the hair from which a white veil would fall at the back and a fan or bouquet might be carried. Whilst the names of those presented have been meticulously recorded in columns of newsprint, those whose nimble fingers contributed to this court ceremony have rarely been considered. Who was stitching the elaborate court bodices or long silk trains? Who prepared the white ostrich feathers? These are women not easily found and yet the fruits of their labour survive in museums around the world, court presentation ensembles frequently kept for posterity, the donor recorded, the makers most often not.

The largest component of court presentation was the dress itself, a garment that fuelled the growth of hundreds of 'court dressmakers'. These included some of the most prominent names in fashion who undertook the clothing of women at court. One of these was Lucile, Lady Duff Gordon, who became one of the most sought-after dressmakers of the early twentieth century. Born into privilege, she nonetheless decided to follow her heart and become a dressmaker, a decision which ironically affected her own standing in the social hierarchy. She wrote in her 1932 autobiography: 'I could never be presented at Court because I was "in trade".' She had established her business amongst the myriad other court dressmakers on Hanover Square in spite of the misgivings of her family. After creating a wardrobe at short notice for the 'coming out' of a young society girl in Dublin, Lucile acquired a reputation for her presentation ensembles and soon it seemed every mother in London required her attention. 'Before long I was running a special department for debutantes' dresses, and our house was the first in London or even in Paris to do so . . .' Lucile wrote of her 'discreet little fitting rooms' which were soon thronged with wealthy patrons choosing their gown in the first step of the lengthy process. Subsequent fittings and choices would be made at the home of the customer, the fitter often travelling in a carriage with a liveried footman to the grand London houses.

One such fitter was a young Irish girl named Mollie. Lucile offers a glimpse of her young employee who visited the then Duchess of York, the future Queen Mary, at St James's Palace. She travelled there with the head fitter and a selection of gowns, bringing back a colourful account of her visit. After telling how she had advised the Duchess about dealing with a baby's cold, Mollie described to Lucile her more surprising impressions of the future Queen of England: 'And isn't it a wonder now that the Duchess wore only ordinary cotton underclothing with Swiss embroidery on it like my very own Sunday ones. I'm thinking she keeps her silk for best.' It seems that Mollie was a hit with Lucile's royal patrons, visiting both St James's and Kensington Palaces on subsequent occasions. Lucile wrote: 'I sometimes wonder whether her shrewd wit and ready observation delighted the august ladies as much as they did me, for she was very popular with them.' We know nothing more of Mollie – of her life outside her work as assistant fitter at the House of Lucile. Nor can we know about her hopes for the future, what her dreams amounted to. She occupied a private space between realities, where confidences might be shared. Lucile wrote: 'There are more secrets told in fitting-rooms and hairdressers' cubicles than anywhere in the world, and all women have to confide in somebody.' Mollie spent her days measuring duchesses in their underwear and her nights perhaps sharing a bedroom with a sibling or as a tenant in a boarding house.

For all her eccentricities and privileged connections, it does seem that Lucile was genuinely fond of those women she employed in her workrooms, relying on their skill and their loyalty. Many stayed for years in her employ, suggesting that as dressmakers went, she was one of the more sympathetic. Early in her career, she wrote: 'It was about this time that I took on a little fourteen year old apprentice, Celia, who used to run errands and match silks.' Over the course of the next decade,

Celia would become indispensable, becoming Lucile's 'right hand' as she opened branches in New York and Paris. The other young women that Lucile had employed were also remembered with great fondness: 'I engaged Margaret and Elsie, two of the best saleswomen I ever had, and Edith, who was a wonderful fitter. They all remained with me through nearly the whole of my career as "Lucile" and I was deeply grateful to them for the loyal service they gave me.' Most such women have been overlooked as court dressmaking became an anachronism, and employers rarely acknowledged their fitters or trusted saleswomen. There are countless Margarets and Elsies and Ediths populating the records of the early twentieth century and without surnames they are impossible to trace, yet their contributions to the presentation ensembles Lucile created were of vital importance to the success of such a business. Where they measured and fitted and listened to the secrets of their young clients, so the resultant gowns glittered under the lights of the Throne Room at Buckingham Palace.

Whilst the grandest of court dressmakers might clothe the aristocracy and even the Queen herself, the expansion of the presentation system meant that countless other small dressmakers began to offer their services to those hundreds of young women whose station in life permitted them access to the drawing rooms. Even in 1958, this was still the case. Fiona MacCarthy, along with all of her friends, had been hauled to Harrods for their season's wardrobe but she recalled: 'Besides the department stores, mothers and daughters went on searches in the local "Madam" shops. Our mothers' favourites were Nora Bradley in Knightsbridge or (slightly more downmarket) Wakeford's in King's Road . . .' Thus, to advertise as a 'court dressmaker' did not mean that you were making garments for royalty themselves but rather that the business had previous experience of making dresses for a court occasion. From December to June each year, these smaller concerns would operate at full capacity to meet the needs of the London Season. Contemporary magazines are filled with advertisements for these dressmakers, all seeking to profit from the whirl of the court. A small rectangular box of print would aim to capture the attention of potential clients.

The wonderfully named Madame Amelia Blazeby was typical of this trade. Her small ad indicated that she was a court dressmaker with premises at 21 Great Portland Street. 'Good fit, style and punctuality guaranteed' it informs the reader. 'COURT GOWNS from 16 guineas' it concludes. Madame Amelia Blazeby was not a dressmaker of French origin but had adopted the title as a strategic nod to the level of her skill set, a popular fiction used by many small West End court dressmakers. Far from the bright lights of Parisian couture, Amelia was in fact born in 1849 in rural Cambridgeshire. She and her five siblings grew up in Wisbech where their father, John, was a shoemaker. Here then was her introduction to the needle trades and the wardrobes of other people. By the age of thirty, Amelia had moved to London to take up work as a dressmaker and milliner; she was the tenant of a family in Marylebone, a boarder like so many thousands of other young women across the city plying their needles to forge a career. Twenty years later, Amelia had made her mark on the world of dressmaking. No longer a boarding house tenant, she now occupied her own premises on Great Portland Street, an address to tempt those in search of a court gown. She was the head of her own household, a woman with a cook and a housemaid. Her niece Henrietta had moved in and was training as an apprentice to Madame Blazeby, learning how to fit the bright white gowns and long embellished trains to the young women crossing their threshold.

These are women who have been, for the most part, hidden behind the names of the more prominent fashion houses of their era and yet were successful entrepreneurs at a time when it was not an easy prospect. I was intrigued by one name that was included amongst a list of well-respected court dressmakers of the late nineteenth century, since it seemed at odds with the grander houses of Worth, Lucile and Redfern. It simply read 'Miss Dust, 5 Brook Street'. Nobody that I can find has written about Miss Dust. I found a single illustration of one of her Regatta Costumes featured in a July 1887 edition of the *Lady's World* but other than that she was entirely absent from later studies of the fashionable world. Amongst hundreds of other business names on a single page of the 1890 *Post Office London Directory*, she appears beneath Eisen Dusseldorfer, a steel wire manufacturer, and above William Dust, an oilman. There she sits, 'Dust, Lucy Rudd (Madame), dressmaker, 3&5 Brook Street, Hanover Sq, W'. So to see if it might be possible to illuminate just a part of the life of one of these women, I set off in search of Lucy Dust. Lucy was born in 1846 in the town of Godmanchester, seventeen miles from Cambridge. Her father, Thomas, was a rag merchant; their household operated on limited means and her mother, Sarah, worked hard to clothe and feed and keep house for Lucy and her siblings.

We find Lucy next at an entirely different address and one that would eventually lead her to success in her own right. The 1871 census describes Lucy as an 'assistant' and her address was given as 247, 249, 251 Regent Street. Multiple numbers such as this can mean only one thing in the second half of the nineteenth century. A department store. From 1841, this address belonged to the London General Mourning Warehouse, otherwise known as Jay's. As a young assistant at Jay's, Lucy would have been introduced to the luxury of shopping. Henry Mayhew, contemporary journalist and advocate for social reform, described a visit to Jay's in 1865, capturing the opulence of the grand Regent Street premises. After passing through a long vestibule, he described the tasteful window displays and the massive mahogany tables flanking the doors. He went on: 'Let us walk upstairs into the spacious showrooms. Here we can lounge about on the most comfortable of sofas and easy chairs; we can look at ourselves in the most dazzling of mirrors; and . . . we have a bevy of bright eyed fair damsels, clad in black silk, who will lay before us every description of mourning we may require to purchase . . .' Lucy Dust was one of these black-clad damsels, storing away all of her acquired knowledge about selling clothes to wealthy customers as she served them on Regent Street. Within ten years, with all her experience she had set up her own establishment, and so at the age of thirty-five she lived in the premises of her dressmaking business at 86 Gloucester Road. Here she employed ten people, including Ellen Howton as manager; Martha Hardwell, Emily Gower, Heinrich Bingham, Clara Plaster and Winifred Ballham as assistants; and Helen Hogg and Clara Adams as 'showroom apprentices'. She was mistress of her own destiny, gaining a reputation for her court ensembles that would eventually take her to the even more impressive address at Brook Street, only a short stroll from her department store days.

At the age of forty-one, Lucy Dust was married. Her husband, William, was a mercer – a merchant of fabric – and so it is tempting to imagine that a romance blossomed during negotiations over the purchase of cloth for her court gowns. William was certainly a modern man, for Madame Dust continued her business for years after their marriage, trading under her maiden name until the early 1900s. It is a remarkable success story, one that was replicated all over the city, and yet she is largely invisible. Maybe one of Madame Dust's court presentation ensembles survives, folded between layers of tissue in an attic or museum, a fragment of her legacy remaining in the pale silks of her trade.

Whilst Lucy had moved on from her days as a department store apprentice, the growing influence of these grand emporiums saw department stores cash in on the court presentation market, creating their own special services for the budding debutante. They employed skilled dressmakers by the dozen in their workrooms, women such as Ann Cheriton. She was interviewed in 1972 at the age of ninety, a rare opportunity for a snapshot of that world. Ann Poole was born in Plumstead, to the south-east of London, in 1882. Her father, George, was a tin plate worker supporting a family of six children alongside his wife, Eliza. By the age of fifteen, Ann and her sister Edith were both working locally, apprenticed to a court dressmaker in Plumstead. She recalled that she received no pay during the course of her apprenticeship and when she had completed her training and might be considered a skilled seamstress, her employer offered her a paltry half a crown a week to remain in post. She refused, deeming the offer unfair, and instead sought work with some of the larger retailers in the city. She eventually found herself at Swan & Edgar, one of the largest and most popular of the London department stores. They had opened a court dressmaking department and along with six other girls, Ann was employed as a bodice hand. She earned twelve shillings and sixpence a week (ten shillings more than her former employer had offered), rising after a time to fifteen shillings. She was not entitled to holiday pay. She explained that 'we lived at home, otherwise we could not have managed'. Unlike Lucy who, as a shop assistant, lived on the premises in one of the attic dormitories kept by the department stores, Ann as a young dressmaker had to travel to work each day on the train from Plumstead. Her hours were long. She would work at the elaborate bodices from 9.00 a.m. to 7.30 p.m. but to save money she and her friends would catch an early-morning workman's train to Charing Cross costing only fourpence, spending an hour before work strolling around Covent Garden. They brought lunch with them from home and were given tea with bread and butter for their break. 'At 7.30 there was a stampede as they raced all the way from Piccadilly Circus to Charing Cross to catch the 7.40pm train . . . The ticket collector held the gates open for them . . .'

This was a period of modular construction as far as expensive gowns were concerned. At Swan & Edgar, like most of the other large stores, there were separate rooms for the different parts of an ensemble – a bodice room, a skirt room, a sleeve room. Ann described the long tables at which she worked, covered in white sheets which would be carefully folded over the work in progress each evening before they left. Over the top of their own long skirts and bodices, Ann and her fellow dressmakers wore white overalls to protect the garments that they fashioned. In 1907, Ann married her first husband, Charlie Waller, a carpenter from Plumstead, after which she no longer caught the early train into the city but remained at home, living with her widowed father-in-law, her days consisting of the 'unpaid domestic duties' so often recorded on census entries. It was a life never forgotten, however. At the age of ninety when she was interviewed about her dressmaking days, the interviewer wrote: 'Mrs Ann Cheriton does beautiful patchwork, joining up with firm, even stitches the bundles of scraps of dress materials sent to her by Swan and Edgar . . .' Over six decades after she had left the firm, the flutter of dress fabric and her careful stitches could still recall her former life.

In addition to each of the workrooms, Swan & Edgar would have sold the accessories required of court presentation. The most visible of these were the snowy white feathers. Feathers had become a requisite of court dress in the eighteenth century and remained a feature of the unique ensemble. For such an ephemeral object, one that might catch a breeze and flutter away, the feather industry in London in the nineteenth century represented globalism and profit on a grand scale. It was also one dominated by thousands of Jewish girls and women who worked in premises across East London, fashioning feathers into the foamy white creations beloved of society women. A fancy trade card dating to 1837 announces the talents of Mr R. Manning, plumassier to the royal family. 'Court and installation plumes mounted as usual' it assures potential customers, in addition to which: 'Feathers cleaned, dyed and dressed with care and punctuality.' Mr Manning might have been the royal plumassier but he was just one of thousands dealing in the valuable and fashionable commodity. Such was their value that at the peak of the industry, the most prized feathers were almost equal in worth per pound to diamonds. London had become a global hub of the feather trade, where they would be inspected by feather dealers after arriving in bundles from southern Africa. Men like Myer Salaman whose father Isaac had built one of the largest ostrich feather wholesale companies in the world. He would visit storage spaces such as the Billiter Street Warehouse on Mincing Lane and there inspect the feathers that were to be sold at auction, casting his practised eye over the bundles and noting which he would purchase. From the bustle of auction, the feathers would find themselves in one of the myriad workshops that crowded the East End, part of an industry that employed more than 20,000 feather workers at its peak in the early years of the twentieth century. Workers such as Clara Mobbs, the eldest of four sisters who lived in just two rooms at 145 Southgate Road, Islington. Clara and her sisters Amelia and Matilda were all ostrich feather curlers, one of the most skilled of the jobs associated with the trade.

Before the feathers founds themselves in front of Clara and her sisters to be curled, however, they had to undergo a myriad of treatments. Young girls in small single-room premises would first be given the task of stringing the feathers, unfurling them from the bundles in which they had travelled and tying them to lengths of twine before passing them on to yet more 'unskilled' women whose job it was to wash the plumes, ridding them of any impurities and storage matter that might have accrued from farm to workshop. Once washed, the dying and bleaching process might begin, a job considered odious by the Board of Trade who inspected such works. It required an experienced hand and was one of the few treatments undertaken by men. Men such as Cornelius Brown who lived with his wife and three young daughters in three rooms at an address in Hackney; or Charles Canter who, in 1911, had been married for less than a year to Alice and who lived in just two rooms at another address in Hackney, like Cornelius described as an 'ostrich feather dyer'. These men would manage the dying of up to eighteen boiling vats filled with thirty pounds of feathers, malodorous and heavy work. Only then, after up to ten days of stringing, cleaning, bleaching and dying, were the now bright and brilliant feathers ready to be curled into showy plumes by women such as Clara Mobbs.

Clara was born in Poplar in 1875, the East End district of London that flanked a great loop of the Thames. Around that bend of the river, the great barges carrying the feathers she would one day spend her life curling and shaping would sail up to the riverside warehouses. Her father, James, was a cooper and the family moved north to Edmonton, following his work as his family grew. By 1891 and aged only sixteen, Clara was already working as a feather curler, contributing to the family coffers. Ten years later her two sisters had joined her in the trade, still living at home with their parents, the family having moved to Bermondsey where James was working as a brewer's cooper, fashioning the barrels to meet the needs of a thirsty populace. Such was life for families such as the Mobbs and countless others like them. They shifted with the nomadic nature of such work, chasing employment and housing where they could. By 1911 Clara was the head of her own household, the two rooms on Southgate Road that she shared with Amelia, Matilda and Ethel. Although the feather industry was reported to be less prone to seasonality than other needle trades, it was still a sweated industry imbued with hazards for the young female workers. Clara and her sisters would have been exposed to the dust and fluff from the stripping of the feather flues in their small and potentially poorly ventilated workroom, and resulting incidences of tuberculosis were high. Steam was required to curl the feathers into their snowy arcs and so the atmosphere might be damp as they shaped and sculpted each wisp of white. Photographs of their New York counterparts show groups of women sitting on hard wooden chairs in front of crowded trestle tables loaded with their necessary tools and the clouds of feathers. At the end of each long day, Clara and her sisters might have been tempted to enhance their wage further, taking their work home with them in contravention of labour laws but a practice regarded by many as the only way to boost their small income. It is entirely possible that some

Feather workshop in New York.

of the many thousands of ostrich feathers that Clara Mobbs curled would have ended up in the showroom of one of the court dressmakers or other high-end retailers far from the East End workshops. In preparation for her day at the palace, some other young woman would have the nodding feathers fixed to her perfectly coiffed head and curtsey deeply before the Queen. The luxuriantly curled feather would complete the ensemble but Clara, Amelia, Matilda and Ethel remained invisible, unknown.

In 1939, newsreel cameras were permitted access to Miss Vacani's school of dance, the only place for the prospective debutante to learn deportment and the art of the curtsey. In perfectly clipped instructions, Miss Vacani, in feathers and chiffon, instructs her 'gels', as they sink to the floor in their silk gowns: 'Keep your head up, bow your head, come up and finish on the back foot, slide, cross, slide. Again.' Should the young ladies have ordered their court presentation ensemble from Debenham & Freebody, their order comprised not only the garments but also a packing service, and advice and instructions on how to maintain a curtsey and negotiate the train. They were preparing for something of an ordeal. In 1863, the magazine *London Society* had described those awaiting presentation, 'pushing as only fine ladies can push, frowning and dragging as only the British dowagers can', whilst *Punch* outlined some of the experiences of young women that year where dresses were allegedly torn in the melee: 'We were driven from one bitterly cold room to another . . . one had many fellow sufferers and these poor creatures pushed against us and fought with us.' By 1958 and the last of the debs, Fiona MacCarthy felt the oddity of the occasion: 'It had a mad, sad beauty, this long chorus line of privilege.'

Behind this mad beauty of presentation were those countless makers, spinners of fantasy, whose names were almost never a part of the ceremony to which they had contributed. Forgotten are the Lucy Dusts and Amelia Blazebys who stitched and sketched and worked over the designs for presentation gowns. Almost invisible are the Mollies, Margarets, Ediths and Ethels who fitted the young girls into their pale dresses. Lost amongst the countless other nimble-fingered feather workers are Clara Mobbs and her sisters, toiling in their tiny workrooms amongst the clouds of bleached ostrich feathers and the thousands of skilled Jewish immigrants whose labour was so invaluable to the needle trades. At ninety years of age, Ann Cheriton would sit and stitch her patchwork of scraps, reminiscing about her department store days. It is indeed a patchwork of labour. Each skilled occupation added to the complexity of the whole from the feather to the gown to the sweep of the train. Behind every deep curtsey in front of the Queen there stretches a shadowy line of men and women who each deserve their own nod of recognition.

CHAPTER 4

All That Glisters . . .
Harold Goodship and the Diamonds

Ask any child to draw a picture of a king or a queen and they will inevitably include a crown. It is the visual code that places the monarch apart from their subjects, historically the indicator of the person anointed by God to rule on earth. Royal tomb effigies are distinguished by their crowns. Portraiture captures the bejewelled regalia of royalty and in 1840 the first British postage stamps featured the disembodied, crowned head of the young Queen Victoria, sending out her regal image to a global audience. For coronations, weddings, state events, anniversaries and balls, the Crown Jewels and personal gems of the British monarchy have been photographed, filmed, written about, argued over and analysed ad infinitum. They have a genealogy of their own; gemstones and jewellery handed down through the generations, crossing oceans and borders. They have passed from one royal family to another. Books have been written and films have been made about these most splendid of objects so that we might easily trace who wore what and when. These are material objects with which we are all familiar, that form part of the collective memory. Beyond the glittering occasion, however, they become harder to track. There might be a detailed visual record about the generational wearing of a jewel but less information about its creation, its maintenance, its life beyond the royal body. Similarly, the pedigree of royal jewellers is well established, names like Garrard and Cartier conjuring visions of opulence, but to find those men and women chiselling, filing and setting in the workshops behind the name is, for the most part, a challenge.

There is nothing relatable about the jewellery of a royal family. Where some illusion of common ground might be found in other sartorial choices from coats to shoes to gloves to hats, diamonds, pearls, emeralds and rubies set into tiaras and necklaces are beyond the imagining of all but the wealthiest. It was an issue of which Queen Elizabeth II was keenly aware, especially during the post-war world of the 1950s. In her analysis of the royal jewels, Suzy Menkes wrote: 'Jewels are so flamboyant a sign of opulence that the Queen has been anxious to damp down their glittering fire.'

Where once the precious stones encased in gold or platinum settings might have been admired uncritically, their origins are often rooted in troubling colonial contexts, with forced labour and the cruelty of empire casting a long shadow beyond the faceted sparkles. They have become synonymous with monarchy, visited by millions in the Tower of London, hidden during war and celebrated during moments of national unity. Beyond their public brilliance, who are the keepers, the designers, the menders and the preservers of these uniquely complicated gems?

Unravelling the origins of just two of the multitude of precious gems in the Royal Collection reveals their complexity beyond the satin-lined cases in which they now rest. In 1850, Queen Victoria was presented with what was then the world's largest diamond, one whose journey could be traced back almost a millennium to its first recorded ownership in 1112. Discovered in a mine in Hyderabad in India, it would become one of the treasures of the Mogul emperors, passing through generations of hands, won and lost in conflict and the subject of myth and mystery. It was named the Koh-i-noor, the mountain of light, a peerless stone which bore legends of bad luck. Leslie Field wrote of its reputation,

All That Glisters . . .

that 'as it was passed from man to man its history became a saga of murder and bloodshed'. It became associated with dynastic conflict, carving a violent path through history. By the 1830s it had passed into the hands of Maharaja Ranjit Singh in exchange for his protection of its former owner Shuja Shah and from here its ultimate connection with the British Empire would be forged. After the second Sikh War of 1849, the British annexed the Punjab, part of their inexorable expansionist ambitions, and in the peace treaty that followed, Maharaja Duleep Singh, the eleven-year-old son of Ranjit Singh, relinquished his rule of the region. One of the clauses in the treaty specifically referenced the great diamond, stating: 'The gem called Koh-I-Noor shall be surrendered by the Maharajah of Lahore to the Queen of England.' Duleep Singh himself travelled to England and lived as a popular member of high society, favoured by the very Queen whose empire had driven him from his home. Whilst Victoria announced that the diamond was not to be treated as a personal gift but rather one which would belong to the Crown, to be worn by subsequent monarchs, its ownership was disputed. A relative of Duleep Singh referred to the Queen as 'Mrs Fagin', referencing the popular story of Charles Dickens's Oliver Twist and the unscrupulous thievery of Fagin and his gang. Protest came to naught, however, and today the diamond remains on public display, one of the most famous gems at the heart of the Crown Jewels, encased in the platinum clasp of a diamond-encrusted crown.

Four years after the death of Queen Victoria, the Koh-i-noor would lose its title of the largest diamond in the world to another corner of the empire and the mines of South Africa, remote locations that employed over 130,000 labourers in appalling conditions. In January 1905, legend has it that the bright winter sunset shone upon a stone caught in the wall of one of the mines. It weighed an unprecedented one and a half pounds and remains to this day the largest diamond ever discovered. Named after the owner of the mine, Thomas Cullinan, the stone was immediately offered to King Edward VII as a display of loyalty by the Transvaal people, the legacy of the Boer Wars looming large in the political landscape. Unusable in its raw state, the stone was sent to the most renowned diamond cutters in the world, the Dutch firm of Asscher's in Amsterdam. They studied the lines of the stone for three months, deliberating where best it might be cut. It took craftsmen four days to forge a groove in the diamond to facilitate the blow of the cleaving knife, a blade that was eventually wielded by Mr J. Asscher himself. The moment was captured in a photograph, Joseph Asscher standing at his specially made clamp, a white apron tied about his neck and his shirtsleeves rolled back, cleaving knife held aloft as he prepared to strike. The first blow broke the blade and it was only at the second attempt that the stone was successfully split, after which Mr Asscher was reported to have fainted. Their work was nowhere near complete, however. 'Over the next eight months, three men worked for 14 hours a day to cut and polish nine large stones from the original diamond.' In the years that followed, and through a series of diplomatic gifts from South African governments to the British monarchy, all of the almost one hundred fragments from the original Cullinan stone would find their way into the Royal Collection where they are now variously mounted in the state regalia, necklaces and tiaras, worn by successive kings and queens for the last century, far from the bleakness of forced labour and colonial mistreatment. There is, perhaps, a greater willingness in the twenty-first century to acknowledge these marginalised histories and to examine such objects with greater criticality as they sparkle in the Tower of London, the material expression of empire and acquisitiveness.

Once the innumerable jewels had passed into the hands of the Crown, their function as pieces of jewellery, to be remodelled and maintained, fell under the responsibility of a variety of high-profile goldsmiths and royal household employees. These were the men and women whose job it was to design, care for and keep secure these priceless objects that would variously emerge to adorn the royal body before once again disappearing into their cases and into the vaults. The earliest firm to hold such a position under Queen Victoria was Rundell, Bridge & Rundell.

The company had been founded in 1787 by goldsmiths Phillip Rundell and John Bridge, and within a decade they had been appointed as one of the goldsmiths to King George III. By 1804, they were Principal Goldsmith to the monarch, their headquarters located at 32 Ludgate Hill. The firm was responsible for the design and setting of the diamond diadem that would grace the head of the young Queen Victoria for her first postage stamp in 1840 and of Queen Elizabeth II likewise on all the stamps of her long reign until 2022. After the firm was dissolved in 1843, one of its long-standing former employees decided to write its history, in what is believed to be one of the earliest known business histories. George Fox was born in 1779 and by 1806 he was working for Rundell & Bridge in their London workshop. Whilst the business prospered, the salesrooms being enlarged to exhibit a set of plate ordered by the Prince of Wales, Fox was able to offer a snapshot of his work. He proved less than complimentary about his employers. Mr Rundell, Fox wrote, 'was naturally of a violent disposition, very sly and cunning and suspicious'. He was known to be an incredibly hard worker and also had a canny eye for good jewels, often purchasing from French refugees in desperate need of money before selling for a profit to the aristocrats of England. Luckily his business partner, Mr Bridge, was a 'complete courtier' according to George Fox, better able to flatter wealthy clients than the more curmudgeonly Rundell.

In 1818, Richard Rush, the American ambassador, paid a visit to Rundell & Bridge and described it in his published memoir: 'Outside it is plain, you might pass by without noticing it, but on entering the articles of silver were piled in heaps, even on the floor.' Fox, having been promoted to superintendent of the workroom, was unimpressed at his employer's general appearance, wary of the impression it might make on their wealthy clientele. He wrote in his memoir: 'Mr Rundell was generally a great sloven himself and might mostly be seen in his shop til after the middle of the day with his shoes down at heel, the knees of his breeches unbuttoned, his hands and face unwashed and his hair matted with Pomatum.' In spite of this rather unsavoury description, reminiscent of a character from Dickens, Fox admired Rundell's attention to detail. He wrote that the craftsmen in his workshops always had all of the materials they needed, an important aspect that was overlooked after Philip Rundell retired in 1823. George Fox stayed in post until the firm's closure when he was disappointed to receive only three months' wages after almost thirty-seven years of service. Rundell retired a millionaire.

The loss of the monarch's principal jeweller meant that Queen Victoria had to appoint another firm in its place. The warrant was eventually awarded to R. & S. Garrard & Co. and for the first time the formal post of Crown Jeweller to the monarch was established, encompassing not only the sourcing of new pieces, but the maintenance of its existing collection as well. The complexity of such a role, working to maintain the condition of the jewels as well as ensure their safety, meant liaising with members of the royal household and the Tower of London's Yeomen of the Guard when various of the Crown Jewels were required to be moved. In 1847 a complaint was lodged with the Lord Chamberlain's Department by Walter Lunn, Gentleman Porter of the Tower of London and the man responsible for accompanying jewellery from the Tower to either the Crown Jeweller or a royal residence. He reported that the department 'was in the habit of sending an ordinary one-horse hackney cab to collect the crown and, as there were three persons travelling with it, he was forced to sit on top with the driver' – from where he was unable to see any would-be thieves. Noting his concern, the Lord Chamberlain ensured that future trips would be undertaken in a larger cab.

Garrard was responsible for the setting and construction of many notable pieces, their workshops captured in short snippets of newsreel

All That Glisters . . .

footage. Spanning less than a minute, an excerpt from 1937 focuses on unnamed workers, men and women in crisp white coats, working intently on a host of crowns, coronets and jewelled settings for the coronation of King George VI. There is no sound to this particular reel of footage and so they work silently, the noises of their trade lost to the modern viewer, but the dexterity of their craft captured in precious seconds. So must a whole host of other Garrard's craftsmen have worked in the decades preceding this newsreel, leaning over their workbenches, a jewel held in the jaws of a wooden clamp to be filed or soldered and set into place.

Garrard were not solely responsible for the making of royal jewellery at this time, however. For many of the most elaborate pieces, they commissioned another firm, that of E. Wolfe & Co., known in the trade as 'the Tiara Makers', to design and construct a range of glittering pieces including Queen Alexandra's coronation crown in 1902, the Cambridge Lover's Knot tiara which would become a favourite of Diana, Princess of Wales, and the Imperial Crown of India for the 1911 Delhi Durbar. The company was founded by Johann Jacob Wolff in 1850, working from a property in Bedford Square. He gathered a team of highly respected designers and makers, building a reputation for the finest craftsmanship. Partnered with his nephew Ernest, Wolff was soon employing over fifty people, and commissions from other establishments began to roll in. The company archive reveals the extent of their artistry in the survival of the exquisitely drawn designs. Thick brown paper serves as the backdrop to the drawings, fine pencilled lines capturing every detail of every gem. The handwritten notes in curling copperplate record measurements and construction notes in a perfect template for the eventual maker.

As the decades marched on, so did taste in jewellery and Wolff's designs reflected these shifts, echoing the romantic swirls of art nouveau followed by the geometry of art deco. It was into this transitionary period that two young men would find themselves a new calling in the aftermath of war. William Cornelius was born in Kentish Town, London, in 1893, eldest child to his father, Reuben, who was a farrier and his mother, Julia. By the age of seventeen, William still lived at home and contributed to the family income through his work as a clerk at a local print shop. Within another three years he had joined the army, signing his papers as a young Rifleman in the London Regiment, and in 1914 crossed the Channel to fight. His service record, like countless thousands of others, describes the dimensions of the man being sent to war. William was five feet six and a half inches tall with a thirty-five-inch chest. Not very tall, not very broad. His physical development was described as 'fair', an unconvincing word for a young man about to enter the most violent of arenas. As a mother of young men myself, I try and imagine Julia bidding farewell to her boy, this young clerk who still lived at home and ate dinner with his family every night. Within months, William was in the thick of the action. He fought at the Battle of Mons before sustaining a gunshot wound to his knee on 18 April 1915, an injury that brought him home.

Another soldier, another William, this time a William Davies, who at the age of fifteen was already describing himself as a jewellery designer. It is likely that he worked for his father's business; William senior is described as a jewellery manufacturer on the 1911 census. The household included two French boarders, both described as diamond mounters, and so from his childhood young William was surrounded by the sparkle of the trade. He too was injured during the war. In search of work following demobilisation, both of the Williams found themselves at E. Wolff & Co. In the mid-1920s the two young men travelled to Paris to study jewellery design. One of the company legends has it that whilst there, they dined out with a fellow designer and such was the inspiration that the restaurant tablecloth was covered in their ideas for new pieces. In 1932, the last remaining Wolff, Monty, was ready to sell the business. The two Williams, Cornelius and Davies, secured loans and bought the firm that had contributed to their rehabilitation in those early post-war years, bringing other family members on to the payroll, embarking on new challenges in design along the way. The advent of war once again saw E. Wolff & Co. turn over their manufacturing to support the war effort, tools of an entirely different nature filling their workshops. William's son Alan recalled: 'One of the floors was filled with heavy machinery – grinders, lathes and milling machines. Gauges and obscure parts of even more obscure weapons in copper, steel and sometimes silver, were made by day and by night shifts.' Despite a near miss during one of the then frequent air raids, the firm survived, its precious drawings remaining intact and royal commissions continuing.

Besides the designing and manufacture of jewellery for the monarch, one of the other roles performed by the Crown Jeweller has traditionally been that of maintenance, i.e. cleaning and repair. In 1901, on the death of Queen Victoria, her then Crown Jeweller at Garrard made a complete inventory of the royal jewels, handwritten in a leather-bound volume which was kept tucked away in the company office. Within the pages of this volume, successive crown jewellers would keep a running written commentary of the additions and alterations of the various pieces: which were broken up and fashioned into something new, which needed replacing and updating. It was the biography of a collection, charting the evolution of its contents which could be traced back through the decades.

One of those pieces was the George III fringe tiara, originally made in 1830 in a sunburst of graduating diamonds George III had owned, that could be worn either as a necklace or wired on to the frame of a tiara. Queen Victoria wore it in Winterhalter's 1851 portrait *The First of May*, holding her son Prince Arthur in her arms, a vision of both mother and queen. Queen Mary was photographed wearing the tiara in 1910. Elizabeth the Queen Mother wore it to a coronation ball in 1937 and her granddaughter Princess Anne wore it for her wedding to Captain Mark Phillips in 1973. It was on the morning of Thursday 20 November 1947, however, that the tiara almost shredded the nerves of the then Crown Jeweller, Cecil Mann. Princess Elizabeth was dressing for her wedding to Philip Mountbatten in a second-floor room of Buckingham Palace. As the crowds gathered, so various makers hovered nearby in case of last-minute adjustments. As the hairdresser placed the fringe tiara on Princess Elizabeth's carefully waved hair, the jewelled headpiece collapsed. According to the Queen herself who recalled the event, it was the catch of the original necklace that had given way: 'And I didn't know it was a necklace, you see . . . I thought I'd broken it . . . We stuck it all together again, but I was rather alarmed.' This was the royal 'we' which in this case meant Cecil Mann, haring across London under police escort to his workshop where he repaired the clasp and reinforced the tiara before returning it to the royal bride.

Six years later, alterations of another kind took place, with the preparations for Queen Elizabeth's coronation. The Imperial State Crown needed to be remodelled to fit the young woman whose reign would start so much earlier than she would have imagined. Press interest in the preparations, including the Crown Jewels, led to a whole host of articles about the work being undertaken. One of those publications included a close-up photograph of the crown under construction, an earnest-looking jeweller peering at its skeleton structure. The jeweller was Harold Goodship, foreman diamond mounter to the Goldsmiths' & Silversmiths' Company, who was tasked with creating the new structure for this traditional piece. Harold had been born in Notting Hill in 1908 and grew up in three rooms at 63 Portland Road. When Harold was a child his father worked as a dressmaker's packer, enveloping Edwardian frocks and tailor-made costumes in tissue for delivery around London. Harold trained as a jeweller and by 1939 was describing himself as a diamond mounter, married now to Nellie and still living with his parents. A whisper of war presents itself in the 1939 register, his father, Cuthbert, now approaching sixty, working as a salesman but also described as a stretcher bearer for the Wandsworth area that had become their home.

I wonder how the Goodships fared during the war? They lived in 17 Plymouth House on the East Hill estate, a building that is coloured in black on the London County Council bomb-damage maps that were created to chart the impact of the Luftwaffe's air raids. On the colour key, black meant total destruction. Plymouth House was hit in April 1941, contemporary photographs showing the gaping expanse of a building destroyed, wallpapered rooms and cosy fireplaces exposed to the world. One young resident recalled the experience of the Wandsworth raids: 'The air raids never seemed to stop. Our favourite game in the morning after a raid was to go out to the yard still in our pyjamas and see who found the biggest piece of shrapnel!' Where were Harold and his family during those destructive nights in April? What stories did he tell of that

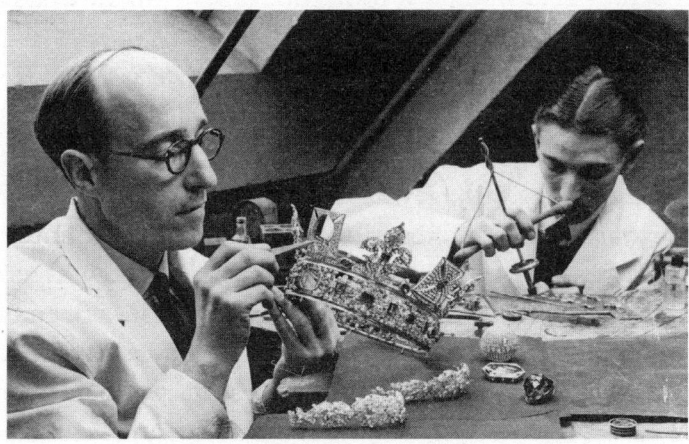

Harold Goodship inspecting the Imperial Crown, 1952.

period of his life, experiences that were universal to the London population? Within a decade, the reconstruction of Wandsworth was complete and Harold was mounting diamonds to one of the most famous objects in the world.

War would shape the fortunes of another maker whose artisanship would impact the life of Elizabeth, Princess and later Queen. When Elizabeth and Philip announced their engagement in July 1947, the engagement ring sported by the Princess had been the subject of detailed plans. Philip had inherited a diamond-studded tiara from his mother, Princess Andrew of Greece, and he chose stones from this headpiece to be made into a new ring. He commissioned the firm of Philip Antrobus to make the new piece on the advice of his uncle, Earl Mountbatten, a commission that landed with two of the company's most skilled craftsmen, diamond mounter George Taubl and setter Harry Marchant. George Taubl was born on 14 June 1910, son of George Wendeline, an Austrian, and Lily, who was from Croydon in Surrey. George Senior spent the entirety of his working life in London as a waiter and had been working consistently for over twenty years when war broke out in 1939. His Austrian heritage would raise questions for the authorities, however, in spite of his long residence in the country. Both he and Lily, who was described as Austrian by marriage, had to submit to investigations regarding their liberty as a male and female 'enemy alien'. As more and more German-speaking civilians were interned around the UK, so George and Lily must have had an anxious wait to learn of the outcome. Records show that they met the requirements for exemption from internment although their names remained on file. Their son George was, by this time, married and had undergone an apprenticeship to become a diamond mounter. His nimble fingers were put to an entirely different use in 1939 and during the war he worked as an aircraft fitter as preparations for aerial combat gathered pace. I wonder if he waited anxiously for news of his parents as he worked on the aircraft that would shortly take to the skies, distracted at the thought of their possible detention whilst his hands were busy with tasks that differed so much from his usual occupation? At the war's end, he returned to the artisanship for which he had been trained and along with Harry, the setter, he helped to complete the smooth diamond ring, set in platinum, that would grace the Queen's finger for the next seven decades.

Today the role of Crown Jeweller resides with a different company. Since 2012 the firm of Mappin & Webb has served in the official capacity as carer of the royal jewels, the head of their workshop, Mark Appleby, the official holder of the title. Following the death of Queen Elizabeth II in 2022, it seems likely that there will be fewer opportunities to study the expansive and sparkling collection, not least because of pressures in a twenty-first-century landscape for the royal family to appear more relevant to a population recovering from an economic crash, austerity policies and a global pandemic. The days of colonial acquisitions are long gone, although the gems themselves cast long shadows. Beyond the moral dilemmas of the Crown Jewels, however, are the industries that have continued, heritage companies who have trained generations of young jewellers to mount and set priceless stones. Men and women whose deft fingers and keen eyes can repair and maintain these historic objects. People who have lived ordinary lives at the very same time as working their magic on extraordinary jewels.

CHAPTER 5

Coats of Many Colours
Of Norwich Shawls and Hardy Amies's Tailor-mades

One of my earliest memories is of waving at the Queen. I don't know if it is a real memory, or one constructed from a thousand similar televised experiences of Queen Elizabeth touring around Britain, planting a tree or opening a hospital, snipping ribbons or pulling a silky tassel attached to a little velvet curtain to reveal an inscribed plaque. And yet I have this snapshot tucked away amongst my childhood recollections, of sitting on my dad's shoulders and watching a black car process past the crowd, a pale-clad Queen sitting inside with a matching hat. Research tells me that the Queen visited our nearest town, Newton Abbot in Devon, in 1980. I would have been six years old. For so many people this is their real-life encounter with a royal family otherwise distant and only accessible on screen. These public, civic duties are the bedrock of the modern British monarchy and so we have very often witnessed queens in their coats. Unlike the pomp of more formal occasions, the outer garments adopted by royal women for public engagements are recognisably like our own. More expensive certainly. Far more plentiful of course. Accompanied by matching accessories perhaps. Yet they are familiar wardrobe staples that soften the differences between Queen and country.

Outerwear has always served a specific purpose in royal wardrobes, partly to support textile industries, to protect against inclement weather and to be visible to the gathered crowds. The Queen famously stated: 'I have to be seen to be believed', an adage to which she subscribed for many decades with her coats and hats of many colours. Behind each of these public garments, however, are the lives of the makers – the weavers of shawls, the tailors of woollen cloth, the silk braid makers and the fitters who flitted about the royal body. As the clothing beneath changed in silhouette, so the outer layer was shaped to accommodate it, the shawl shrinking to a mantle, expanding to a cape and finally narrowing to a form-fitting overcoat. Where these objects survive, the lives behind their creation remain opaque, so who were these weavers, tailors and braid makers?

On 14 June 1851, Queen Victoria recorded an account of her visit to the Great Exhibition in her diary. From amongst the many hundreds of displays and manufacturers, she noted: 'Went first through one or two of the French courts and then upstairs to examine in detail the Norwich shawls, of the lightest Cashmir material, also of silk with beautiful designs.' Shawls formed an essential component of the mid-nineteenth-century wardrobe, growing ever larger as the circumference of the skirts beneath widened. Norwich already had a decades-long industry devoted to the making of fine shawls by the time Queen Victoria visited the Great Exhibition. The *Norwich Mercury* reported in 1804: 'Norwich manufactured shawls are in such high repute that one manufacturer in the city has received an order for not less than 42,000. Such an order must necessarily give employment to a great number of men, women and children.' Shawl making did indeed employ many thousands in the city. A report of 1839 recorded more than 4,000 hand looms working in and around Norwich, most of which were operated from the homes of the skilled journeymen weavers themselves. It was highly skilled and time-consuming work. Local newspaper reports sought out the most respected weavers in the months leading up to the Great Exhibition in order to ask them about the process of weaving the great squares of fashionable fabric. One of the most respected of these, although sadly unnamed, spoke of the five weeks it took to prepare his loom for a shawl pattern. If the pattern 'took well' he might then spend more than half of the year producing shawls of that specific design, weaving one shawl per week for which he was paid twenty-four shillings and tenpence. The money was not all his own, however. From his wages he had to cover all of his expenses, which included the paying of a 'winder' at two shillings and sixpence and a 'drawboy' working on the loom to lift the threads for a further six shillings. Working long hours required candles, 'three a night' he explained, at a cost of fourpence each. The weaver was left with eleven shillings and fourpence for his long week amid the hurtling of shuttles and thread-by-thread emergence of the beautiful and complex pattern.

There was a symbiosis to the work of shawl making between master and weaver. The cottage-based workforce would take their finished shawls to the factory, hand delivering the valuable squares before collecting their wages and the yarn for the next piece of work. One master weaver was known to carry the great beam of his loom to St Clements Alley in Norwich where the finished shawl would be cut from its web of thread. This weaver was William Armes, one of the few named artisans whose work survives today. A six-foot-square swirl of fine wool in the familiar pine pattern, alternating bands of red and green, forming a fringed backdrop to the expansive design, forms part of the collection of the Norwich Museums. William was a native of Norwich, born in 1821 as the shawl industry was beginning to make its mark on the city. On Christmas Day 1851, he married Elizabeth Fish, daughter of another weaver, James.

It was so often the case that children followed their parents into a trade, generations of the same family incrementally acquiring the skills to work the draw looms that formed the centrepiece to many a living space. William and Elizabeth moved to Priory Yard, the same address as her parents and younger siblings. There were hundreds of such yards in Norwich. Entered via a narrow passageway from the street, the yards were usually built around a central space, shared pan toilets and a communal water hand pump providing the sum of their sanitary facilities. The yards were often poorly ventilated and dark, multiple households crowding the small, cobbled square. A reporter from the *Norwich Mercury* visited one of the yards in the 1890s and offered a vivid description of the experience: 'The stranger gropes his way up one of these passages, and his olfactory nerves soon let him know he has entered upon a new land – a land of stinking slops and refuse of all kinds.' Echoing across the cobbles of Priory Yard then, was the repetitious rattle of looms, those of William and Elizabeth Armes, of James Fish and others, filling the enclosed space with their racket and producing shawls fit for a queen.

In 1855, Queen Victoria purchased two such shawls from one of the leading Norwich manufacturers, Clabburn Sons & Crisp, the same firm presenting the newly married Alexandra, Princess of Wales, with a pair in the colours of her Danish family in 1863. One weaver who created shawls for Clabburn has been immortalised in sepia, a rare photograph that connects the elusive weaver to the manufacturer who employed him and the shawls that he wove. Much like William and Elizabeth Fish, James Churchyard had been born into a weaving family, his father, Isaac, mother, Julia, and three of his siblings all described as weavers on the 1851 census. Ten years later James had married Susannah and like William Armes, they too lived in a yard, Rose Yard, named for the nearby public house. A 1945 line drawing of Rose Yard captures the two- and three-storey buildings, the long narrow windows that would have cast what little daylight there was into a room dominated by the loom visible in the illustration. Here James worked with Susannah as his drawer, assisting in the movement of warp and weft and spinning into life the dizzying pattern of softest, finest wool. By the turn of the century, James was still living in Rose Yard. Susannah had died in 1881 and he lived alone. Despite the often poor living conditions, community spirit was strong. A former resident of Rose Yard, recalling her experiences before the post-war slum clearances of the city, described a collaborative life: 'Everybody looked out for each other, what little people had, they were willing to share with each other.' James, as a decades-long resident of the yard, would, I hope, have been the recipient of the neighbourliness prompted by living at such close quarters. He continued to work until the end of his life in 1913. The black-and-white photograph catches James at his loom, peering around the gathered vertical web of threads descending towards the surface of the cloth. He stares intently at the camera, black cap perched above his ears, his white beard just brushing the dark linen of his smock. Fourteen of James's

James Churchyard, Norwich silk shawl weaver, *c.* 1910.

shawls have survived, precious family heirlooms that memorialise this unique industry. Woven in Rose Yard, perhaps with Susannah at his side, these wondrous garments rose from James Churchyard's loom to grace the figures of royalty.

Names of makers are rare and photographs rarer still. The vast majority of those who contributed in some way to the outerwear garments chosen by royal women have remained nameless thanks to the very nature of their work. Cocooned in conservation conditions in an American museum lies an 1870s dolman. A dolman was a short cape-style garment, briefly fashionable during the bustle era of women's fashions, and shaped to fit over the shelf of the skirt. This dolman bears the label of a French maker, Dieulafait & E. Bouclier, and it was purchased by the then Princess of Wales, Alexandra. The cream wool foundation of the cape is almost entirely obscured by a particular decoration, scrolls and curlicues of applied braid in a convoluted design of pale gold and brown. This was the work of the trimmings makers. Their skill is in evidence across countless surviving garments in museums all over the world.

The trade, known by the French term of passementerie, had become ever more popular in the second half of the nineteenth century as clothing embraced new complexities made possible by the invention of the sewing machine. Tassels, cords, braids and fringe in all manner of styles and colourways were applied to bodices, skirts and jackets, an aesthetic mirrored in the upholstered interiors to which the passementerie workers also contributed. It is a sad irony that whilst so many of their creative endeavours remain, the makers themselves are almost entirely invisible. Passementerie was, for centuries, a sumptuous expression of wealth, still visible in the swags and furnishings of grand residences. Furniture historian Annabel Westman, author of one of the few books on the subject, writes: 'The stupendous sums spent on such ornaments can come as a shock to those unaware of their importance as a strategic status symbol over the centuries.' The 1861 edition of the *Post Office London Directory* reveals upwards of 100 passementerie makers in London and whilst many focused on the furniture trade, two thirds of them were related to ornaments of dress. Their skills fell into three main categories: the spinning and winding of cord or rope; the weaving of fringes and braids; and the turning of wooden moulds over which silk floss would be wound. It is in this diversity of skill and the multiplicity of design that the people themselves are lost.

The difficult vocabulary of their labour has prevented subsequent explorations of their lives, and the piecework nature of the looped silks and lengths of braid has meant that countless men and women toiling in their small lodgings in London's East End or along Tottenham Court Road are lost to us. The census can lift a corner of the veil, however. Through those carefully inked columns, doorways open and names spill forth. Names like Ethel Oatham who in 1911 lived at 1 Sedgewick Road with her parents and four siblings. Her father, William, was a paper hanger and decorator, his son working alongside him as he painted

Detail of a jacket by Dieulafait & E. Bouclier, late 1860s.

houses and pasted wallpaper. Ethel, aged seventeen, worked with her sister Delia on ladies' dress trimmings for a local manufacturer. It is a tantalising description in that it gives so little away. Did Ethel twist and loop silken cords or weave the dizzying varieties of braid? Perhaps she sat with her older sister and constructed the bands of fringe ready to be stitched to the hem of a fine gown. Their wage would have made an important contribution to the household income and just maybe every so often Ethel was able to purchase a yard or two of the very trim that she made in order to decorate her own garments.

The same year, in another part of East London, Louisa Marriott was living in two rooms on Gotha Street with her husband, Samuel, who was a male nurse in a nearby workhouse. Louisa and Samuel had been married for five years, living at their South Hackney address with their four-year-old son, Victor. The starkly completed column asking how many children have been born alive to the respondents shows the number 2. 'Children who have died. 1.' The careful recording of facts and figures briefly illuminates grief and loss whilst at the same time Louisa was working as a 'dress trimmings maker'. Unlike Ethel and Delia, she was working from home, somehow managing to fulfil her piecework at the same time as watching young Victor in the two rooms that they occupied. Did she sit in that confined space knotting silk fringe and mourn her lost child? Wound on to notched cards or large reels, the fashionable fripperies would be sent either to a haberdasher or direct to a dressmaker to be applied by other hands. Industrialisation and changes in taste saw the industry reduce dramatically so that by the early twentieth century only those making passementerie for interior furnishings remained.

Until very recently there were six passementerie makers in the UK, all devoted to furnishings, and one alone, Brian Turner, holding the Royal Warrant. I spoke to Brian at a pivotal point in his career, the very day that he was closing his doors for the last time. Brian's grandfather had acquired the business in 1889, taking on the complex trimmings work from a French maker. He described to me the 131-foot-long rope walk in his premises where silk floss would be twisted into shining multicoloured cords on the same hand-operated machines that had turned for over a century. In the background I could hear the sounds of the workshop being dismantled. There was nobody to take on this unique business. Brian had been making trimmings for the royal family for decades, recalling the vibrant colours that the Queen had chosen for her private sitting room in the mid-1980s. His exquisite work gained him the Royal Warrant but this will now lapse without a successor. 'I'm seventy-one this year and my landlord decided he wanted a fifty per cent increase in rent,' Brian explained above the noise of the shed. 'I certainly can't buy the yarn to make trimmings from for the price of the finished product coming from overseas.' As we spoke, I scrolled through the kaleidoscope of colour on his website, picturing the gimp braids, cords, rosettes and tassels that had been his stock in trade for so long. He was selling the remnants of his work and so I purchased some antique wooden reels still wound with magenta silk as a souvenir of his craftsmanship. They sit on my desk as I write and I imagine all of those workers before him whose fingers would have deftly turned this silk into countless lengths of braid.

Connections such as this that are made through dress can be tenuous but persistent, as I have found over my years spent in museums and archives, studying garments and poring over documents. One of my earliest experiences in a dress collection takes me to 1993 and the first time that I worked as a volunteer. Aged nineteen, I had no sense of how I might forge a career in such a niche area of historical research. All I knew was that the clothes worn by people in the past held a unique fascination for me, these shells of their former human inhabitants offering tantalising glimpses of lives past. I learned so much there. Once a week I would drive my old Mini up to the staff car park of Killerton House, sign myself in and walk past the modern offices at the back of the property, through a seemingly magical doorway into the public face of the house. To be there when it was closed felt like stepping into another time and for those precious few hours each week I was allowed to help with the care of this enormous collection of historic dress and, once a year, the mounting of its exhibition. In dimly lit rooms, boxes filled with acid-free tissue would spill their secrets as the display took shape. Mannequins would take on the silhouettes of another age, bodices and skirts carefully lifted on to the dress form to live fleetingly once more. Alongside me were two other older volunteers, Margaret and Sheila. They had been coming to Killerton for years, both hugely keen and knowledgeable women who maintained an interest in the world of fashions past. Margaret especially was the cheeriest of companions. A small and stocky figure, short straight hair cut into an uncompromising iron-grey pageboy shape, her stories were endlessly entertaining.

Years later, I was sitting in a curved, book-lined room in the Royal Archive examining the wardrobe accounts of Queen Alexandra, noting the names of the many suppliers who had contributed to her complicated and varied wardrobe and one took me straight back to Margaret and the tales of her youth. In the later years of her life, Queen Alexandra had ordered from the London department store of Marshall & Snelgrove as a convenient means of acquiring multiple items which included outerwear. I was first introduced to the name when Margaret regaled us with the stories of her employment there in the late 1940s, and sitting on the leather-cushioned chair, gazing out from the narrow window of the round tower in Windsor Castle, I was struck by those ephemeral threads that follow us through life. I couldn't have recalled the details of her memories more than ten years later, but luckily she had published her reminiscences in a journal. Margaret was just one of thousands of young shopgirls selling and packing garments in the department stores of the UK, thousands of lives long forgotten. Her short memoir is an irreverent, often hilarious account. Of the formidable buyer heading up their department she wrote: 'Miss T was a hard drinking woman who could – and frequently did – swear like a trooper.'

Margaret was only two years out of school when she left the security of her home in the south-west of England for her new job as a junior at the London department store, inexperienced but desperate to enter the world of fashion. 'I was to live at Debenham's Ladies' Club, a tall terraced house in Bulstrode Street.' Ongoing rationing and austerity measures meant that it was a meagre place yet one that still cost her thirty shillings a week out of her forty-five-shilling wage packet. Her role included the dressing of mannequins in the latest model gowns, one that must have echoed down the decades as she clothed the static figures at Killerton House. She was also responsible for parcelling up the purchases of the wealthy clients, filling the black flower-patterned boxes from a small room that overlooked the umbrella, haberdashery and lace departments. 'I really enjoyed tucking tissue paper carefully between the folds of skirts, turning the sleeves neatly back and folding the bodice to the top with a twist of tissue for padding to give it a realistic appearance when the purchaser opened the box.' Her descriptions lay bare the often hidden world of these women behind the glossy shop floor, short vignettes of otherwise anonymous lives. She recalls with fondness the under buyer 'Mintie' who acted as intermediary in the frequent squabbles that broke out, and 'Miss Beard, our chief fitter, a chirpy little Londoner who had her own domain upstairs in the labyrinth of steamy workrooms on the top floor of the building'. Her tenure at Marshall & Snelgrove began over a quarter of a century after the death of Queen Alexandra but it remained a popular store, trading until its absorption by Debenhams in 1972. In 1999, during the course of my MA in the history of textiles and dress, I contacted Margaret to ask if I might write an essay about her collection and so I visited her bungalow in East Devon where she took me on a tour of the rails and boxes that filled her home, an eclectic mix of historic garments and accessories amassed over a lifetime. So it was that

Dressing the Queen

Queen Alexandra, Margaret Trump, Marshall & Snelgrove and myself were united momentarily and became a part of my own story.

Coats of many colours have become a more prominent feature of the royal wardrobe in the twentieth and twenty-first centuries with the concept of 'the walkabout'. During a royal tour of New Zealand and Australia in 1970, Queen Elizabeth II had decided that to simply cruise past the gathered crowds in a car did not do justice to the efforts of well-wishers and so she asked to walk along the street. In a white-trimmed lemon wool coat designed by Norman Hartnell, she stepped out of her car to greet people lining the route and so a tradition was born.

Whilst the Queen had long awarded patronage for many of her most glamorous garments to Norman Hartnell, the tailoring prowess of another London designer had caught her eye. Hardy Amies had spent a lifetime around fashion. His mother worked for the well-known turn-of-the-century fashion house Miss Gray, and Hardy spent happy hours in the workroom there amongst the fabrics and threads of its seamstresses. By the late 1940s he was making under his own name, operating from premises on Savile Row. In 1950 he received a visit that would change the course of his career. His loyal fitter Betty Reeves was on hand when Princesses Elizabeth and Margaret came calling: 'The collection was shown privately in my office, with only Betty and myself present from the Savile Row staff.' Following their visit, Amies received his first royal commission for the Princess's upcoming Canadian tour – two overcoats, two day dresses and two evening dresses. 'I was particularly known for my tailoring; so there was no trouble with the coats. I already had the idea that royalty should be dressed like royalty, so I used rich materials.' Skilled though he was in his designs, his memoir is threaded through with acknowledgements to the team that worked alongside him. As he strove to build his business he wrote: 'I began to realise how little power a designer has to keep his customers without the fitters and tailors to whom his clientele is accustomed.' These fitters and tailors appear often in his recollections but they can be frustratingly absent in other records. The formality of addressing tailors by their first name generates a trio of shadowy figures in the shape of loyal Mr Ernest, Mr Leonard and Mr Michael, all of whom worked for Amies for many years, overseeing the cutting of the Queen's coats.

The women who worked as vendeuse and fitter for Amies were drawn in more detail. During the war his chief confidante and head saleswoman was Miss Campbell, or Cammie, as he usually called her. Cammie was in her seventies and was often at war with the tailors and fitters but her knowledge was invaluable. 'In the true court dressmaker tradition, she knew the lineage of anybody who was anybody,' he wrote, along with a sharp vignette: 'Usually dressed in black, with very high heeled shoes, I have never seen her with anything other than four rows of pearls and a large imitation cabochon emerald ring.' He gives the role of vendeuse credit for the clientele who would find their way to his door, including the Queen.

The fitter occupied a unique place in the world of bespoke dress. Already skilled as a dressmaker, the fitter would then ensure that a garment was perfectly proportioned for the customer. One of his longest-serving fitters was Maud Beard. She had started her career in the same workroom as Amies's mother at Miss Gray's but during the war had left the fashion world to oversee the making of parachutes. When Hardy Amies had started out on his own he asked Maud to work for him: 'Although she had known me since I was two, I knew very little of her work, but no sooner had she started with us than we saw what a genius she had for the handling of all fabrics.' A smartly tailored Maud features in Amies's images, standing next to the designer and tweaking the cloth on a mannequin, a line of young seamstresses seated in front of them. Maud was born in Lambeth in 1902, following her older sister Mabel into dressmaking to supplement her father, Alfred's, house-painting income. By the age of fourteen she was apprenticed to

Miss Fowler, a skirt fitter for Miss Gray, and so found herself within the orbit of young Hardy. Forty-five years later, she was photographed processing with Amies, another fitter Betty Reeves and the tailor Mr Leonard into the back of a large black car, accompanied by dress bags and sketches destined for Buckingham Palace. The fittings took on a certain pattern. They would arrive at the palace and be taken to a waiting room, next to the large fitting room that had been established by Queen Mary as suitable for the swishing of broad skirts. Amies would wait outside whilst the fitter attended to the Queen, glancing at his sketches and awaiting the verdict. 'Fittings are prepared in the workroom on stands, but it is impossible to judge the effect until it has been put on a body. So intent are we all on our work that there is very little time for chat. However, there is no strain during this silence; the atmosphere is relaxed and it is fair to say that we look forward to our visits.' Countless press photographs attest to the success of those fittings and his name became synonymous with sharply tailored coats and ensembles, a working relationship that endured for over three decades. They were cut by Mr Leonard and fitted by Maud Beard.

If Queen Elizabeth instituted the royal walkabout, Diana, Princess of Wales brought star status to her own version of it. Her lack of preparedness for the role she would occupy meant that she was often learning as she went, including the fashioning of her public self. It was Diana who brought the overcoat to new heights of popularity and she did so with the help of a young French designer, Catherine Walker. Walker had started her career in London making a range of children's clothes. Recently widowed, she had to forge a living to support her two young daughters and so she started the Chelsea Design Company. She employed women who were similarly in need of money and flexible working hours. 'Helen was pregnant when she answered our advertisement for a machinist in 1978, and shortly after that time she separated from her husband,' Walker recalled. Helen was able to take piecework home with her and work around the needs of her young child. Carmelita was a Portuguese machinist who stayed with Catherine for many years, and Susannah was married to an estate agent but wanted work of her own, answering the advertisement placed by Walker as she expanded her business. She called them her 'gifted part timers'.

In 1981, Walker had been commissioned to make a maternity blouse for the young Princess of Wales but assumed that would be the sum total of her contribution to a royal wardrobe, 'I was therefore astonished in the autumn of 1982 to receive a telephone call from her lady-in-waiting telling me that the Princess wanted me to suggest some designs for coats for her formal engagements.' Walker had never embarked on anything like a tailored coat before but nonetheless accepted, with some trepidation. Recognising her complete lack of skill, she began to scan the Yellow Pages in search of somebody who could help. 'I don't know if it was luck but after only two days I found a wonderful tailor on the third floor in South Molton Street. Anthony was totally eccentric and despite nearing retirement age he was completely unset in his ways which was just as well because I think he thought I was mad.' With Anthony's expertise and Walker's design flair, she developed what would become her signature style: 'Within a few weeks I had it: a long-line fitted coat with a defined shoulder in a traditional military style, a mix of French cut and English sentiment.' She employed a second tailor, George; he lived in Oxfordshire and so she rarely saw him, but they would meet at Junction 6 of the M40 and reverse their cars tailgate to tailgate in order to hand over the precious fabrics that would clothe the world's most famous woman. She talks of her 'petites mains' embellishers, her technicians and her cutters but, presumably for discretion's sake, they remain nameless in her memoir. A single photograph captures them, however. In May 1997, Diana invited Catherine and her team to Kensington Palace. Clad in snowy white coats, twelve of Catherine's various makers surround the Princess and Catherine herself. These were the makers behind the coats which, by the 1990s, had become a part of this most famous of wardrobes. By way of thanks for their hard work, Catherine wrote: 'A few days later each member of the staff received a framed and signed photograph as a memento from the Princess. Each parcel was carefully wrapped in navy blue paper and tied with a silk bow.'

During the final few years of Queen Elizabeth's life, her brilliantly hued coats and hats became one of the most memorable facets of her public appearances. Catherine, Princess of Wales, has followed suit and, perhaps by way of tribute to the mother-in-law she never knew, often chooses Catherine Walker coats for her daytime duties. These outer shells are both ordinary and exceptional not least because of the teams of makers who contributed to their creation. I doubt whether William Armes or James Churchyard ever gave much mind to the ultimate destinations of their shawls, preoccupied as they were with eking out a living in the yards of Norwich. Edith Oatham and Louisa Marriott were just two of the countless trimmings workers whose ephemeral fancies have survived where their life stories have not, and Brian Turner has turned off the lights to his passementerie workshop for the last time. Maud Beard retired from her job as fitter at Hardy Amies and I wonder if, during the later years of her life, she ever told anybody about those hours spent with the Queen fitting the tailored coats to her satisfaction. I am thankful that Margaret Trump told her story, recording that brief period of life where she parcelled up coats for customers at Marshall & Snelgrove. I shall always remember how our lives were briefly connected and that her tales live on.

CHAPTER 6

If You Want to Get Ahead . . .
From Straw Plaiters to Palace Milliners

On 23 March 1863, just thirteen days after their wedding, Edward and Alexandra, the Prince and Princess of Wales, ventured out for a walk around the London Zoological Gardens. Word had spread of their public outing and the diarist William Hardman took a stroll in the hope of seeing them, and recorded later: 'We were quite close to them several times, just standing aside as they passed.' His friend Miss Thackery, who had missed her chance of seeing the celebrated newlyweds, asked immediately: 'How was she dressed?' to which Hardman was able to give a detailed reply, capturing the colour and trim of her gown and her 'handsome shawl'. He went on: 'A white bonnet with a transparent white veil, only plain net, covered her face, so we saw her quite well. She is quite as tall as the Prince, and with a very long dress and a high bonnet looks more important than he does . . .' Herein lies the significance of the hat for royal heads. The fashion writer Colin McDowell has described hats as 'the most unnatural of all items of clothing', going on to say that 'they are the least necessary but the most powerful'. Hats are transformative, hence, he states, 'why power and ceremony are normally hatted'. The hat has replaced the crown in all but the most ceremonial of events. On the occasion of Queen Victoria's Golden Jubilee in 1887, she was resolved not to wear her crown or robes of state in the procession through the city of London, but was determined instead to retain her usual mourning bonnet. Despite the entreaties of her daughter-in-law Alexandra, who reported back to the family that 'I was never so snubbed in all my life', Victoria stuck to her intentions and appeared in the open carriage bonneted as usual.

The hat has retained its prominence in the royal wardrobe long after it has ceased to be a standard of anybody else's. These confections of straw and felt mark decades of work and a myriad of contributary trades. Stephen Jones, milliner extraordinaire who has himself hatted many a royal head, reveals the complexity of his world: 'The Bias, egg irons, wire. Stiffener, buckram, blocks. Feathers and flowers. Felt and straw. Furs. Silks. Ribbon . . . The millinery workroom is a strange and unusual place. Half Aladdin's cave and half artist's studio, hats are coaxed into life with 90% perspiration and 10% inspiration.' Behind the celebrated milliner then, are those for whom the making of hats was their livelihood. The straw plaiters, the flower girls laced with arsenical powder, the mercury-infused hatters and the bonnet sewers – the countless men and women who steamed, pressed, wove and stitched the head-turning creations find their voice here.

A fashionable straw-based hat is nothing without its raw material. The surviving bonnets of Queens Victoria, Alexandra, Mary and Elizabeth began their journey in the fields of Bedfordshire and its environs, tall stalks of wheat that could be sold for a good price to service the straw plait industry around Luton. The straight, hollow lengths, at least nine inches ideally, were perfect for the workers who, over the course of two centuries, mastered the art of plaiting. At its peak, almost 50,000 straw plaiters produced in excess of 6,000 yards of plait a year, loops of gold braid ready to be fashioned into bonnets and boaters. The *Queen* newspaper described the work of a plaiter to its readers in 1861. Having received the bundle of bleached straw, 'she splits the straw . . . and then moistens the splits (this is mostly done

If You Want to Get Ahead . . .

Girls straw plaiting, photographed by Godfrey Bingley, 1890.

with the mouth), in order to make them more pliable. The plait is begun with the end nearest to her, and soon the braid starts to form in her nimble fingers.' The plaiter would hold the bundle under her left armpit and use her mouth to draw out the next split, leaving her fingers free to braid each strand into a gleaming, sinuous length. A straw plaiter might be identified from the permanent scarring to the right-hand side of her lips caused by the continuous pull of straw in the mouth over years of labour.

A surviving photograph catches this moment for posterity. It shows Sarah Jane Cook sitting and wearing a jaunty, flower-trimmed hat, presumably constructed from her own plait. Over one arm is a coil of the plait that she has already made, whilst under her arm rests the bundle of splits. There is a straw protruding from her mouth and she stares intently at the stalks in her hands through thick round spectacles.

Sarah Jane Cook was a straw plaiter from Ivinghoe, an entrepreneurial woman who spent her life making plaits, selling plaits and teaching the braiding of plaits at her own school. She was born in 1862. Her father, George, was a labourer for a local brewery and her mother, Fanny, worked as a straw plaiter. By the 1880s, the skill had cascaded down to her two daughters, Sarah Jane and Mary Matilda, all three contributing to their family's income through their busy fingers. Plaiting dominated entire villages and it is likely that Fanny and her daughters were accompanied by dozens of other women locally. Unlike other textile trades, plaiting might be carried out anywhere from the cottage to the street. Nineteenth-century photographs show lines of women, either bonneted in a straw hat of their own plaiting or wrapped in plaid shawls, white aprons fastened at their waists. They are talking, watching the world go by, laughing. But all the while they are plaiting. The convenience of the labour gave rise to some unease around the 'respectability' of the neighbourhoods – women who were so frequently plaiting were not keeping up with their domestic duties or caring for their children. The vicar of Abbots Langley found morals were 'at very low ebb' amongst his female parishioners, criticising their ignorance, idleness and 'gossipy habits'. These were independent women, the sort that vicars found troubling.

At the age of ten, Sarah Jane is described on the 1871 census as a 'scholar and straw plaiter', implying that she perhaps undertook a few hours of plaiting around her studies, but this was likely to be far from the case. Plait schools had evolved alongside the booming trade and were in fact little more than nursery workshops. Children as young as three would be enrolled in a plait school, overseen by women who were, in theory, supposed to offer them a rudimentary education but who, in reality, taught them to plait. Rather than their ABC, these children learned the local rhyme: 'Under one and over two; pull it tight and that will do.'

If You Want to Get Ahead . . .

The Children's Employment Commission set out to expose the iniquities of child labour and in 1867, Mr J. E. White, the commissioner for the Luton area, interviewed seven-year-old Sarah Ann Meagher from Berkhamsted. She told him: 'I go to Mrs Scott's plait school three times a day, from 8.30 to 12.00, from 1.00-4.00 and from 5.00-8.00. Mother sets me five yards to do in each school, one yard at dinner and one at teatime. Often I have to get up in the morning at 7 or 6.30 and begin work, because I have so much to do. If I do five mother says I am a good girl; she doesn't hit me. The mistress does sometimes.' I was curious about Sarah Ann. What a life to have led before she had even reached her tenth birthday, a childhood dominated by yards and yards of straw plait, her existence a grim fairy tale straight out of Rumpelstiltskin. I wondered if I might find her to see whether she was destined to plait for the rest of her life, lips scarred and fingers callused. In fact Sarah Ann did not become a plaiter but left that world behind and on the 1871 census, just a few years after her interview with the commissioner, she was employed as a housemaid for a local dentist, Mr Edwin Winterbottom. And from there she fled – taking ship to America where she married Samuel Pearson in New York in 1884. I wonder if she described her life as a plaiter to Samuel? Perhaps she drew on her former skills in her new life or maybe she left them behind. I do not know.

By the age of forty-nine in 1911, Sarah Jane Cook was the head of a large household consisting of younger siblings, nieces and nephews. She was, by this time, a straw plait dealer and had started her own plait school. By this date, the plait schools were not the labour workshops for the under-fives that they once had been, but encouraged older girls to learn to plait in small groups at the same time as acquiring a basic education. When Sarah Jane died in 1934, she left behind a skill that was already waning, an industry no longer employing the thousands it had in her childhood. The women standing in the plait markets, arms laden with their handmade wares, were already only a memory.

Dressing the Queen

A plait stall in Luton.

So what became of the shining plaits braided in the villages of Bedfordshire? Once sold at the plait markets around Luton, they would wend their way into the millinery industry, to factories and workshops and single rooms of countless milliners engaged in the business of crafting the finished hats. It was a brutal industry for its long hours and poor working conditions. Milliners in London might expect to work a fifteen-hour day, more if the Season demanded, in poorly ventilated rooms. The atmosphere was stultifying, the hiss of steam mingling with the potency of glue, whilst fingers darted with needle and thread stitching hat bands,

If You Want to Get Ahead . . .

ribbons, net and flowers. Fanny Burney's 1814 novel *The Wanderer* sees her protagonist Elinor at work as a young milliner, 'a whirl of hurry, bustle and loquacity and interruptions . . . the goods which required most work, most ingenuity and most hands were last paid'. From amongst this cacophony of fabric and fashion, voices emerge from those for whom their work took them into the unexpected world of the royal supplier. Mary Perryman was born in 1844 in St Pancras, London. Her father, Francis, was a carver and gilder, an artisan of some distinction working with fine tools and gold leaf to support his large family of eight children. By the time Mary had reached her fifth birthday, her father had died and she lived with her mother, Lucy, her older brother Charles and her sister Emily in a tall brick stuccoed house on Newman Street, Marylebone. The once graceful Georgian town house was home to seven other families in 1851. Their neighbours included an upholsterer, a printer and a cabinetmaker, skilled workers inhabiting two rooms each at the shared address. There were also three milliners.

Perhaps it was through these connections on Newman Street that Mary found her trade, for she too would become a milliner. It was a long-serving apprenticeship, complex hierarchies ensuring that everybody knew their place. More than a century later, the royal milliner Aage Thaarup wrote of his own apprentices and practices that would have been recognisable to Mary. His girls spent 'one year making tea, one year going to the post office, one year sewing headbands'. By her late teens Mary was able to describe herself as a milliner. At some point now unknown, fate would send her across the path of Sarah Ann Unitt. Unitt had been working as a dressmaker to Queen Victoria since the early 1850s. Whether Mary Perryman was employed specifically for her skill in making hats is impossible to say, but when Sarah Ann Unitt retired in 1876 Mary Perryman, along with another employee Caroline Parsons, was well placed to continue making the royal bonnets. One of their creations still survives. It is a rarity, a small silk mourning bonnet designed to sit towards the back of the Queen's head. Fashioned from black and white silk, beaded and with two lace streamers hanging down behind, it bears the printed label stitched into its lining 'Perryman & Parsons'.

By the early 1880s, both women lived at their premises on 20 Brook Street, a far cry from the cramped rooms of Mary's childhood. They employed a servant and three other young milliners working from the same address. The ultimate accolade was accorded to them in 1882. On 4 October the Warrant of Appointment was issued to Mary Frances Perryman and Caroline Elizabeth Parsons 'as milliners to the Queen'. In support of their application, the Queen's dresser Miss Dittweiler wrote that 'they have worked for the Queen for many years', cementing their place in a hierarchy that had taken them some distance from their years of apprenticeships and crowded workrooms to three-storeyed splendour in Mayfair. The two women along with their employees worked for the Queen for another decade but there the trail runs cold until 1911 and a now sixty-eight-year-old Mary living in Richmond. Details are scarce. She remained single and she still described herself as a milliner working on her own account. The house had seven rooms but she clarifies in the records that she only lived in two of them. No lodgers are in evidence. Perhaps she retired to the relative peace of Richmond when they gave up the lease on the Brook Street workshop and there worked as a milliner to the middle-class suburban ladies. Did she tell anybody of those confections of silk that were fit, literally, for a queen? Perryman & Parsons were an unlikely partnership then, forged through a mixture of skill and luck. Where so many other young women toiled in the basements of a thousand poorly run workshops, Mary and Caroline managed to follow an altogether different path.

Toxicity infused the worlds of millinery and hatting, as the trade for more masculine hats was known. When Professor Alison Matthews David studied casts of hand-painted hands belonging to Parisian hatters

If You Want to Get Ahead . . .

from the late nineteenth century, she described the impact of the chemicals used in the trade. The permanent staining of the nails revealed the young man's long-term exposure to toxins: 'His nails are clubbed: they bulge slightly, a shape that indicates chronic oxygen deprivation.' He was a victim of mercury poisoning. Animal pelts had long been utilised in the fashionable world of hats, used to create robust and waterproof head coverings. In order to achieve the smooth and felted fabric, however, the hairs had to be removed from the skin and this relied on a variety of processes that included chemical solutions. As cheaper furs replaced more expensive choices such as beaver, so the chemical requirements to treat them became more invasive and the process of 'carroting' – the breaking down of the keratin in the hair by brushing the pelt with a solution of mercury was developed.

One of the Victorian period's most beloved fictional characters was said to hail from this poisonous industry in the shape of Lewis Carroll's 'Mad Hatter'. Aside from the physical impact of mercury poisoning on the skin and lungs, it was also found to be responsible for deteriorating mood disorders, the implication being that hatters were sent mad by the mercury that had invaded their bodies. It was not only the hatters who were affected by the desires of the fashionable world. Countless workshops were filled with hundreds of young girls all employed in the dusting of silk gauze with a beautifully realistic, fresh green powder to create foliage that might trim a bonnet. The lifelike fronds might be interspersed with silk flowers and berries to meet the demands of consumers keen to display ensembles inspired by the natural world. There was nothing natural about these leaves, however, for that brilliant-hued powder was made from white arsenic. The nails of the flower girls would turn a bright green, as would the whites of their eyes. It was a condition that proved fatal. Philanthropic organisations demanded action and in 1862 the chemist Dr A. W. Hoffman was commissioned to analyse the arsenical content of these objects. *The Times* published his findings, recording: 'The expert concluded that an average headdress contained enough arsenic to poison 20 people.' Whilst studies such as these began to prompt change in the industries, I can't help but think of Mary Perryman and the path of her career. Many a young milliner before her had not been so fortunate, their lives cut cruelly short by the tools of their trade.

The steaming, stretching and stitching that would have been so familiar to Mary Perryman and Caroline Parsons in their work for Queen Victoria, had barely changed in decades and would have seemed much the same when a young Danish milliner arrived in London in the early 1930s. Aage Thaarup had been fascinated by cloth since he was a child growing up in Copenhagen, fashioning small objects from scraps of fabric and making a little hat when he was six years old. After a long apprenticeship in a leading Copenhagen department store, selling hats to the women of his home city, he spent some years roaming Paris, Berlin and Bombay before setting up a small workroom near Berkeley Square. As is so often the case with makers, who might have no clear idea of where their inspirations could take them, luck played its part in his life as a milliner. Thaarup came to the attention of Cecil Beaton and was asked to make a hat for his friend to wear to Royal Ascot – this hat appeared in *Vogue* two months later and so his star began to rise. He recalled in his autobiography the first time that he was asked to consider a royal commission. He received a telephone call from the then Duchess of York, later to be Queen Elizabeth, consort of King George VI. She wanted to visit his salon. 'I put down the receiver, not quite in a panic, but not very calm. I simply thought I must make everything as nice as I possibly could.' Whilst his small salon was reasonably presentable, his workroom consisted of bare boards and spare furnishings. 'Quickly I borrowed a little strip of red carpet and secured it with drawing pins.' The visit was successful. Hats were ordered, and when they had been completed, Thaarup himself took them to be fitted at the Duchess's residence at 145 Piccadilly.

If You Want to Get Ahead . . .

Whilst Thaarup's own story is a fascinating one, a career in London that spanned decades and many subsequent royal hats fashioned over the course of his life, he remains sadly tight-lipped about the women who contributed to his success. He acknowledges their efforts briefly amongst descriptions of his celebrity clients: 'The girls who actually stitch the hats together are invaluable. They are craftswomen and I should be lost without them.' He writes of his good fortune in finding his talented girls, several of whom stayed with him for many years: 'They not only stitched well but were able to translate my directions with real feeling.' Unlike Hardy Amies, whose memoir was littered with fond reminiscences of the men and women who populated his workshops, Thaarup never names any of these trusted women. They are his 'girls' who were able to bring to life his often whimsical designs, but they remain anonymous. A single grainy photograph depicts the interior of his workroom but it is difficult to discern anything from it. Shadowy figures, who have stopped their work at the table in front of them momentarily for the photograph, remain nameless.

A solitary British Pathé newsreel from 1957 follows Thaarup through the design process as he sketches the outline of the Royal Albert Hall in a quest to create one of his famously quirky hats. He lays his sketch on a small table strewn with artfully placed reels of thread and lengths of buckram from which the hat will be moulded into shape. Sitting at the table in a neat brown suit, his milliner winds the buckram around the mount in front of her, pinning and stitching fabric to the canvas beneath. Her fingers work swiftly, turning the emerging hat, spinning it to life. The clipped commentary mentions her not at all and so she is both nameless and voiceless in her act of creation though not invisible. She gives a slight smile and a nod to her employer as he whisks the hat from its stand and packs it with a flourish into a lavish hatbox. It is undoubtedly staged for the camera, but it is a glimpse all the same of the labour behind the designer. I rewatch the film and wonder if she felt nervous about

Dressing the Queen

Milliner Aage Thaarup at work by Tim Gidal, 1940.

her moment in the spotlight. Did she take the bus home that evening and describe the experience to her family? Perhaps she went to the pictures and watched the short film, all two minutes and thirty seconds of it. These illuminating pieces of newsreel are sometimes all that remains of lost worlds, footage that was shown to filmgoers to enjoy before the main feature at the cinema.

A year later, another famous London milliner, Otto Lucas, allowed the cameras into his workrooms to follow the progress of a hat. 'Heady Stuff' offers a more realistic view of the milliner's workspace, one that would have been familiar to generations of makers past. The narrator, in tones of best BBC received pronunciation, announces: 'We were so intrigued by all this ingenuity that we asked to be shown behind the scenes.' Cut to a crowded room of long tables filled along each side with thirty or more women, each bent over a canvas head. Each head is crowned with a froth of tulle or ribbon or net. Each pair of hands is busy with pins, scissors and needles. The tables are overflowing with materials and trimmings, long meadows of silk flowers and curling chiffon. 'The actual materials and equipment are very simple,' the viewer is informed, 'but it takes years of experience before you reach the stage, as this house has, of being the biggest single dollar earner in the business.' The camera moves from the trimmings room to a steam-filled space where the hats are moulded with egg-shaped irons, moving swiftly around brims to sculpt them into submission. The male hat blockers, shirt sleeves rolled back, force the crown of the hat around the mould. A former employee recalled that these two or three hat blockers were always 'cockney men' but their names have gone unrecorded. In total, a mere seventy-six seconds is devoted to the workers in Otto Lucas's employ, but it is a rare and revealing moment. Stephen Jones acknowledges that the practices in millinery workrooms have barely changed in a century, so to watch these men and women at work is to imagine generations of milliners whose days followed a similar pattern.

Curiously, Otto Lucas never made hats for the royal family, in spite of his reputation as the best milliner in London. He did, however, employ apprentices who would themselves go on to become royal milliners, designers such as Frederick Fox who learned from Otto about the structure of a successful workroom. Otto himself had learned from the model couture milliners of Paris, bringing the hierarchical formation with him, his rooms overseen by two 'Modellistes' – who were always referred to as 'Madame' – and then the thirty or more milliners, those women stitching away so assiduously for the British Pathé cameras. Frederick Fox left Otto Lucas and in time started to work for Hardy Amies, making his first hat for the Queen in 1968. By 1974 he had been awarded the Royal Warrant and would make more than 350 hats for the Queen over a thirty-five-year period. Whilst little has been written about Fox and nothing about his milliners, their legacy remains in the careful preservation of his creations in the Royal Collection.

The variety of hats worn by Queen Elizabeth became one of the defining features of her style in the later decades of her life. The bright coats were always complemented with matching millinery, combinations that were configured by an in-house team of makers. Angela Kelly, the Queen's dresser, described the collaborative nature of this later working royal wardrobe in her memoir: 'We have Stella, who is our milliner. Stella makes Her Majesty's hats based on my designs and I often ask for her input on which trimmings work best together – I really value her ideas and suggestions.' I wondered about Stella and the very visible contribution she had made to a wardrobe that was so prominent in the public arena of the Queen's working life. Social media can be a useful tool and I managed to find Stella McLaren on Instagram and messaged her, asking if she might talk to me about her life as a modern-day milliner. I was hopeful but not optimistic until a reply pinged into my inbox. Stella was delighted to be asked – she had not often had the opportunity to really talk about her own career – and so we arranged to speak on the phone.

It was a delightful conversation. Stella told me that she had always loved to sew and her needlework teacher at school suggested that millinery might offer an interesting career path. The year was 1967 and apprenticeships were still more abundant than they are today. Stella visited the Youth Employment Office with her mum and was offered a place at a millinery establishment to serve her apprenticeship. She earned five pounds twelve shillings a week out of which she gave her mum one pound two shillings for bed and board. She must have been a natural, as her needlework teacher had guessed she would be, and by the 1970s she was working for Frederick Fox: 'To me he is the most talented, he was the one who designed and made the hats. I was really good at draping.' She continues: 'So I started doing the Queen's hats at Freddie's and it stuck.' It would prove to be the defining moment in her life.

After Fox died, Stella was headhunted by another royal milliner, Philip Somerville, which was where Angela Kelly first noticed her talent. 'Angela said to me: "What are you going to do when Philip retires?" and I said: "Panic!" and she said: "Don't! We'll give you a job at the palace."' True to

If You Want to Get Ahead . . .

Angela's word, Stella was offered a full-time role as the Queen's personal milliner and started her new job on the dresser's floor at Buckingham Palace. It was a world that she grew to love, forging a fond relationship with the Queen herself. Her millinery room occupied a space on the floor above the Queen's bedroom and she would often pop downstairs to try the fit of a hat. 'I knew the Queen's head inside out so I would just take something down and try it on.' She built up the working space into a contemporary millinery workshop, one that would have been familiar to Freddie Fox and Philip Somerville, carrying forth the years of her apprenticeship into the inner circle of the royal wardrobe.

As the Queen aged and her stature became more diminutive, Stella had to accommodate a different physicality. 'As she got older and more stooped we had to change the brims and cut down the neck.' Her days were always varied. Sometimes she would take shopping trips to buy fabrics, often she would spend time forward planning with Angela to cater for forthcoming trips. She recalled the warmth of her interactions with the Queen. 'The Queen liked to be surrounded by normal people,' she told me. 'We weren't posh like the ladies-in-waiting.' Stella spent much of the first lockdown with the Queen at Windsor in 2020, standing in as a dresser during that surreal time, and said goodbye to the Queen at Balmoral in 2022 just weeks before her death. 'She said: "Thank you so much for coming and looking after me." I came home to London and I cried for two weeks.' Her sadness is still palpable, even over the phone. I asked if she was still creating lovely hats now but it was to prove the end of an era for Stella too, 'I've got no room and no equipment,' she explained. 'I love it so much, I just miss it.' As we said goodbye, I felt the poignancy of those words. Her hats might have been photographed by a thousand paparazzi but, like the milliners before her, Stella's creations were forged behind doors and her own life unremarked upon. I was happy to have heard her story.

Hats would become the most obvious element of the queenly

wardrobe in the twentieth and twenty-first centuries. The diminutive stature of Queen Elizabeth gave the hat greater significance, its role in increasing her public visibility an important one. As the function of the hat to impart royal status grew, so rose the stars of celebrated milliners like Aage Thaarup and Frederick Fox. For each name I include here, however, I am mindful of those I have left out. Names such as Simone Mirman who made hats for many members of the royal family in the 1960s and more recently Rachel Trevor-Morgan who held the Royal Warrant from 2014. I know that when I write about the straw plaiter Sarah Jane Cook, she is one amongst thousands of women all undertaking the same arduous work, their scarred lips a testament to their skill. When I imagine Mary Frances Perryman fashioning wisps of silk into bonnets for Queen Victoria, she does so at the same time as countless other hands stitching similar creations across the country. Child labour reports and newspaper exposés decrying the toxic flower trade shine a brief light on to the plight of workers, the vast majority of whom are anonymous, whose stories we shall never know. The British Pathé newsreels at least make the milliners momentarily visible, and if we cannot hear their voices we can witness and marvel over their artistry as they glance shyly at these unfamiliar cameras. Stella was able to tell me a little of her own story, one whose industry mirrored that of others before her. To hear her tell it in her own words felt like a special moment indeed. And the hats themselves survive as a legacy not just of the wearer but the makers too. In every shade, in straw and leather and felt. Fashioned from chiffon, from net and from silk, they chart decades of collective memories. They remain intact, imbued with the love and labour of the plaiter, the blocker, the flower girl. The milliner.

CHAPTER 7

Best Foot Forward
The Shoes of Gundry and of Rayne

Shoemakers past are elusive creatures. I have vivid memories of the fairy story 'The Elves and the Shoemaker' as retold by Vera Southgate in the 1965 Ladybird storybook. Illustrator Robert Lumley painted the most sumptuous shoes fashioned by the elves by night to help the poor shoemaker. By morning they were gone, leaving their magical footwear behind them. Museums have become the repositories for similarly stunning creations. Paper labels attached to the insoles or stamped in gold reveal the identities of the primary retailer of the shoes and boots worn on royal feet but, like the talented elves of legend, they give away nothing about the army of men and women who measured, cut, shaped and stitched the silky slippers and elegant boots. Unlike hats, the shoes worn by royal women are an altogether quieter affair. For centuries shoes have been symbolic of a person's place in the world, used to demonstrate wealth and status. King Louis IV of France famously sported red heels in a show of sartorial power, an affectation that was forbidden to anybody else. Shoes are complex objects with dozens of different processes that must be followed along the path of their creation. They can transform the wearer, elevating them both physically and psychologically. They root us to the ground and ensure our equilibrium. They can be comfortable or treacherous, functional or flamboyant. We leave traces of wear in our shoes, the material moulding to the unique outline of our feet, and so they can be intimate objects that carry ghostly remembrances of wearers past.

The potentially fetishistic element of footwear and the knowledge that particularly decorative shoes were often favoured by stage performers may account for the relative soberness of shoes worn by royal women over the last two centuries. Where hats and coats and dresses were expected to dazzle, their shoes were operating on a more discreet level, carrying the Queen forth without fear of distraction. To read a list of the shoe and bootmakers awarded the Royal Warrant from Queen Victoria and beyond takes no time at all, so few are the names that appear. Gundry & Son, Joseph Box, Joseph Sparkes Hall, H. & M. Rayne, Anello & Davide – from queen to queen, these shoemakers feature time and again, demonstrating that in this aspect of their wardrobes at least, the tried and tested was preferable to the new and unknown. In part this may be a question of loyalty and discretion – after all, feet are very much on display and where clothing might create illusions for other parts of the body, the feet are harder to disguise. Young Edward Rayne, working for the family business that had been supplying shoes to a succession of queens for decades, was unfortunately caught out during a working trip to New York in 1950. A keen journalist with a generous flow of Martinis resulted in Edward divulging the size of the Queen's feet. Panic ensued along with the very real expectation that all royal orders would cease henceforth. Edward was summoned to Buckingham Palace to explain himself to a formidable Press Secretary. He was reprimanded for his loose tongue but thankfully for the company the patronage continued.

Queen Victoria's feet were hardly on display, given the nature of the skirts that covered them for the duration of her reign, but the shoes themselves survive, more visible now perhaps than ever they were in her lifetime. Straight cream slippers, square-toed and be-ribboned, bear the oval paper disc pasted inside the shoe, proclaiming Gundry & Son of 1 Soho Square as the maker. Richard Gundry had been making shoes for the Princess Victoria from as far back as 1824 and the firm would continue to do so until 1898, almost the end of her life. In 1840, the year that the company made the ivory silk bridal shoes for Queen Victoria's wedding to Prince Albert, the firm of Gundry was well established at Soho Square under the leadership of Richard's son William who lived there with his wife, Ann, and their growing family. The many-paned windows of his shopfront were surmounted by the golden arms of the Royal Warrant, impossible for those strolling by to miss.

Like hundreds of other shoemakers at this time, Gundry's premises were multi-purpose, serving as a retail space, workshop and accommodation all in one building. William employed both men and women in his workshop, their designated roles a reflection of the different requirements of each stage of the shoemaking process. Male shoemakers were

Gundry & Son evening slipper, 1840s.

responsible for the early stages that involved skills such as the carving of the shoe last – the wooden mould around which a style of shoe would be crafted. This was an expensive but necessary component for every shoemaker, pieces of beech wood shaped to each individual type of footwear in order that the leather sole and material of the upper could be fitted to its dimensions. Photographs of celebrated shoe designer Salvatore Ferragamo's workshop in the mid-twentieth century capture row upon row of wooden lasts carved uniquely for each of his famous clients, Sophia Loren's nestled up to Marilyn Monroe's in a who's who of celebrity feet. A paper pattern would be taken for the shoe, taking in the shape of the sole and the various pieces of its upper known as the vamp and the quarters, essentially the toe and the sides.

Next came the 'clicker', the name given to the skilled craftsman whose job was to cut the leather for the sole, the insole and the upper. It was a skill that required experience and imagination for the maker had to take into consideration not just the dimensions of the shoe but how each of its components would stretch; how the grain of the leather might change the fit of the shoe; and how each of these elements would work in harmony. Once the clicker had completed his tasks, the pieces were handed to the 'closer'. This was often a job undertaken by women and consisted of the joining of the pieces that formed the upper part of the shoe – the leather or fabric that enclosed the foot. This had been a process worked entirely by hand until the middle of the nineteenth century when, as with so many other textile- and dress-related industries, machinery began to offer up new working practices and a change to the traditional methods. The final major step in the process was to complete the making up of the shoe, attaching the sole, the insole and the upper to the last and stitching them together to form the final, wearable object. It is a much simplified description of a trade that comprised in reality dozens of different moments of making and accompanying tools, and I have found myself scouring YouTube for tutorials that spotlight the complexity of traditional shoemaking.

Shoemaking, old and new, line drawing, 1911.

By 1851, William Gundry employed forty-four men and twelve women to meet the needs of his growing customer base, all with their distinct roles in the business, wielding sharp 'clicking' knives, leather-punching awls, scissors, needles and sturdy thread. These were the men and women who fashioned the dainty slippers worn by Queen Victoria for almost her entire life, and which remain intact as testament to their labour. The vast majority of them are sadly nameless but there is one woman, living under William's roof, who performed a slightly different but crucial role in the daily operations of William Gundry – his sister-in-law Sarah Holt. Sarah had been living with William and Ann for at least ten years, for she appears on the 1841 census in 1 Soho Square, but by 1851 there is an explanation of her place in the household. She was the shop woman. Shop work was a growing arena of employment for women in the second half of the nineteenth century. By 1900, a quarter of a million women worked as shopgirls, finding not only employment but often accommodation and food as part of their conditions of work. This did not mean it was an easy life. The hours were long and in the larger department stores the accommodation and food were basic. Sarah Holt, of course, was a family member in a much smaller establishment, but as an unmarried woman of thirty-four years of age, her place must have felt precarious. She would have served behind the wooden counter of Gundry's shop, seeing to the needs of customers, assisting with shoe fittings and wrapping up goods to be delivered. The shoemaker Joseph Sparkes Hall described the workings of a shop in his 1847 publication *The Book of the Feet*: 'A lady or gentleman requiring boots or shoes, pays a visit to a respectable shop, and the measure is taken either by the master or the clicker; the order is entered in the order-book, and the time named when they are to be ready.' I wonder if Sarah was given charge of the order book, entering measurements, customer details and prices all recorded in careful cursive? Did she ever package up a pair of shoes that she knew were destined for the feet of the Queen? Sarah would go on to live a somewhat nomadic life, always subject to the support of her family. By the age of seventy-five she was living with her niece, Alice Gundry, who had grown up in the Soho Square shop. Did the two of them reminisce about life on the periphery of the royal shoemakers and marvel at the exquisite footwear their family had produced?

Gundry were not the only shoemakers to Queen Victoria. Joseph Sparkes Hall was a pioneering and passionate shoemaker who had been determined to bring innovation to his creations. He spent many years developing boots that had elastic sides for both comfort and convenience. Of his early ideas he wrote: 'My first experiments were a failure, as the manufacture of elastic materials was not so perfect as they are at the present period and the necessary elasticity could not be gained in any material I could meet with.' By 1837 he had come up with a successful combination of India-rubber and wire and patented his elastic boots at the same time as presenting a pair to the Queen. 'Her Majesty has been pleased to honour the invention with the most marked and continued patronage; it has been my privilege for some years to make boots of this kind for Her Majesty, and no one who reads the court circular, or is acquainted with Her Majesty's habits of walking and exercise in the open air can doubt the superior claims of the elastic over every other kind of boots.' Such innovation saw Joseph's star rise and, like William Gundry, Joseph had employed his sister-in-law, Elizabeth Hill, as a bootmaker's assistant and shop woman. For her bed and board, Elizabeth, like Sarah Holt, would have undertaken a whole host of daily tasks that would have included some of the finishing processes of the boots and shoes as well as her behind-the-counter role. Sarah Holt and Elizabeth Hill lived only a mile apart. Both depended on the good grace of their respective sisters' husbands and both were involved with the finishing and selling of shoes to Queen Victoria, which makes me wonder if they ever met. There is no evidence to suggest they did and yet what similar trajectories their lives had taken, surrounded by the smell of leather and glue, by the noise of the hammer and the awl, in the knowledge that the carefully wrapped footwear would soon be gracing the feet of the world's most famous woman.

Bespoke shoemaking in smaller retail premises that combined the workshop was becoming rarer by the second half of the nineteenth century. The vast majority of shoemakers were working in larger establishments as new machines intensified the volume of production. Where formerly most makers worked in their own homes, assisted by their wives and older children, the size and requirements of the new equipment meant that the cottage-based industry was no longer sustainable. In the UK, one of the most significant towns associated with shoemaking was Northampton. For centuries its fame as a centre of the trade had seen thousands of local people earn a living from the leather shoes it produced. In 1725, Daniel Defoe wrote in his book *The Complete English Tradesman* that shoes were, 'from Northampton for all: the poorest countryman and the master'. By the 1860s, the industry had changed beyond recognition – closing machines allowed for the joining of the uppers, a press machine could cut the leather and a blocking machine was able to shape the shoe fronts. Contemporary photographs capture the sheer scale of manufacture in Northampton. Clicking rooms are filled with rows of smooth tables covered in leather, over which lean aproned, bespectacled makers. Closing rooms are populated with treadle machines operated by row upon row of women. Vast lasting or making rooms display ranks of almost completed shoes and finishers stand alongside piles of white shoeboxes ready to fill them with glossy footwear. In the 1830s, one manufacturer alone made eighty thousand pairs of shoes.

It was a far cry from the well-appointed shopfront of Joseph Box, a bootmaker who had also been awarded the Royal Warrant by Queen Victoria. His premises at 187 Regent Street featured a modern plate-glass window filled with gleaming boots, the golden crown of his warrant prominently displayed. At the very top of the grandly porticoed building peep the upper floor windows, and it must have been here that Henry Harvey and John Smith lived. They were both bootmaker's assistants for Joseph Box and lived in as part of their employment. Names such as theirs are not conducive to easy discovery in the records. There are 58,749 John Smiths on the 1861 census in London alone and so beyond the fact that he was born in 1843 in Paddington, I can glean little of his life. What we can say is that at the age of eighteen, he would already have been working for some time in the trade, perhaps serving an apprenticeship with Joseph Box before his role as an assistant saw him learning the art of the clicker, closer or maker. Every day he would cut, shape and stitch. By night he would sleep in the eaves of Regent Street. Perhaps if he looked out of his window he could just make out the top of the magnificent golden crest that proclaimed their status as makers to royalty.

A name that would become synonymous with specifically royal footwear and provided shoes for three generations of queens was that of H. & M. Rayne. The widespread media coverage of the young Princess Elizabeth from the 1930s onwards meant that her shoes have perhaps been the most visible of all royal footwear, and for many years Rayne was her label of choice. The story of Rayne has theatrical origins, filled with colourful tales of entrepreneurial spirit, ambition and loss. Mary Ann Clark was born south of the river in Lambeth in 1863. Her father, William, was a potter's labourer, perhaps working on Lambeth Walk, that street teeming with market stalls which would attain its own kind of fame when music hall star Alec Hurley sang about the 'costers' and the 'pearlies' and the cockney strut that went along with it in 1899. By the age of seventeen, and like so many girls of her age and stage in life, Mary Ann had left home and was working as a housemaid for a builder in Clapham, sharing her working life with a slightly older maid and shouldering many of the daily duties of the household.

On 28 September 1884, Mary Ann was married. Her husband was Henry Edward Rayne, a young waiter who had been born in Plymouth and had made his way to London in search of fame and fortune. At the age of twenty-one, serving food and beverages, that must have seemed an unlikely outcome to his life and yet their domestic and professional partnership would take an unexpected turn. Mary Ann and Henry would join the ranks of the Lambeth stallholders amongst whose colourful stands Mary Ann must have trotted as a child. They had chosen to trade in the ephemera of theatrical costuming, located in close proximity as they were to a whole host of theatres, not least the Old Vic. I wonder what prompted their choice of goods to retail? It seems a leap from anything either of them had known before and yet it would prove to be a canny choice. By 1895, they had attained enough of a business to be recorded in *Kelly's Directory*, described as 'theatrical costumers, shoemakers, hosiers, wigmakers and theatrical perfumers'. Their premises were located at 115 Waterloo Road, an address that would expand over the next twenty years to include the buildings next door, advertisements describing them as a 'theatrical store'. Prominent stage performers became famous clients, women such as the music hall star Kitty Lord. The Museum of London has in their collection a beautiful pair of long, pink, embroidered satin boots of hers made by H. & M. Rayne, a portent of the objects that would make them a household name. It is heartening to see the prominence of Mary's name and influence on the business at a time when, as a general rule, married women with children would have been expected to remain at home. However, the toll of multiple pregnancies and an expanding business proved too much. Mary Ann is absent from the 1901 census, her youngest child only three years old. She had suffered a breakdown and was admitted to Banstead Mental Asylum where she died on 17 February 1911. She was forty-eight. Mary Ann herself would never see the ultimate royal fruits of their work, from its roots in the markets of Lambeth to a Royal Warrant on Regent Street.

Around the time of Mary Ann's death, the firm had begun to specialise more in the creation of fancy footwear, the shoes and boots manufactured in workshops at the Waterloo Road premises. Of the dozens of young men and women employed by the company in the making and finishing of the shoes, one rare account survives of a maker for H. & M. Rayne. Keturah Filmer was born in 1896 and lived with her parents and her seven brothers and sisters at 31 Albert House, one of the imposing tenement buildings on Blendon Row in Walworth, before finally moving to Townley Street, directly adjacent to the East Street markets of Mary Ann Clark's childhood. Keturah described her house in her memoir, recalling: 'There were four rooms and a scullery which had a stone floor . . . There were no decent bedrooms or a bathroom.' The rent was a constant struggle. Her father was a hard-working scaffolder but his work was not always regular and so the children were expected to contribute as early as they could. As she approached the end of her schooldays aged thirteen, Keturah had to find work. She was able to clean doorsteps for threepence a step, she said, but fate took her in a different direction. Her friend Bessie was the head machinist for H. & M. Rayne and secured a job for Keturah in one of the workrooms of the boots and shoes department. 'I was very nervous on my first morning at H. M. Rayne . . . What kind of work will I do? I wondered.' Bessie told her that she was to sit next to a girl named Molly who would tell her everything. 'The first thing I had to learn was how to hand stitch a button hole and it was Molly who showed me how.' Perfecting the buttonholes meant she would be able to work on the tall satin boots that had eight buttonholes each – this piece of cloth was called a 'fly'. When she had perfected the fly, she handed it to Bessie who would stitch it to the uppers. 'After three months of practising sewing button holes, Bessie came over to me and took my "flies" for the Forelady, Lottie, to see.' She was declared competent and became a professional buttonholer. Her eye for colour prompted a promotion for Keturah. She learnt the art of hand dyeing the ribbons to match the boots. 'So now I was also a professional dyer of ribbons for which I got a rise of one shilling, making my weekly wage four shillings and sixpence.'

Her life might so easily have carried on in an upward trajectory at the firm. In fact her quick intelligence and acquisition of new skills had been noted and after a year of working her buttonholes and dyeing her ribbons, she was called to the office by Mr Rayne himself. Legs shaking, certain that she was being reprimanded for some unknown mishap, she was met at the office by Mr Rayne's secretary, Miss Fisher, who delivered some startling news: 'Mr Rayne has brought you down here for me to tell you that you are just the girl who later on, when I retire in a few years' time, has all the potential to take my place . . . Mr Rayne says that you will make a fine businesswoman.' Miss Fisher would train her up for the role and another year passed with glowing reports for Keturah as she achieved all that was required of her in the new and responsible job. But, as was so often the case for women during a period when social care was non-existent, her path was to change: 'One night when I came home from work my mother was in bed. She had had a heart attack.' Faced with costly bills, Keturah informed the doctor that she would look after her mother herself, leaving her job at Rayne's. 'I wrote to Miss Fisher telling her the sad news and thanked her for her kindness to me but I knew that my mother and family needed me.' Keturah would go on to marry and have a family of her own, a happy marriage by all accounts, and it was after the loss of her husband in 1977 that she was persuaded by her niece to record the memories of her younger days. How different might her life have been had she been able to take up the opportunities offered by Rayne? I picture her sitting at her table, laughing (as she apparently often did) at one of Molly's jokes whilst they stitched their buttonholes, surrounded by the silks and satins and ribbons of Rayne's footwear, bright and carefree before life came crashing in.

By the 1930s, and through the stewardship of Mary and Henry's son and grandson, H. & M. Rayne was selling exclusive footwear from premises at 58 Bond Street to such an extent that it had reached the notice of Queen Mary. The first of their Royal Warrants was awarded by her in 1935 and like so many other warrant holders, the cachet it afforded the firm contributed to the rising of their retail star. The emergence of shoe designers as a specific branch of luxury manufacture had gained credence with makers like Ferragamo and later names such as Roger Vivier, matching his glittering pumps to the confections made by Christian Dior.

At Rayne, by the 1950s, the mantle was handed to another young and ambitious woman, Jean Matthew. Jean was one of the first students to graduate from the Royal College of Art's new 'Fashion' pathway and the only one ever to have taken that route into shoe design. By her mid-twenties she was working at the firm's King's Cross factory and was interviewed by *Picture Post* journalist Cynthia Judah, appearing in their September 1954 issue. Cynthia captured the force of nature that Jean Matthew appears to have been: 'She designs and adapts models and sees them through to production. And she is in charge of advertising and publicity. Her office which she shares with two men and hundreds of shoes at all stages of manufacture looks out over the factory floor.' Cynthia continued: 'During the day, she will probably discuss new leathers, fabrics and designs; draw and adapt to the Rayne last and market some fabulously elegant kid pumps from Italy; modify another already in the making; and hurry through a special order for a couture house.' She would send prototypes to *Vogue*, hurry over to the Bond Street store to fulfil other tasks, talk to the buyers 'and, in her spare moment, punch studs into a new model, because someone has to get it done by that evening'.

In 1953, British Pathé filmed some of the work undertaken at Rayne. It is barely a minute long but there is Jean Matthew, hand-decorating the heels of one of their popular styles with rhinestones. There can be little doubt, given her boundless energy and knowledge of every detail, that Jean would have had a hand in the royal orders. Queen Elizabeth (later the Queen Mother) ordered twenty to thirty pairs a year from Rayne, costing eight guineas a pair, and both of her daughters, Princesses Elizabeth and Margaret, began wearing Rayne shoes from the late 1930s onwards. They favoured pale sandals for many of their public outings,

A still from the British Pathé film *Jewelled Shoes*, Jean Matthew working at Rayne shoes, 1953.

culminating in the ivory silk pair made for Princess Elizabeth's wedding in 1947. Rayne would continue to provide shoes for the new Queen after her accession in 1953 as she settled into what would become the familiar black court shoe that became something of her trademark. Small design details were factored into her footwear. A soft suede arch support was included for extra comfort and the soles were carefully scored to prevent any slips. I do wonder if this is the kind of thoughtful knowledge that one woman would bring to another and that maybe Jean Matthew, as a pioneering shoe designer, quietly worked her magic. There is little in the public domain to acknowledge her contribution – she was another talented young woman to add to the many at H. & M. Rayne whose skills are now largely forgotten.

When Rayne ceased trading in 1994, Queen Elizabeth was forced to adopt a new shoemaker and so it was that Anello & Davide became the face, or the foot, of the Queen's shoes for almost thirty years. She would order multiple pairs of shoes in advance, for one specific reason, as her dresser Angela Kelly explained: 'As has been reported in the press, a "flunky" wears in Her Majesty's shoes to ensure that they are comfortable and that she is always good to go. And yes, I am that "flunky".' Angela explored a range of different makers during these years of the Queen's public life, choosing neutral colours for practicality. 'Her Majesty tends to use cream, white or black for her shoes as one pair will match, and be worn with, many different outfits.' The shoes were quietly performing their part amongst the complexity of the modern royal wardrobe.

The wearers might have changed but the processes have remained the same. Anello & Davide held the wooden lasts belonging to the Queen, just as Richard Gundry possessed those for Queen Victoria a hundred and fifty years earlier. A clicker from Joseph Box or a closer from Joseph Sparkes would recognise the details undertaken in their respective roles, then as now. Bessie, as head machinist at Rayne's in the early years of the twentieth century, would have been familiar with the closing and finishing skills possessed by Jean Matthew. Electric lighting might have replaced shivering candlelight, but they would cast a glow over the same tools, the same ribbons and rhinestones. In the making of sturdy and comfortable footwear fit for a Queen, this is also a tale of resilient women. Sarah Holt and Elizabeth Hill both worked at the whim of their brothers-in-law, forced to rely on their continued good nature for a roof over their heads. Mary Ann Rayne was a seemingly fearless entrepreneur whose business grew from the seeds of a market stall to one of the best-known luxury footwear brands in the world and yet eight pregnancies and little support meant that her mental health suffered irreparably. Where today she would have been cared for, then she was incarcerated. Keturah Filmer, young and spirited and clever, had an exciting future mapped out for her, taking her from buttonholes to beyond, but the family's low income forced her to care for her sick mother when nobody else could do so. Jean Matthew would become one of the first female shoe designers and an indomitable employee with her finger on the pulse of H. & M. Rayne at every stage. The shoes remain. These objects that were coaxed into being by so many people stand in silent, rhinestone-trimmed satin tribute to all of those lives.

CHAPTER 8

Fashioning a Silhouette
The Art of the Dressmaker

Not all queens like clothes. In September 1905, Mary Duchess of York, wife of the future King George V, travelled to London three weeks before a planned trip to India in order to choose garments for their visit. She wrote to her husband that it had been 'a hard day's work at tiresome clothes', an aspect of her role that she disliked. A few days later George replied: 'I am delighted to hear that you have now finished trying on all yr dresses & I hope they fit well. In all the papers I see long accounts of them.' For Mary, the necessary acquirement of a public wardrobe was a chore that she could easily have lived without at the same time as recognising that there was a public appetite for her choices. On the other side of the sartorial coin were the challenges of interacting with a royal customer. Jean-Philippe Worth, son of the couture legend Charles Frederick Worth, recounted a dress fitting with Queen Alexandra: 'We made only one dress for the Queen of England . . . she came in for the fittings herself and three ladies in waiting accompanied her. Alexandra had scarcely stepped on the tiny stage to be fitted before these gadflies began: "Don't tire Her Majesty", "Be careful of that pin", "Don't stick Her Majesty", "Watch out now!"' Jean-Philippe continued his description of the experience: 'The poor fitter dripped with perspiration and trembled with nervousness and in the end hardly knew whether she dared use a pin, let alone where to put it. Alexandra herself was pleasantly pliant and agreeable and, being rather deaf, missed all the uproar of solicitude going on around her.' Even Alexandra herself, who was so famously elegant and would spend a lifetime ensuring that her clothing was suitable for every occasion, could get frustrated with the whole business. In 1873, she wrote to her sister Dagmar in Russia, whilst preparing for a state visit, about 'our <u>unbearable</u> dress nonsense which is boring me beyond description'.

Serving as a dressmaker to the Queen could be the making of a career but also a source of no little stress, working under more unusual

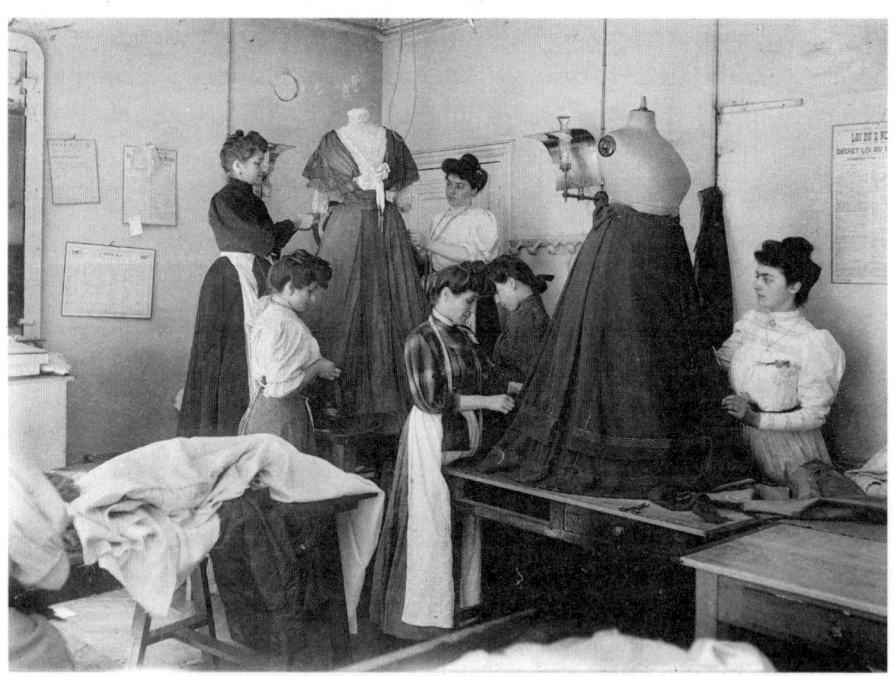

Seamstresses at the House of Worth salon, 1907.

conditions than usual. Perhaps more than any other of the needle trades whose skills contributed to the royal wardrobe, the dressmaking establishments serving Queens Victoria, Alexandra and Mary in the nineteenth and early twentieth centuries were emporiums of almost exclusively female labour. These were women who often began their lives away from the metropolis and came to London in search of work. And what work they found, fitting and fashioning silk and lace and chiffon for the most famous women in the world. These were not the women who would necessarily become the most renowned fashion houses, however. Who now has heard of Mary Bettans or Elizabeth Gieve or Martha Dudley? Even those whose royal patronage brought them some contemporary celebrity have faded largely into obscurity now, the names of Morin Blossier, Madame Clapham and Handley-Seymour relegated to the woven labels stitched into their garments that lie sleeping in museum stores. There are photographs in their thousands of these queens in their clothes, beyond which are the hundreds of women who made them.

A whole group of women served specifically as Queen Victoria's dressmaker, about whom there is hardly any surviving documentation, simply echoes here and there of their work. Their creations predated the custom of attaching a maker's label into the waistband of a garment and so there is not even that silky signature to mark their contributions. One of the earliest of Victoria's named dressmakers was actually chosen for her by her mother the Duchess of Kent, featuring in the Duchess's accounting records as a new maker in 1824 when the Princess Victoria was only six years old. Her name was Mary Bettans. Mary was born in Southwark in 1798 and in 1817 married Samuel Bettans who was twenty-one years her senior. The hows and whereabouts of Mary's apprenticeship as a dressmaker are lost but her reputation as a seamstress was such that by her mid-twenties she had secured royal patronage. It is likely that she made one of the most celebrated and best-recorded dresses of the period, the cream satin gown that Queen Victoria wore for her wedding on 10 February 1840. By this time she was well established at 84 Jermyn Street with eight dressmakers living under the same roof with her and Samuel. They included Louisa Clarke whose name appears underneath Mary's on the 1841 census, and who leaves another trace thanks to official documents of the government commissioners reporting on the conditions of child labour in the mines and manufactories of Great Britain the same year.

Perhaps because of her association with royalty, Mary Bettans's establishment was chosen as one of those visited by the commissioners. In summary, the visiting official wrote: 'This has the appearance of a well-conducted establishment. The work-room is airy and pleasant and has three large windows.' We hear the voice of Mrs Bettans herself as she describes the hours that her apprentice girls work and the conditions of their employment, during the busy season commencing at 7 a.m. and not finishing until 10 or 11 p.m. but in the quiet season, 'they often leave off at tea-time or in the afternoon'. Louisa Clarke was interviewed by the commissioner and asked about her position, to which she replied that she had sufficient food and everything was of the best. She dined with the family, was provided a cooked dinner on a Sunday and was very properly instructed in all branches of the business by Mrs Bettans. 'The sleeping rooms are comfortable. The work-room is very airy. The work does not try her eyes and has no cause of complaint.' I wonder if it was Louisa who was responsible for the collection of scraps pasted into an exercise book that only came to light in a private collection in the 1990s. Roughly cut swatches of silk, of velvet and tiny snips of lace were glued into its pages with handwritten notes about the gowns they had become. Identified as an unknown employee of Mary Bettans, I imagine Louisa, after her cooked dinner on a Sunday and with an hour or two to spare, making this tactile memory book of the royal commissions she helped to stitch.

Mary's workshop had closed by 1844 and whilst she was not the only establishment serving as dressmaker to the Queen she had certainly been responsible for some of the most important garments in young Victoria's early reign. Where Mary had her husband Samuel as a support during her working life, a pattern that emerges from many of Queen Victoria's named dressmakers is one of single independence. At different times from the 1850s up until the 1890s, Sarah Ann Unitt, Elizabeth Gieve and Martha Dudley all operated their own businesses making clothes for the Queen and all were masters of their own destiny. Sarah Ann Unitt had been born in Staffordshire in 1808 and by 1851 was the head of her household, employing eight dressmakers from her premises at 21 Grosvenor Street. They included the wonderfully named Honorina Pranger from France as well as a host of other dressmakers, two milliners, a cook and a housemaid. From her Mayfair address, Sarah Ann conducted her household of women from top to bottom, the sleeping, eating and the all-important making of gowns. At the same time Elizabeth Gieve, originally from a small farming town in North Devon, ran her dressmaking business from 28 Davies Street, employing two other dressmakers; whilst thirty years later, Martha Dudley ran an enormous household from 11 Bruton Street, which included ten dressmakers, a specialist milliner, a mantle maker, a showroom assistant for packing parcels, a page and a porter.

Including her domestic servants, Martha coordinated the work, the rest, the sustenance and the discipline of twenty-one people in her house and like the others before her, she did so as an entrepreneurial businesswoman. Martha was the maker whose gowns are distinctive, not because they bear a maker's label, but because she made many of Queen Victoria's dresses that almost came to define the lasting image of the ageing monarch – the black silk gowns of her widowhood. As a young curatorial assistant, I worked in a collection that had two of Queen Victoria's 1890s dresses, and preparing them for exhibition was always an instructive experience. The combination of her diminutive stature and her expanding waistline meant that there was no dress form that would easily accommodate the dress and we would have to wind yards of museum padding around a display torso until it matched the garment's dimensions. Then it was as if she had taken form in the room, this significant figure. At that time I didn't give any thought to the maker. There was no label and so Martha Dudley was absent from this later recreation of her work, but there in the tiny stitches, the black silk fringe and the rustle of the silk were the sartorial fingerprints of Martha and her seamstresses, Sophia Smith, Frances Clayton and Lydia Dewey.

I hope, but do not know if, like Mary Bettans, Sarah, Elizabeth and Martha ran well-conducted establishments with employees who felt that they were looked after well by the standards of their day, but it was certainly not a guarantee. One of the most notorious cases of the mistreatment of seamstresses covered in the national press involved the prestigious dressmaker Madame Elise – who would one day receive a Royal Warrant of Appointment from Alexandra, Princess of Wales. In the middle of the nineteenth century, concerns about working conditions in the needle trades had been increasing as factory reports and commissioners' findings revealed some dreadful statistics. In 1863, the plight of seamstresses was brought to a wider audience with the death of a young dressmaker named Mary Ann Walkley. Mary Ann worked for Madame Elise and, like the other women in her employ, had been undertaking horrifically long hours in a bid to meet the orders placed during the busy London Season. The cause of Mary Ann's death, as reported in the press, was 'long hours of work and insufficient ventilation'. Following her death, one of the other dressmakers working for the firm wrote an anonymous letter to *The Times* in which she described their conditions, from the minimum eighteen-hour working day to the single-room workspace to the sharing of a bed in a windowless room.

Within a month, *Punch* published a cartoon by John Leech entitled 'The Haunted Lady or the Ghost in the Looking Glass' which depicted a fine London lady admiring her reflection in a tall mirror, the unscrupulous dressmaker standing behind her, whilst to her horror, she sees in the reflection not her splendidly clad self, but an exhausted seamstress. The firm of Madame Elise was founded by Elizabeth Marie Louise Jaeger who had been born in Frankfurt. In 1851 she was working for a milliner on Regent Street named Jane Clarke, and when Clarke retired in 1859 Elizabeth and her husband Frederick Isaacson took on the business. Whilst Elise Isaacson has become notorious for the death of one of her seamstresses, it was by no means a rare set of circumstances. It is likely that she herself would have experienced poor working conditions as a young milliner, just another young woman plying her trade as part of the industrial status quo. By the early 1870s, she was advertising her Royal Warrant and went on in later life to publish books and articles about fashionable dress but I wonder how the experience of 1863 marked her? The John Leech caricature had depicted the 'Elise' figure in a wildly anti-Semitic light and whilst she would go on to have a celebrated career as a royal dressmaker, did that experience shape her in some way?

Madame Elise was not the only prominent female dressmaker whom Alexandra would patronise in the course of her long career in the fashion limelight. During a period in the later nineteenth and early twentieth centuries when male designers had been making their mark on the new world of 'couture', Alexandra steadfastly chose female makers. One of her favourites was the now little-known Morin Blossier. Contrary to many press reports at the time, as well as subsequent biographers, who maintained that Alexandra always patronised British makers, she did in fact commission most of her formal gowns from French dressmakers. She ordered frequently from Morin Blossier, a firm founded by two sisters in Paris, Victoire and Marie Morin. They had both started their careers working as forewomen for other dressmakers before moving to Vienna in 1873 and establishing their own label, garnering a number of wealthy clients in the city. There, Victoire married Albert Blossier and together they began to trade under the Morin Blossier name, Albert taking on the business side of the venture whilst Victoire and Marie focused on the making. In 1884, there was an in-depth feature published about the fashion house that appeared in newspapers around the world, offering a tantalising picture of life in this high-end fashion establishment. The author described the Paris premises, a house on the corner of the rue de la Paix: '[They] furnished it charmingly in Genoese velvet, with old hangings and great mirrors in carved wood frames.' The sisters employed between two and three hundred men and women: 'Some of these employees take their meals in the basement, where there are kitchens and dining rooms for the common folk.' The ground floor included packing rooms for the garments being sent to clients and some living quarters for the male employees, then a floor inhabited by the sisters themselves along with the governesses for their children. On the first floor was a large high reception room where the customers were received, the glamorous salons for enjoying the wares produced by the needlewomen of Morin Blossier. 'The second floor holds stores of dress-goods, brocades, velvets, silks, embroideries, furs, gauzes, flowers and lace, metal ornaments and bead garnitures of all sorts.' It is a dizzying description of the variety of materials required for such a venture as theirs. Each department had its own tasks and specific skill sets: 'The corsage-maker never sees the skirt, the sleeve sewer never sews a dart, the draper never cuts the gores and the designer never has shears in her hand.'

Although Alexandra did visit Paris from time to time, the firm of Morin Blossier did not require in-person fittings, thanks to the measurement system they had in place: 'In the corsage department is to be noted a vast wardrobe with pigeon-holes, where every client has a fitted lining kept in a numbered and ticketed case.' Corsage was the contemporary description for the bodice, the unnamed journalist from the article reporting that: 'One sister has a talent for fitting corsages, probably unequalled at present in all Paris.' It may have been Morin Blossier's skill in this particular department that appealed to Alexandra for a very specific reason, one that only came to light relatively recently. In 2011, I was awarded the Gervers Fellowship at the Royal Ontario Museum in Toronto, an opportunity to research the garments belonging to Queen Alexandra that they hold in their collection, and amongst the garments there was a glorious court gown made by Morin Blossier. Yellow chiffon was dotted all over with hand-applied rhinestones and I could imagine the materials being chosen from that array of supplies on the second floor of the rue de la Paix. The dress was decorated with large hand-painted purple irises that bloomed from the hem of the skirt and on to the bodice itself, but herein lay a mystery. When fastened at the back, the painted irises did not sit straight. They were misaligned in such a fashion as to appear poorly constructed, which did not make sense given the quality of the garment and the reputation of the makers. Shoddy workmanship would not have passed the eagle eyes of Victoire or Marie, so what had happened to Queen Alexandra's bodice? I contacted a former curator at the Metropolitan Museum of Art who had mounted some of Alexandra's dresses some years earlier and she confirmed that these, too, never fitted standard dress forms comfortably. I needed to look further back into Alexandra's past for some clarity. In 1869, Alexandra, Princess of Wales had suffered from what was described at the time as a 'rheumatic fever' following the birth of her daughter. She was gravely ill and daily updates were printed in the newspapers as she eventually began to recover. She was left, however, with a stiff knee joint and would limp for the rest of her life. By the time Morin Blossier made the iris gown for Alexandra in 1903, she had been limping for over thirty years. I contacted an orthopaedic surgeon to ask about the long-term physical impact this may have had and his answer made sense of it all. She would almost certainly, he said, have developed a degree of scoliosis – a curvature of the spine. Here was a woman approaching her sixties who was still at the forefront of public life and who wanted to maintain some discretion around the realities of her body. She entrusted the fitting of her dress and the uniqueness of her shape to the expert corsage makers at Morin Blossier, women who would craft a garment fit for her and her alone.

An address in Paris or London was generally the most common location for dressmakers associated with royal patronage, but there were some businesses in regional locations, unusual though that generally was. One such dressmaker who made her mark on the world of fashion in the late nineteenth century was Madame Clapham. Like so many others in her world, the 'Madame' was a nod to her skill as a maker rather than denoting French origins, for Emily Clapham was based not in the rue de Rivoli or in premises on Regent Street but in the East Yorkshire town of Hull. Emily was born in Cheltenham in 1858, middle child of Walter and Rhoda MacVitie. Walter was a house painter and the family subsidised their income with female boarders. By her early teens, Emily had left the family home and began her apprenticeship as a dressmaker in a branch of Marshall & Snelgrove in Scarborough. She lived on the premises under the supervision of the shop manager, James Dippie, and his wife, Harriet, along with seventy-nine other employees. It is hard to imagine that life. Two hundred miles away from the rest of her family, Emily would live amongst the milliners, shop women, drapery assistants and clerks. She picked up pins from the floor and incrementally learned the skills of a dressmaker at the same time as navigating the hierarchies of life in a department store.

In 1886 she married Haigh Clapham and a year later the couple pooled together their savings and invested them in number 1 Kingston Square in Hull. Here the dressmaking salon of Madame Clapham quickly made its mark. Emily had a reputation for her Parisian-inspired gowns and attracted clients from around the region to her door. She made wedding dresses, court presentation gowns and dinner ensembles. Her elaborate designs survive today in UK collections, not least those of Hull museum. By the mid-1890s her success was such that she added number 2 Kingston Square to the Madame Clapham salon and could also boast of clients from further afield. Queen Maud of Norway amongst other European royal women began to order garments from Emily Clapham. Daughter of Queen Alexandra, Maud was famously stylish and so her patronage cemented Emily's unexpected place in the fashion hierarchy. She never received a Royal Warrant for her endeavours but the regal associations lent the business all the glamour it needed to fill its order books. She was known as something of a formidable woman and her ambition appears to have impaired her judgement to no little extent when it came to her employees. As her star continued to rise, so too did the pressure on her seamstresses and they complained about the long hours they were forced to work with few breaks, echoes of the Madame Elise scandal sounding across the decades. As a mark of some progress in the working conditions of women dressmakers, Madame Clapham was found to have violated the Factory Act and fined for her practices. Whether or not this led to any material changes in Emily Clapham's workrooms, her reputation remained intact and she continued to expand, adding a third neighbouring property to the establishment just before the outbreak of the First World War.

A photograph of Emily in her middle age depicts an imposing figure, 'redoubtable' as she was described by contemporaries, stoutly posed in a dark tailored costume with a fur stole draped across one shoulder and a feathered hat balanced on her curled and coiffed head. Small spectacles attest perhaps to the many hours that she once spent peering at the stitches in front of her before her own name was above the shop door. The fortunes of the business faltered during the war and although Madame Clapham continued to clothe a broad clientele, it was much

Madame Clapham.

reduced. Remarkably, the firm managed to continue, however, through two world wars, only finally closing its doors in 1967. She stands as one of the few makers outside London to have secured such a prestigious client list – and all from such unlikely beginnings.

If you drew a line across a map of the UK east to west from Emily Clapham's Hull you would find yourself in the seaside town of Blackpool, where, in 1868, Elizabeth Fielding was born. Not unlike Emily, Elizabeth was born on the coast of the North of England into a working family. Where Emily's father painted houses, Elizabeth's father constructed them; over the years he was described variously as a stonemason and a builder. The family fortunes changed when, on 24 February 1882, James Fielding died. Elizabeth's mother, Rachel, took on the mantle of breadwinner and opened up her house to tenants, becoming a lodging-house keeper to support her still growing family. Elizabeth undertook a dressmaking apprenticeship, working in Blackpool establishments until her early twenties, but the bright lights of London were calling. She moved south and managed to forge not only a business but a relationship too, marrying fine art dealer James Burke Handley-Seymour on Boxing Day in 1901.

By 1908, Elizabeth had begun to design her own dresses with the help of four dressmakers. Within three years the business had outgrown itself and Elizabeth had not only to employ more staff, but also to move to larger premises on Bond Street and enlist the business support of her husband. Here she would receive her first court commissions from Queen Alexandra's daughter-in-law, the soon-to-be Queen Mary. By 1938 and in a story familiar with other dressmakers to benefit from royal patronage, Elizabeth Handley-Seymour had expanded to the extent of employing more than two hundred women all charged with the creation of Madame Handley-Seymour's gowns. Descriptions of them appear in the detailed diaries kept by Queen Mary's dressers, written in the shorthand necessary to keep track of garments and jewels worn on any given day. A typical entry for 8 May 1933, regarding an evening entertainment at the London Palladium, reads: 'H. Sey Beaded lace gown. D. comb. With carved emerald. 3 rows of Ds. Large E brooch. Green Chinese coat.' In 1932, the house of Handley-Seymour had made for Queen Mary a red velvet gown, a powder-blue crushed velvet, a silver lamé coat, an ivory embroidered dress, a beaded cream chiffon, a periwinkle georgette and a lace with painted roses. She was responsible for significant garments at significant moments in the royal calendar, including the wedding dress of Elizabeth, Duchess of York, in 1923 and her coronation dress when she was crowned alongside her husband, King George VI, in 1937. However, Elizabeth Handley-Seymour was not necessarily the greatest of designers. Her skills lay in her ability to see the talent in others.

As early as 1914 Elizabeth was advertising those Parisian fashion houses with whom she had reached an agreement to produce licensed copies, including the great Paul Poiret. This was a practice that she would continue throughout her career. The Victoria & Albert Museum holds almost five thousand of her hand-coloured fashion drawings bounds in forty-eight volumes, sketches that would have been distributed to clients. Each season this menu of garments was offered for selection, many of which were copies of those emerging from the major houses in Paris. It was not illegal, nor was it uncommon, and for Madame Handley-Seymour it would work in her favour as a sound business strategy that successfully contributed to her reputation.

Another wise business decision that would serve her well over the years was the employment of a young Australian apprentice named Avis Ford. Avis was born in Adelaide in 1888 where her father was an English surveyor of mines. The family returned to London when Avis was seven. In 1911 she can be found on the census, working as a 'costume saleswoman' and living in Putney with her aunt, but not long afterwards she was apprenticed at Handley-Seymour and would go on to become head designer and fitter. In fact, it is Avis who is credited with the design for the royal garments with which Handley-Seymour would become synonymous. In February 1949, Australian journalist Elene Foster wrote a piece about Avis Ford for the *Sydney Herald*, titled 'The Mysterious Miss Ford'. The article states that Avis had been making garments for the royal family for many years, including at this point for the young Princesses Elizabeth and Margaret, and whilst she says that some London dressmakers refer to her as the 'mysterious' Miss Ford, 'Avis Ford simply keeps to herself and dislikes publicity. She is regarded at Buckingham Palace as a family friend and sometimes has lunch there.' Foster describes Avis Ford as 'a little woman with mouse-coloured hair, blue eyes and a schoolgirl complexion'. She goes on to list the many designs for which the name of Handley-Seymour would become famous but which came from the imaginative mind of Avis Ford. It seems to have been a successful collaboration and indicative of the flair for fashion business that Elizabeth Handley-Seymour clearly had. She could spot talent, it seems. Whether via the designs of the Paris greats or the quieter brilliance of young Avis,

Fashioning a Silhouette

Avis Ford, designer at Madame Handley-Seymour, *Sydney Morning Herald*, 1949.

Elizabeth made a huge success of her name even without necessarily designing the garments herself. From Blackpool to Bond Street, Elizabeth made her mark.

As visible, tangible reminders of lives lived in the public eye, dresses bring forth the silhouette of their former inhabitants. Writing in her introduction to the book *In Royal Fashion*, Museum of London curator Kay Staniland wrote of royal dress: 'It offers an actual contact with its original owner, an outer skin which is still strongly permeated with the bodily characteristics of that personality.' That was certainly the case when displaying the distinctive black dress belonging to Queen Victoria, creating a silhouette that emerged into the room, a presence still felt in the threads of the bodice created by Martha Dudley. If the surviving dresses are infused with the personality of the wearer, then they stand too in tribute to their maker, even if they remain nameless or obscured by the more obvious label of their employer. We may catch a glimpse of those early dressmakers who fashioned the garments worn by Queen Victoria, either in snippets of text or in the rustle of the silk they left behind.

Dressing the Queen

Queen Alexandra's dressmakers were the first to advertise their skills and their status as warrant holders through the fixing of silk labels to the waist tapes of their creations, taking ownership of their brand for the first time. But they kept secrets too – Madame Elise using the royal arms to distract from her earlier brush with scandal and the terrible working conditions for so many exploited seamstresses, and Morin Blossier holding fast the secret of Alexandra's curved spine. Their dresses maintained the facade of upright youthfulness that the Queen was determined to retain, the skill of their construction fashioning her public armour. From the regional spaces of Hull and Blackpool came Emily and Elizabeth, women from working-class backgrounds whose clothes would appear on the world stage, with the quieter influence of makers such as Avis Ford adding their own contribution. Ultimately, these seem to be stories of female success. Against a backdrop of undoubted misogyny, oppression and the established patriarchy, here were a handful of women who stepped out of their lane and somehow managed to stamp their name above the door, across the label and into the royal records. Here might they find themselves celebrated once again.

CHAPTER 9

Fits Like a Glove
Dents of Worcester and Cornelia James

On a light June evening in 2009, I encountered my first (and only) gloved, royal hand. I didn't touch the hand (we were instructed that a bow of the head was sufficient) but it was the soft navy blue fabric gloves worn by the Princess Royal that I remember most about that evening. The event was a celebration of the Textile Conservation Centre, established at Hampton Court in 1975 and then relocated to the Winchester School of Art where I was undertaking my doctoral research. That evening at the Clothworkers' Company had an otherworldly atmosphere, as we stepped into the wood-panelled hall, glass of wine in hand, waiting for the announcement of the arrival of Princess Anne. Her dark blue gloves matched the details of her scarf and were a counterpoint to the bright yellow silk coat she wore. I was struck by the anomaly of the indoor glove. As objects, they inhabit our wardrobes today for reasons purely driven by the weather and have long ceased to function as symbols of status for almost everybody. Except royal women. Gloves have formed a staple of the royal wardrobe for centuries, performing roles as varied as the spiritual and symbolic to the purely practical, acting as a barrier between the royal body and everybody else.

The Heritage Crafts Association, champion of a whole host of traditional artisanal practices, has placed the technique of glove making on to their red list of endangered crafts. An ageing workforce, lack of apprenticeship places and competition from low-cost producers elsewhere have severely impacted the viability of glove making as an industry. Now there are fewer than a hundred people working in this trade which once supported thirty thousand in the town of Worcester alone, glovers and gloveresses whose livelihoods depended on the labour-intensive, handmade processes of the industry. The ubiquitous nature of gloves meant that they were often purchased by the dozen from high-end outfitters or department stores, sourced for the Queen's wardrobe as an accessory that had frequently to be replenished. The uniformity of the glove might suggest mass manufacture and an identikit process of mindless making, yet nothing could be further from the truth. A conservative estimate records over seventy different processes contributing to the manufacture of a pair of leather gloves, from tanning and dyeing to the final distinctive, decorative stitching across the back of the glove. It involved a variety of tools and spaces, of men and women, of machine and hand.

Gloves do not really change. Where shoes and hats might alter according to taste and fashion, gloves remain the same. Even grandly ceremonial gloves are almost interchangeable with one another. Queen Elizabeth I's coronation glove – a marvel of white leather with a deep wrist panel of golden embroidery in the gauntlet style – is almost identical to the coronation glove worn by her namesake Queen Elizabeth II centuries later. These ceremonial gloves were, and remain still, an important part of the symbolism of monarchy. The single coronation glove has long played a role in the ceremony and embellished gloves were often historically given as gifts both to and from kings and queens. They can be potent reminders of the wearer. In the varied collections of the Ashmolean museum in Oxford, there is a rather battered and well-worn buff leather glove. It is described as a hawking glove, decorated with unusual swirls. It is stained on the fingertips and creased where the fingers curved within. Out of context it might seem an unlovely object and yet its great age (it dates to the sixteenth century) and its provenance (it was King Henry VIII's hawking glove) lend it an altogether different quality. The ghost of the hand remains in its moulded shape, the outline of a larger-than-life historical figure left behind in the silhouette of a single glove. Ghostly too, are the glovers whose livelihood depended on the social conventions of sartorial etiquette. What was life like for them?

A company that looms large in the records of royal glove making is Dents. The business was established by John Dent in 1777, manufacturing leather gloves from a small property on Wood Street in Worcester. A combination of high-quality materials and some canny business strategies meant that within seventy years, Dents had become the most successful glove manufacturer in the world, making twelve million pairs annually. Leather gloves had to have an inherent stretch without being too elastic and so the complex tanning processes and choice of leather were crucial to ensure the best fit. There was a surprising element to the softening of glove leather, however, one that Mrs Henry Wood described in her 1862 novel *Mrs Halliburton's Troubles*. A morality tale of toil, labour and social status, Mrs Wood painted a picture of the glovers and gloveresses in her home town of Worcester, including the unusual ingredient so crucial to the end product: 'When the skins came in from the leather dressers they were first washed in a tub of cold water. The next day warm water, mixed with yolks of eggs, was poured upon them, and a couple of men, barelegged to the knee, got into the tub and danced upon them, skins, eggs and water, for two hours.' Large manufacturers such as Dents used a million yolks a year, the eggs imported from China to meet the great demand. These yolks plumped and softened the skin prior to its

Dressing the Queen

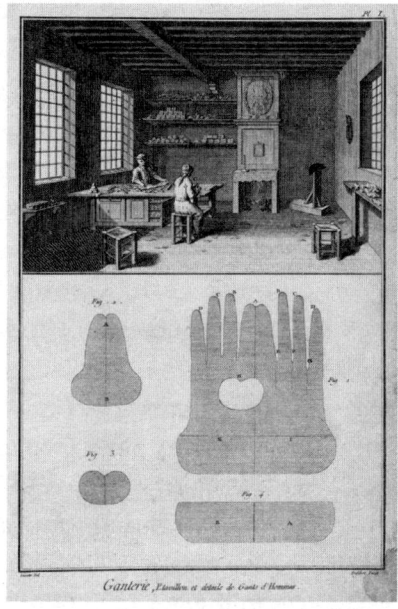

Glove-making diagram in Diderot's *Pictorial Encyclopedia of Trades and Industry*.

drying, a desirable property for leather gloves, suppleness being key to their success.

When the skins had been fully prepared and softened, they would be dampened slightly and left overnight, staked or stretched, so that they would be at maximum elasticity when the glove cutter was ready to begin the process of shaping the glove. To be a glove cutter was to be regarded as a skilled craftsman, the apprenticeship a full seven years in the nineteenth century. Even in the 1920s, when mechanisation had changed methods of manufacture, a trainee glove cutter would serve four years as an apprentice before he was considered a master of the art. It was a gendered division of labour – all cutters were male, and contemporary photographs of the Dents factory capture be-whiskered men, shirtsleeves rolled up, dark waistcoats fastened and aprons tied at the waist as they prepared the skins. Cutters would cast a practised eye over the skins which had been stretched overnight to determine how to cut and thus achieve the best fit. It was a process that remained almost unchanged over the course of centuries. Diderot's famous *Encyclopedia* of 1764 includes an illustration of a glove workshop, the tools of which would have been as familiar to a Dents cutter a century later, as would the drawings of the various parts of the glove to be cut. It is a magical-sounding glossary of terms: the hank or hand-shaped piece; the fourchettes, strips of leather between the fingers; the small triangular quirk to allow more space for the fingers; vents and welts and thumb pieces all cut from thousands of squares of stretched leather ready to be stitched.

It was a craft that supported many thousands of families in Worcester alone. Page after page of census records list 'glover' and 'gloveress' in the town, sons and daughters following fathers and mothers into the trade. Thomas Harrison lived on Bromyard Terrace in Worcester. He and his wife Margaret had six children to support. Their eldest sons, sixteen-year-old Thomas and fourteen-year-old Walter, were already working at Dents, contributing to the family's income via the glove factory that was the centre of their working lives. Each day Thomas senior and his older sons would have walked a little over a mile from their red-brick terraced house, crossing the River Severn to South Quay and the vast four-storeyed Dents factory. Each morning they would have left Margaret as she readied eleven-year-old Ernest, eight-year-old Mary and little five-year-old Margaret for school, leaving her at home with two-year-old Eliza. For most women at this time, factory work would have been more difficult with a small child at home, but Margaret's occupation illuminates one of the more unusual realities of the industry. She is listed as a 'gloveress'. Unlike so many other of the needle trades in the second half of the nineteenth century, outworking remained central to manufacture and so, with baby Eliza pottering around her, Margaret could stitch gloves at home by the dozen. It was a practice that continued well into the twentieth century, described in detail by a glove worker in the 1940s: 'Most of the stitching was done by outworkers as we called them, virtually all women in their own homes around the area. Many of them sort of came in weekly to collect their work and get their wages for the amount that they'd made the week before and take on next week's work.' The author continued: 'Those who didn't or couldn't come into the factory were delivered to: often by a boy coming in after school, riding an errand boy's bike taking the goods out to them and bringing what they'd completed back again.'

Either by hand or at a treadle sewing machine, women by the thousand would sew the glove components delivered to them in bundles, attaching each part to form the shape of the glove before adding the decorative stitching. Each process required a different technique, Eldred Ellis keen to stress in his 1921 volume on the glove trade that: 'Thus, "pointing" or the decoration of the back of the glove, stitching in the thumbs, fourchettes and gussets, closing of the glove, making of button holes, sewing on of buttons, welting and finishing are often done by different operatives and frequently on entirely different classes of machine.'

One of the ten thousand outworkers employed by Dents was Ethel Wale. Ethel was born in 1880, living with her parents, Nathanial, a porter, and Ellen, who was a gloveress, as well as her two brothers Bertram and Harold. The family were long-time residents of Dandy Row, a street of nine terraced houses in Worcester. Each house had a small front living room with an oven grate and a little back room. The family had two bedrooms and a strip of garden at the front. Whilst Nathanial, Bertram and Harold went to work each day, I wonder if Ethel and her mother sat in their small living room, stitching gloves? Did they talk as they worked, assembling the fashionable objects or

Fits Like a Glove

A Dents gloveress at work, 1890s.

running the decorative pointing stitches? Did they ever wonder who might draw the soft leather gloves on to their hands or were all of their thoughts directed purely to the speedy completion of as many pairs as possible? Pay for outworkers was low and so volume was of the essence to enhance the weekly wage packet. Ethel was still living at home with her brothers in 1911, still stitching her gloves and living with her family on Dandy Row, supporting her now retired parents through her employment at Dents. How many thousands of pairs of gloves passed through Ethel's hands, I wonder, during the more than twenty years of her employment? Just as she fashioned the supple gloves for equally soft, unseen hands, so must her own have become hardened through the labour of stitching.

Leather gloves were not the only type of glove favoured as a fashionable accessory. Increasingly, fabric gloves became a popular and practical object in the royal wardrobe, dominated for more than seven decades by one name. Cornelia James. The story of Cornelia James is one of success through adversity, and of manufacture that has defied the odds in a world of mass production and fast fashion. Cornelia was born in Vienna and after school, began to train as a glove maker at the Viennese College of Art. Turbulent times were ahead for her and her family, however. Her daughter Genevieve described to me her mother's recollection of this period in Austria, of Vienna in the 1930s and increasing hostility towards its Jewish population. Living in a non-Jewish district of the city, the family's neighbours turned on them. 'She had to scrub graffiti off the pavement of their house,' Genevieve recalled, 'and then they got out on forged passports.'

Escaping the Nazi regime, Cornelia arrived in England where for a time she was interned. Of the few possessions she was able to bring with her when they fled their home, one of the most pivotal was a case of her precious glove leather. It was not the most auspicious of beginnings to a life in design. Following her release from the internment camp, Cornelia spent time during the course of the war working with wounded soldiers, using the skills that she had learnt at art college to offer rehabilitation to these damaged bodies. Stitch became a means through which these men could regain the finer movements of their hands. It was a practice that had a royal precedent during the years of the First World War. Sawdust hearts were textile keepsakes that had been made as love tokens for centuries and were often made by soldiers and sailors in conflicts to send home to loved ones. Queen Mary recognised their potential value as a therapeutic practice and organised for kits to be assembled and sent out to injured soldiers on the Western Front. They became known as sweetheart cushions, heart shaped and decorated with glass-headed pins, patriotic symbols and memories of home. Stitching was, then as now, such a gendered practice, but solace was to be found in the mindful making of the cushions. Cornelia brought such solace to shattered bodies and helped their hands to feel useful once more.

The gloom of post-war Britain proved to be Cornelia's salvation.

She returned to her early days as a glove designer and, with the colourful leather that had filled her suitcase, made gloves once more, in rainbow shades. She recognised that whilst rationing was still in force and clothing was expensive, gloves could bring colour and life to a lacklustre wardrobe. The vibrancy of her creations caught the attention of *Vogue* magazine who dubbed her 'the colour queen of England'. It would change the course of her life. The publicity brought her gloves to the attention of Norman Hartnell who, by this time, was already making clothes for the young Princess Elizabeth. Genevieve described her mother's career-changing moment thanks to Hartnell. 'She caught his eye and he started to become interested in her. Her big break came when he was asked to make the wedding gown and he asked my mother to make a whole trousseau of gloves for the honeymoon. After that she became quite well known and anybody who was anybody had gloves made by her.'

Business boomed throughout the 1950s and the company moved to Brighton where they employed local makers to meet the demands of a keen clientele, royalty included. Genevieve remembers her mother as ever present in their small factory, clad in a white coat and involved still in all of the gloving processes. A cultural shift was on the horizon, however, captured in a single photograph of the model Jean Shrimpton at the Melbourne Cup in the shortest of mini dresses wearing neither hat nor gloves. The 1960s cast off the etiquette of accessories but the royal wardrobe persisted where others did not. Cornelia James continued to make gloves for the Queen, the soft white fabric gloves that became synonymous with her royal wave, hand aloft, fingers curved. The company was awarded the Royal Warrant in 1979 and has held it ever since, through the highs and lows of manufacture, changing fashions, rising costs and cheap alternatives.

Cornelia died in 1994, still active in the business of glove making to within a few months of her death. Today it is her daughter Genevieve and her husband, Andrew, who maintain the Cornelia James brand. Genevieve holds the Royal Warrant and has supplied gloves to most of the royal women today. They ensured that the Queen was supplied with her requisite number of white gloves no matter the inconvenience, Genevieve recalling one particularly stressful royal commission. The Queen was leaving for a state visit to Korea. 'On Sunday we get a panicked call, her gloves had not turned up!' It being a Sunday, there was nobody in the workshop but Genevieve managed to find enough pairs and her husband set off for the palace on his motorbike. 'But it was the London Marathon and everything was cordoned off.' Andrew managed to convey the urgency of his mission to a policeman in the vicinity and across a loudspeaker rang out the command: 'Make way for the Queen's gloves!' He was ushered to the back door of Buckingham Palace and duly delivered his important parcel.

In the face of challenging times, it is the retention of some of the older, familiar practices that has served them well. The gloves are die cut using a lever press made by the firm W. H. Hallett & Sons in Yeovil more than a century ago. Their buttonholing machine dates to the mid-1950s. Their workforce is small, having moved from Glovers Yard in Brighton to a farm in East Sussex. There are ten seamstresses, some full-time and some part-time. Outworking is still a part of their process. Transport Ethel Wale and Margaret Harrison through time and into the Cornelia James workroom and I suspect they would feel at home amongst the familiar processes and shapes, able to fashion a pair of gloves at Cornelia James as swiftly and successfully as they did for Dents a century or so earlier. This kind of practice remains at the heart of what Genevieve and her family have sought to retain. Whilst most of their business is online, the service aims to replicate a more intimate experience. 'What we are trying to do in this world of fast fashion is the feeling that you are buying the gloves over the counter with a personal touch,' Genevieve explained. It is a rare endeavour. In global

Cornelia James at work.

north economies, over-consumption has become endemic in fashion and textile retailing, so to run a viable business with mindful making at its heart is no mean feat.

As the wearing of gloves became less fashionable, so the making of them became less lucrative. Gone were the years that saw millions of gloves packaged up and dispatched to department stores far and wide. In the late 1930s Dents moved from its established base in Worcester to the town of Warminster in Somerset, another hub of glove-making expertise. It was with a pared-down workforce that they continued to produce the finest of leather gloves, following the time-honoured techniques. It is an employment that has produced loyal craftspeople, so rare are these roles today. In July 2019, three Dents employees were recognised for their long service with the company. Lily Mundy, Teresa Tryhorne and Sally Norris all started working for the firm in the 1960s, following in the footsteps of the thousands of women gloveresses who had closed fingertips, sewn buttonholes and stitched the lines of pointing before them. Ethel Wale and Margaret Harrison and the countless other women who supported their families with the stitching of supple leather at Dents would find their contemporary counterparts, different and yet the same, in Lily, Teresa and Sally.

There is a connection of my own that I treasure, threads that link projects past and present through the gift of gloves. In February 2023, my husband and I were in London for the launch of *The Dress Diary of Mrs Anne Sykes*. My proposal for a book exploring the lives of royal suppliers had been submitted and recently accepted for publication and I was both overwhelmed and excited at the prospect. At breakfast, my husband handed me a slim black box with the name 'Cornelia James' inscribed in gold, surmounted by the arms of the Royal Warrant. Encased in layers of tissue were a beautiful pair of soft, navy, jersey gloves, along with a little handwritten note from the maker, Libby. Here was the maker acknowledging her contribution in an often anonymous world of creation, and she seemed to stand for all that I hoped I might find. When I told Genevieve about the gift, she wrote: 'Your husband did the right thing, giving a pair of gloves is a gift of love.'

CHAPTER 10

Queens of Couture
The Modern Designer from Hartnell to Parvin

Where dressmakers dominated in the nineteenth and early-twentieth centuries, the age of the great fashion designer was also gathering pace. In a system that revolutionised the dissemination of costly clothing, the emphasis was beginning to move from the client to the maker. Where dressmakers often worked under the instruction of their customer who might provide the cloth and even suggest the style of a garment, the designer began to turn the process on its head and dictate to an avid audience what they ought to wear. Whilst British fashion was often dismissed as the poor cousin of the French industry, there was a thriving and creative band of luxury designers serving monied clients and, of course, royalty. From the early years of the twentieth century, London designers like Mrs Seymour-Howell and Lucile occupied desirable London addresses and began to make a name for themselves as couturiers, occupying a different space from that of the dressmaker. It is a small world, the space of upmarket British couture, and the network of designers who would be granted the Royal Warrant seems to share connections, a common thread of patronage and labour. This gossamer thread of design and endeavour connects Norman Hartnell with Ian Thomas; Ian Thomas with Stewart Parvin; Stewart Parvin with Bruce Oldfield. From the 1930s to the present day these are sartorial narratives that share a regal DNA, navigating the challenges presented by royal design.

Paris had become synonymous with ostentatious fashion, thanks in large part to the quality of its brocaded silk designs in the eighteenth century, but the first designer to truly make their mark in this world, operating out of a glamorous Parisian salon, was, in fact, an Englishman from Lincolnshire. Charles Frederick Worth was born in 1825 in a small market town, son of a well-to-do solicitor and the youngest of the family's five children. His father, William, did not provide the stable home life that might have been expected from a legal career, but rather frittered away all of his money and in 1836 left his wife and children to fend for themselves. At the age of twelve, only a year after his father's abandonment, Charles left home and travelled to London where he started work as a young clerk in a ladies' outfitters. It was here he discovered that, rather than taking down the company figures in an accounting ledger, he much preferred handling the fine fabrics and imagining the garments they might become. In the mid-1840s he travelled to Paris to try and live out his dream of working in the fashion capital of the world, becoming a sales assistant, soon well versed in the language of fabric. His perseverance served him well and by the late 1850s he had entered the world of couture under his own name, first in partnership with Otto Gustav Bobergh and eventually as a solo venture, from the rue de la Paix. In their detailed catalogue of his work, archivists Chantal Trubert-Tollu et al. wrote: 'By 1863 Charles Frederick Worth employed a workforce of nearly 700, and the company had a turnover of nearly twenty million francs.' His legacy was long-lived and even today he is still popularly referred to as the 'father of haute couture'; the designer who created a collection of gowns and invited Paris society to inspect them in his salon so they could thereafter place valuable orders. Ironically for a fashion house that made such an impact, clothing many of the world's most famous women including European royalty, the British monarchy rarely sourced their clothes from Worth. His influence echoed down the decades, however, the first of the long line of celebrity fashion designers who would become household names.

One of the leading lights of the British scene, with whom we have already become somewhat familiar, was Norman Hartnell. Hartnell described his entrance into the world of fabric and fashion at a young age in his memoir *Silver and Gold*. He recalled sitting in his nursery as a small boy where: 'My interest in Fashion began with a box of crayons.' So sophisticated did his sketches become that his cousin Constance asked if she might take one of his drawings and have it made into a gown for an upcoming fancy-dress party. She subsequently won the fancy-dress parade in this first-ever Hartnell design, a portent of the successes that would follow. His path was not necessarily clearly mapped out, however. Fashion was not considered a suitable career path for a young man like Hartnell, but an unsuccessful period at Cambridge convinced his family that convention was not to be. He left university and found work with a court dressmaker, a grand dame of the Edwardian era named Madame Desiree, who hired young Norman Hartnell as a sketch artist for £3 a week. It was doomed to failure, however, the cost of his employment proving too prohibitive for the establishment, and within a matter of months he was unemployed, the business unable to support him no matter how good his drawings were. His first brush with fashion royalty came when he was summoned to the small London studio then occupied by the famous Lucile. Sharing his ideas with her, he was delighted with her response: ' "These are exactly the sort of thing I need," she said and, in one breath, "I trained and made Molyneux. I can train and make you. Are you free? It would mean of course, your travelling to Paris and to New York to work with me," she added almost apologetically.' His excitement was to be short-lived, however. Shortly afterwards, he discovered that Lucile had been passing off his sketches as her own – a final desperate attempt, perhaps, to rejuvenate the fashion house that had been so celebrated two decades earlier.

Hartnell refused to admit defeat. With next to no money but an optimistic view of his talent, he decided to circumvent the usual routes into the industry and set up in his own name. Strolling along Bruton Street, in Mayfair, he noticed a sign indicating some first-floor rooms to rent and took the plunge. He gave a memorable description of that decision: 'No house was ever started in a more unprofessional, amateurish way. To inaugurate such an establishment now, one would have to acquire great financial backing and a number of thoroughly experienced directors.' He continued: 'A London mansion, or even two or more mansions, would have to be found, rented or purchased, in a suitable street and reconstructed in accordance with the rules of the L.C.C., Westminster City Council and the Factories Act, the consideration of ancient lights not being overlooked, then decorated and carpeted sumptuously to please the expected clients.' That was not the end of the challenge, however: 'Simultaneously one would need to engage under contract expert fitters and master tailors, with scores of accompanying workgirls, experienced saleswomen with devoted clientele, furriers, embroideresses, milliners and mannequins.' In describing the realities of a mid-century London couture establishment, he highlighted the lack of all of those things at the very beginning, describing the many roles for which his sister volunteered for want of additional staff: 'I imposed upon the poor girl the combined duties of manageress, receptionist, saleswoman, bookkeeper and stenographer. Her office was a table and a chair behind a grey velvet screen, which kept falling over, revealing her in all her capacities.'

Whilst being aware of his own potential, Hartnell was never in any doubt as to the importance of those he would employ. He recalled a talented dress fitter at Madame Desiree, a Madame Mole, who found herself 'disengaged' and so he swiftly hired her, but he needed more staff. 'With difficulty we managed to engage a few young ladies for the workroom. Miss Holliday, Mrs Leach, Miss Griffin, Violet Durling, Mabel Cox and little Nellie Todd.' Hartnell was quick to realise his own limitations and the importance of these women to his success. Having spent a period of time in the earliest days as a 'matching boy' tasked with trudging about the fabric centres of London to find cloth and trims in the perfect shades, he realised that he was ill suited to the job: 'The matching queue was not my particular milieu and one day my sister engaged a busy little body called Louie. Having devoted her quick wits to my business ever since then, she is now my head stock keeper and a well known figure in the West End world of dressmaking.' Louie was Louise Bowen Richardson, who started working for Hartnell at the age of fifteen, her keen eye eventually taking her around the world sourcing the fabrics that would clothe queens. She became a familiar figure in Buckingham Palace, always referred to fondly as 'Miss Louie' by the various royal women she encountered in the half-century of her employment. Having worked until her late eighties, Louise retired to Paignton in Devon, only half an hour from where I am sitting now, an elegant and expensively dressed older lady as her family recalled. Her niece described the presence of those fabrics that had made her such a fixture in the Hartnell workrooms: 'When we were children, she would have these fabulous silk scarves and silk ties for us to choose from.'

The legendary status of Norman Hartnell as the designer of both the Queen's wedding dress and her coronation gown of 1953, alongside an increasing appetite for 'behind the scenes' tales, meant that numerous Hartnell 'hands' shared their stories of stitching in Bruton Street, the value of the maker unexpectedly appreciated. Betty Foster was one of the four principal seamstresses to have worked on the royal wedding dress in 1947, and gave an interview to author Jennifer Robson in 2017.

Asked about her working day, she described the logistics of post-war life in London: 'I'd go in early, because if you got the train before seven it was cheaper.' She would walk to a Lyons Corner House for a cup of tea and a bun, before the final steps to Bruton Street for 8.30. Her day was spent at Miss Holliday's table with the other seamstresses who worked under the older, senior maker, the same Miss Holliday who had been amongst Hartnell's first, hard-won employees over two decades earlier. Betty described the working relationship between the designer and his valued, experienced 'hands' when he received the request to design and make the royal wedding dress: 'Mr. Hartnell came to our table, Miss Holliday's table, with the sketch that the princess had chosen, and that's when he asked if Miss Holliday would make the dress. Would you believe she was hesitant? She made all the important dresses for him, and she was the oldest of his seamstresses, and had been there the longest. But she did hesitate, because it was such a big responsibility. And we said, "Oh, please, Miss Holliday!" So she gave in, but she made us promise to behave ourselves!' It is an illuminating extract, demonstrating just how central Miss Holliday was to Hartnell's own decision-making. Betty recalled a workroom visit made by the Princess Elizabeth and the unequal bobbing up and down of the seamstresses and their curtseys, despite their earlier practising.

Almost twenty years later, another of Hartnell's hands would reminisce about her time in the same workroom, under the same skylights, undertaking the same close-worked stitching for the same, more established Queen. Jean Harding was fifteen in 1964 when her father simply rang the Hartnell showroom and asked if they might give his daughter a job. She finished her school classes on a Friday afternoon and by Monday morning she was travelling to Mayfair and one of London's most exclusive fashion houses. She served a three-year apprenticeship before being officially named one of the 'hands', at which point she began to work on royal commissions. At the age of seventy-two, she wrote down some

A Hartnell sketch.

of her memories of those years, recalling the realities of the Queen's wardrobe: 'People used to say she only wore something once, believe me that isn't true. She used to send dresses back time and time again to have them readjusted with a new neckline or a different sleeve or a different panel to make it slightly different.' So many young women on so many buses, countless sandwiches in staff canteens and buns in Lyons Corner Houses. They were the workforce that filled the workrooms of Hartnell in Bruton Street, and their recently told stories fascinate.

Betty Foster or Jean Harding, certainly Miss Holliday, would have encountered Mr Hartnell's assistant designer, a young man named Ian Thomas who was appointed to his post in 1953 and worked alongside Hartnell on the designs for the Queen's coronation gown. Fresh out of Oxford Art College, Thomas had specialised in fashion during his last year and now went in search of employment, writing to the secretary of the Incorporated Society of London Fashion Designers who sent him in the direction of up-and-coming designer John Cavanagh. Whilst Cavanagh liked Thomas's sketches, he couldn't afford to pay him a living wage but suggested he wander around Mayfair to enquire with other fashion houses. The first that he came to was Hartnell. He was offered a job the very next day and continued to work alongside the couturier for the next seventeen years. Whilst they were close, Thomas recalled that Mr Hartnell guarded his royal privilege fiercely, reluctant to dilute his influence over the royal style. Eventually in 1970, and much to Hartnell's disappointment, Thomas left to establish his own label, operating a small design business from premises on Motcomb Street in Belgravia. He assumed that any chance of a royal commission was simply not possible following his departure from Hartnell, but he had not counted on the Queen's eye for talent. 'Within six months Miss MacDonald [the Queen's dresser] telephoned on behalf of the Queen and asked him to submit some designs.' Within three years, Ian Thomas would be awarded the Royal Warrant for his continued commissions for the Queen's wardrobe and so completed a triumvirate of designers catering to the needs of the royal calendar – Hartnell, Thomas, and Hardy Amies, favoured for his sharp tailoring.

Whilst both Hartnell and Amies recorded their memoirs for posterity and left a prolific legacy of work, Ian Thomas is less visible. I found around fifty of his sketches in the collections of the V&A, beautiful renditions of designs often with a fragment of the intended fabric pinned to the corner. The Royal Collection protects the actual garments he made for the Queen, carefully packed away as important cultural markers for key occasions, remnants of a working relationship now unknown. But about Thomas himself, or indeed anybody that worked for him, I can find almost nothing. He gave few interviews. He did not write a helpful autobiography. He worked in his studio in London and then would retire as often as possible to his house in Warwickshire with his horses and his dogs, one of which (a corgi) was a gift from the Queen. His discretion, designing in the 1970s and 1980s when the British press was becoming ever more hungry for royal gossip, was perhaps what secured him his continued patronage, and he remained tight-lipped until his death in 1993. Doubtless there are seamstresses and tailors alive today who might recall their days working for Ian Thomas. There are stories to tell about their experience of London high fashion in the 1980s and the creations that were wrought in Motcomb Street.

A designer who would become synonymous with royal style discovered his passion for stitching cloth far from the showrooms of Mayfair. Born in July 1950 in Hammersmith Hospital, Bruce Oldfield was the third child of a single mother, Betty. Oldfield cites that her medical file at the time described her as: 'mentally and morally weak, an epileptic who gave birth to a child with negroid tendencies'. Given the circumstances, her family were not prepared to take on the child. Doubtless Betty's experience would have been a very different one today, but in post-war Britain judgements about illegitimacy and race conspired against her. The brutality of such decisions and the repercussions for countless children and families seem desperately cruel from a twenty-first-century perspective but in 1950 the system was still predicated on a set of Victorian values that castigated women. Bruce was placed in the care of Dr Barnardo's Homes but in February 1952 he was taken into the home of Violet Masters. Violet had applied to Dr Barnardo's for a child who might keep another of her young foster children company and she readily accepted Bruce. Violet lived in County Durham and as a child had not been considered to be academic. She was, however, very creative, and so acquired the skills of a dressmaker. It was in Violet's front room, tailor's dummy shrouded in the corner, that Bruce honed his craft: 'I learned all the techniques, hemming, sewing on buttons and simple embroidery. I patiently brought to life the pale blue outlines of flower patterns on tablecloths and napkins with brilliant Sylko threads.' Bruce practised his new-found skills with offcuts of fabric and would make dresses for his foster sister's dolls: 'She ended up with the best dressed Cindy in town with a complete wardrobe crammed into her red vanity case.'

Bruce was only eight years old but it was an apprenticeship that served him well. Many years later, showing the determination that would see his name amongst the brightest lights of British fashion, Bruce won a place at Central Saint Martins and began to forge a career in London. Like so many makers, before and since, he would come to rely on the expertise of his workroom staff to bring his designs to market. Bruce writes fondly of the experienced Jewish couple who would become pivotal figures in his professional life. Judith and Felix Wolkenfeld had emigrated to London during those febrile years of the 1930s as anti-Semitism marched across the continent of Europe. A *London Gazette* entry from 1967 describes them as originating in Czechoslovakia but now working as gown manufacturers at 10 Scardale House on Evering Road in London. Judith had trained at a fashion college in London to become a highly skilled seamstress and Felix was an expert pattern cutter. Bruce describes his first encounter with the couple who, in the 1970s, were still making a living from their own premises: 'When I met them, they ran their own dressmaking business from Blackstock Road in Highbury where they had a small workroom, essentially a cutting room with four machines where they worked with a finisher. They produced CMT (Cut, Make and Trim work). Felix did the cutting while Judith turned her hand to everything.' They became an integral part of his progress as his star began to rise in the world of high fashion: 'I'd take them the sketches, fabric and patterns then leave them to it, visiting them about twice during the whole manufacturing process just to check how they were getting on. Occasionally slight changes might have to be made to a pattern or I might alter a detail on a sketch but I knew they were so professional and worked to such a high standard, I could trust them to get on with things. With their invaluable skills, skills that were largely dying out by the seventies, they soon became not only essential to the business but very much part of the family.'

By the early 1980s, Oldfield's reputation was such that it would extend into the gilded rooms of Buckingham Palace and the emerging style of Diana, the new Princess of Wales: 'The Palace had asked Anna Harvey at *Vogue* to mastermind the Princess's wardrobe, so various designers were asked to send a selection of outfits along to the *Vogue* offices where the Princess would make her choice.' What followed was a working relationship that made countless newspaper headlines. Diana's youth and inexperience quickly became apparent, forging very different client needs from his other customers: 'This was more a question of dressing a young woman who, to an extent, was relying on us to steer her straight, knowing we wouldn't let her down in the concept of the garment, the way it fitted and the way it was made.' There were protocols to be followed and needs to be met in this era of press scrutiny that would pounce on any fashion fail. Her gratitude was always warm and extended to all of the staff in the workroom, when she dropped by unannounced to deliver her approval in person.

Compared to the stringent, formal expectations of mid-century couture, Bruce described a more relaxed approach to the fitting process, which would take place at Kensington Palace: 'We'd do the fittings in her sitting room, dumping everything on the three seater sofa and putting up the long portable mirror . . . Then she'd give us an hour and a half – long enough for three fittings, a coffee and a chat.' After almost a decade of these coffees, chats, public appearances and casual workroom arrivals, Diana moved on. Her more established status as a fashion icon saw her style evolve and so Bruce Oldfield had to relinquish his royal connection. For the time being at least. In an unexpected twist of fate, Oldfield would eventually form a new royal relationship and for the last decade or more he has been making formal wear for the now Queen Consort, Camilla. Late in 2022, he was commissioned to make Camilla's coronation dress. The white silk coat dress with embellished underskirt included embroidered symbolic tributes in gold. Whilst undoubtedly modern in style, it shared an obvious DNA with coronation gowns past, and those designers who had forged their own royal connections; including Mrs Seymour Howell with Queen Elizabeth the Queen Mother, and her daughter Queen Elizabeth II with the legend that was Norman Hartnell. From Violet Master's sewing table in County Durham to Westminster Abbey, Oldfield's name will sit alongside those ceremonial couturiers that came before him.

The length of Queen Elizabeth II's reign was such that it encompassed the entirety of her adult life and all of the changes to a body that are wrought in that span of time. Hartnell and Amies oversaw her youth into maturity, fashioning cinched-in gowns and suits for her public life as a young woman and then as a young mother. As her shape changed, so too did the silhouettes, the garments in the Royal Collection mapping out her physical self in ghostly outline, decade by decade. As she entered her eighties and after more than half a century as Queen, a new designer would find himself undertaking the unique challenges of clothing her. Stewart Parvin was born in Berkshire in 1966. He remembers as a small child being fascinated by clothes and the garments that women around him were wearing, an enduring interest that finds its echo in the memoirs of Hartnell, of Amies, of Oldfield before him.

By the time Parvin had reached his teens and was in a position to determine a career path, a fashion theme began to emerge: 'When I was doing my A Levels there was a programme, *In at the Deep End*, where each week they offered something for a different career. One of them was going to become a fashion designer.' His challenge was to make a garment for the Berkeley dress show at which he met figures from the industry, one of whom was Bruce Oldfield.' It was a pivotal moment and one that sealed his future career. I spoke to him in the summer of 2024. Already brimful of the stories I was invested in telling about the myriad makers, I added his compelling voice to the many that spanned two centuries of royal style. The familiar determination to succeed in a world that was often deemed too frivolous for serious careers was apparent, from college and beyond: 'When I wrote my page in the yearbook I wrote my little bit, maybe 100 words and if you read those 100 words I wrote in 1989 it is pretty much what I did,' he recalled. He knew from the outset that his interest lay in the world of high-end fashion, making occasion wear for a host of clients. He secured work with those designers in London who had made their mark in this area – Donald Campbell who had made garments for Princess Diana; and John Cavanagh, the London stalwart whose label had made the Duchess of Kent's wedding dress.

He was set on making his own label, however, and found premises on Motcomb Street as his base for Stewart Parvin couture. The location would be strangely prophetic, for it was the very address from which Ian Thomas had worked during his many years of designing, a royal association that Parvin was yet to join: 'The basement was where we had all the fabric and kept all the patterns. Ian Thomas had had a little camp bed there and a funny shower in the corner. Tuesday to Thursday he would sleep there and then go back to Warwickshire.' It was in this space that Parvin was working one day when a lady called into his shop to enquire about possible designs for a client of hers. She wanted to look at the quality of his garments and asked about his work. 'We hit it off instantly. She said, "I can't have anything you have in your collection." She said if I had any fabric from previous seasons or fabric I hadn't used before she would need that.' Parvin offered to cut some samples and make a few sketches for her client to inspect, drawing five or six ideas that she could take away. The following week, he received a phone call from the lady asking for some additional sketches featuring specific fabrics which he duly finished. Then came the grand reveal: 'She came back and collected them and about a week later she rang back and said I have got some good news for you. My client has actually chosen a sketch from each of the fabrics. She asked would you like to know who it is for. It is for Her Majesty the Queen.' The lady in question was the Queen's trusted dresser, Angela Kelly, who had experienced some less positive experiences in her quest to find a maker, before she encountered Stewart. She had visited a number of expensive dressmakers in the vicinity of Buckingham Palace, entering the hushed and carpeted salons of exclusivity, where she was met with less of a welcome. Of one assistant she wrote: 'He peered over the top of his black rimmed glasses and condescendingly advised that the clothing was "couture not retail".'

It is a curious insight into the changing processes of the royal wardrobe, and of the needs of an older Queen still subject to the glare of publicity and opinion. Having agreed to make the garments, Parvin was not allowed to have the Queen's actual measurements but instead was lent some existing pieces of the Queen's wardrobe from which he could draft a pattern. Once the garments were under way, so the fittings began. As with so many dressmakers and designers past, the same protocols were followed. Parvin would visit the palace with his long-serving seamstress, Barbara, and together they would make the adjustments: 'I would do the pinning and she would hand me the pins.' After Barbara retired, Stewart would go on his own, meeting other makers at the same time, usually the milliners who would be matching the hats to the dresses that he designed. It was a working relationship that would thrive and in 2007 Parvin was awarded the Royal Warrant for his continued contributions to the Queen's wardrobe. 'The last thing she wore of mine was the green balcony outfit for the jubilee,' he told me. 'When she came up on the balcony I said: "Oh my God, she's worn that one!" The colour was amazing, the simplicity of it, the punctuation with the buttons.' His reminiscences might have been shared by so many of those who have contributed garments worn for such public occasions, their work surveyed by the watching world.

In July 2020, months into the Covid-19 pandemic, the Queen's granddaughter, Princess Beatrice, was married. Stewart Parvin had been handed the commission to refashion an old dress from the Queen's wardrobe – a beaded satin gown bearing the label of Norman Hartnell. Stewart recalled that piece of work during our conversation: 'It was really interesting to take something that was old and incredible and a famous dress in its own right and make adaptations that could be undone if necessary.' As he described carefully unpicking parts of the embroidery and the joy of reusing something with a shared family history, I couldn't help but think of all of those hands contributing to this single garment across its lifetime. Perhaps it was Miss Louie who had sourced the perfect fabric which was then pooled in liquid satin on to one of the seamstress's tables to be pinned and cut. Miss Holliday may have overseen the careful stitching before passing pieces up to the embroidery studio for the shining embellishments. The dress would have accompanied Mr Hartnell to a fitting at the palace before finally finding its way into the wardrobe of the Queen, only to be dusted off half a century later and emerge from the hands of a new maker and into a different story.

The fortunes of designers can be fickle, much like the industry itself. Fashions change and wearers change. Norman Hartnell became synonymous with mid-twentieth-century royal couture but would find his influence waning as the decades passed. Ian Thomas slept on the camp bed in the corner of his Motcomb Street basement as he created new directions for the Queen's wardrobe, and in that same building in 2001 Angela Kelly found her new royal designer. Stewart Parvin had followed his dream from boyhood to create beautiful clothes, and retained the memory of his teenage self, meeting Bruce Oldfield whose own design legacy has encompassed the icon that was Diana, and the state ceremonial splendour of the coronation gown. Designing and making for

Stewart Parvin at his work table.

the monarchy, for queens whose every sartorial step is so often subject to the curious eyes and critical pens of public and press, can be difficult. The royal seal of approval brings with it a notoriety which can raise up the status of a designer brand but might also dash it down. The only constancy in fashion is change.

CHAPTER 11

A Travelling Wardrobe
The Trunks of Harriet Cave and the Cases of Pendragon

On Friday 23 October 1903, *The Times* reported in its regular Court Circular column that Queen Alexandra was scheduled to leave her Danish family summer gathering in Fredensborg at precisely five minutes past ten, to begin her journey back to London. The brevity of the official update belies the complexity behind the journey. A glimpse of the reality comes a few days later when her luggage was detained by customs officials at the Belgian border. For her five-week stay in Denmark, her specially commissioned luggage train consisted of twenty-nine large trunks. In a letter dated 16 November 1888, Marie Mallet, lady-in-waiting to Queen Victoria, wrote to her stepsister of her recent return from Balmoral: 'Your distinguished relative has safely passed through the manifold perils and luxuries of a Royal journey', recounting a lurching train punctuated by lavish refreshments at their various stops along the way: 'We had a hearty tea at Aberdeen, where royal footmen rushed about wildly with tea-kettles, gazed at by a large crowd.' Moving the monarch and all of the accoutrements required of trips away calls for a vast amount of unseen labour. Clothing must be selected or commissioned to meet the needs of the journey, appropriate to both climate and occasion. Packing must be undertaken logically, planning for the schedule of events and ease of access. Routes must be drawn up and transport arranged. To facilitate all of this, the luggage built to contain the life of a travelling queen had to be sturdy, practical and distinctive. These are the makers, the messengers and the couriers who did not make the clothes but fashioned and facilitated, instead, the wooden and leather shells that safely encased all of the silks and chiffons, skirts and blouses, hats and shoes and coats across counties and continents.

The evolution of luggage design maps on to the developing modes of transport itself. For instance, during the eighteenth and early nineteenth centuries, domed trunks were preferable for strapping on to horse-drawn coaches, their shape preventing the stacking of luggage so that the contents were not squashed, and determined by the mode of transport. It was an industry dominated almost entirely by men, the materials and techniques being associated with traditionally masculine skill sets. Trunk making required the talents of a carpenter and the precision of a leather worker, combining to produce the kinds of well-travelled luggage that still survive in museums and auction houses. Wooden carcasses would be created from planed lengths of okoume, poplar or beech, timbers that were lightweight enough not to add unnecessary bulk to cases that were going to be heavy enough once filled. Leather or canvas would be cut to cover the bare wooden shell and brass studs and corner pieces hammered into place to reinforce vulnerable edges. The sawing, glueing and hammering were activities mostly reserved for men who would undergo apprenticeships to the trade, undertaking their craft in workshops around the country and catering to a burgeoning market of travellers. As the pace of travel changed with the advent of the railways in the mid-nineteenth century, so too did the volume of luggage.

Perhaps the most famous of luggage makers, a brand still synonymous with the production of luxury leather goods, was Louis Vuitton. Young Louis had grown up in the forested region of Franche-Comté and brought all of his knowledge of wood with him to Paris when he travelled to the city in 1837 to become a box maker; he served as an apprentice to the atelier of Monsieur Maréchal and would remain there for the next seventeen years. By 1859, Louis Vuitton had established his own business in Asnières-sur-Seine where the firm remains to this day. As well as the poplar frames and beech reinforcement strips, Vuitton would line his early boxes with fragrant camphor wood as a deterrent to cloth-eating insects or rosewood for its scented grain. His reputation brought him into the orbit of the French Empress Eugénie and he would become her personal packer and luggage maker, securing a position in the luxury market that would remain secure. Some of his early inspirations, however, were drawn not from fellow makers in Paris, but from a more surprising source – from the English luggage firm of H. J. Cave. The H. J. was not a Harold John or a Herbert James but, unusually for so masculine a space, a Harriet Jane.

Harriet Jane Hackett was born on 21 June 1821 in South Audley Street, London. She was baptised by her own father, Samuel, a pastor in the parish of St George's Hanover Square, and grew up with her siblings in the city. In 1841, Harriet married Benjamin Cave and, along with his sister Eleanor, they moved into rooms on Edward Street in Marylebone, sharing the premises with a schoolmaster and a druggist amongst others. It was here that they opened their shop making wicker baskets for those travelling upon the expanding rail network. Within a decade, Benjamin and Harriet had built a successful business as basketmakers and luggage makers operating out of Edward Street to a growing clientele. Whilst Benjamin, as head of the household, was given the status of his occupation on census records, the driving force behind the business was Harriet. Her ambition was given new impetus when Benjamin died, leaving her the sole proprietor of a business traditionally occupied by men and with six children. She was thirty-two years old. Her response to the circumstances would make the company world famous. Moving to 40 Wigmore Street, Harriet ensured that the name of H. J. Cave would be associated with only the finest leather work, producing quality goods that would earn her name an honourable mention at the World Exhibition in London in 1862. Much like the Great Exhibition of more than a decade earlier, this was a fair to celebrate the arts and industries of the thirty-nine participating countries. Across its eleven hectares of exhibition space in South Kensington, exhibitors were able to display their wares. In six months, the fair received over six million visitors and Harriet secured the attention of Queen Victoria. Only a year later, in 1863, Harriet was awarded the Royal Warrant of Appointment to the ever-popular Alexandra, Princess of Wales, charged with the creation of her extensive luggage needs.

Queen Victoria decided to sponsor Harriet to participate in the World Exhibition in Paris in 1867 and here she was able to showcase her flat-topped 'Expanding Travelling Basket', an innovative new luggage option that suited both the rigours of railway travel and the expanse of womenswear at the time. Perhaps it was the female perspective that allowed Harriet to think so creatively about a solution to the problems of travelling with the scale of clothing worn by women in the 1860s. Her idea was recorded in an 1866 volume of the Office of Registrar of Designs, a colourful watercolour illustration demonstrating the various parts of what appears to be more like a black leather-covered trunk than a basket. The expandable lid was able to accommodate 'the more convenient stowage of wearing apparel' according to the copyright description, along with five compartments and a removable tray. Harriet recognised that women's clothing, especially the generously proportioned skirts, was often bulkier after having been worn and so the expanding trunk could more easily account for changes to the garments within. Her innovation earned the company a first prize silver medal at the Paris fair, ahead of Louis Vuitton himself who was awarded the bronze. Vuitton acknowledged Harriet Cave's designs and proclaimed himself inspired by her creations. Harriet lived long enough

Queen Elizabeth II leaving Westminster Abbey after being crowned.

Court presentation ensemble of 1896.

Court presentation ensemble of 1928.

Bonnets worn by Queen Victoria.

'Passementerie Workshop' by Karl Meunier.

A coat by Dieulafait & E. Bouclier belonging to Queen Alexandra.

Boots probably worn by Queen Victoria.

A 1870s pair of shoes belonging to Queen Alexandra.

Wedding shoes of the then Princess Elizabeth (later Queen).

Choosing fabric at the dressmakers: a Victorian watercolour.

Riding ensemble by Morin Blossier.

Genevieve James, glover.

 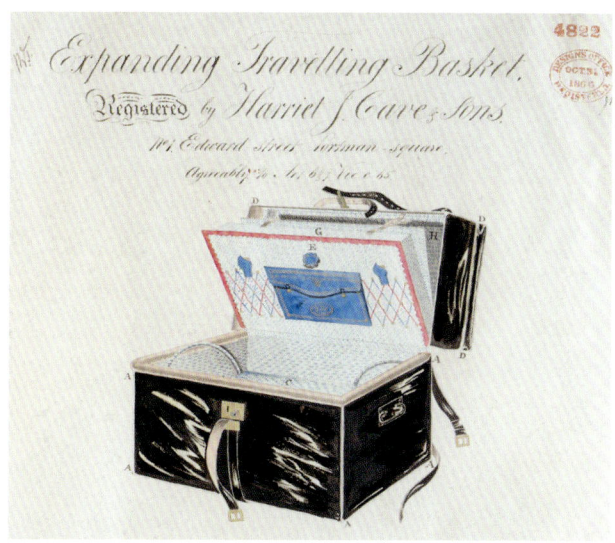

Riding habit jacket by John Redfern & Sons.

Expanding travelling basket by Harriet J. Cave & Sons.

'Cinq Heures Chez Paquin', showing clients visiting the couturier Maison Paquin.

Blue silk and cotton corset by Madame Roxey Caplin.

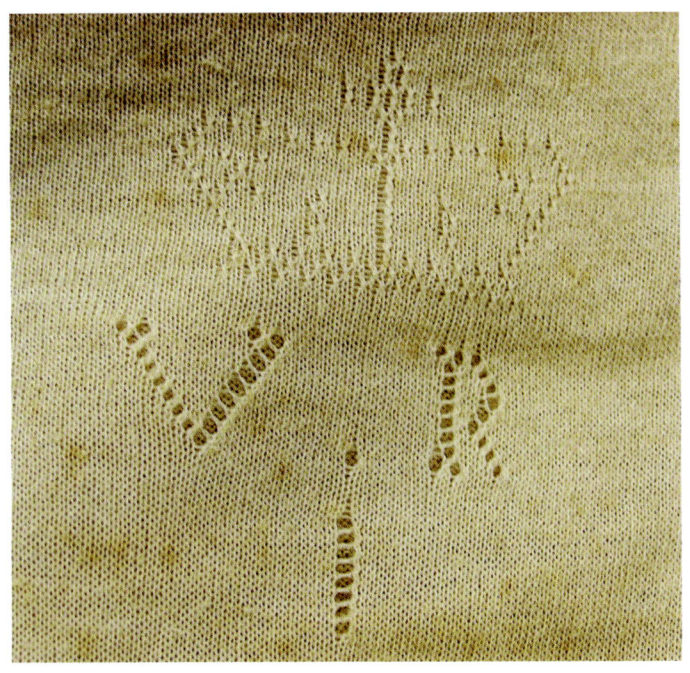

Detail of a pair of cream patterned cotton stockings, initials 'VR' and crown worked at the top of the leg, said to have belonged to Queen Victoria.

Marianne Skerrett.

Queen Elizabeth II wearing an ensemble designed by Hardy Amies for her Silver Jubilee.

The Queen dressed in an outfit designed by Angela Kelly for the Diamond Jubilee.

(*Left*) Mourning dress belonging to Queen Victori

(*Below*) Queen Victoria's dressing room at Balmoral.

A Travelling Wardrobe

to see the business that had flourished in her name become the largest travel goods store in the world. She died on 29 December 1874 at the age of fifty-three but the business continued, her children extending the legacy of their remarkable mother. Amongst the fragrant wood, the supple leather and the brass tacks of a man's world, Harriet had forged her own entrepreneurial path, securing the recognition of royal women as she went.

Were any of the Belgian customs officials to have opened one of Queen Alexandra's trunks in 1903, they would have read the name H. J. Cave stamped on to the interior pocket, her stackable luggage piled high as it awaited its release. The logistics accompanying the luggage itself to ensure a properly attired queen relied upon the services of another unseen figure – the royal courier. During much of Queen Victoria's reign, this role was the responsibility of one man who, for forty years, coordinated all of the royal travels and the complex logistics that accompanied them. His name was Joseph Julius Kanné. Joseph was born in Pilsen, Austria, in September 1819, only a few months after the baby Princess Victoria in London. At the age of thirty-one he travelled to London and by 1857 had secured some occasional courier work in the royal household for the Prince of Wales. Queen Victoria recorded her first meeting with Joseph in her journal, writing on 22 October 1857: 'Bertie brought the courier Kanné to me, whom he so much likes. He is in manners quite like a gentleman, & certainly very nice, very cultivated & speaking many languages.'

By 1860, Joseph was offered full-time employment as courier to the royal family, earning him a salary of £200 per annum. His command of languages and his organisational skills clearly served him well. It is estimated that he oversaw the logistics of five hundred royal trips in his many years of service, undertaking the planning of routes, the transport, the hotels, the security and, of course, the luggage. To ensure the seamless running of the arrangements, he would accompany members of the royal family on their trips, smoothing the paths of onward travel at every stage. Oliver Montagu, a personal secretary to Alexandra, Princess of Wales, kept a journal of the state visit to Russia in 1871 and pasted a newspaper report into its pages that read: 'The whole of the arrangements for the trip from London to Russia are under the control of M. Kanné, Her Majesty's director of continental journeys who attends their Royal Highnesses throughout their visit to the Russian capital and during their return to England.' There are nineteen entries in Queen Victoria's journals in which she notes conversations with Joseph Kanné in preparation for her various journeys. He answered questions about staircases in Italian hotels and lodgings in Germany. During a carriage drive in the mountains above Lucerne in Switzerland in 1868, she wrote: 'The mist began to come down & as we got higher & higher it became very cold & damp. Kanné was in a great state of fidget to hurry us on.' Poor Joseph. Not only had he organised every detail pertaining to the movement of this intractable, powerful woman but here she was on a mountain road in a cold mist. Responsibility must have sat heavily on his shoulders as he tried to hurry the royal party to a safer environment.

The Queen did appreciate the efforts that he took to facilitate her travels so successfully. On their return from Switzerland, she wrote from Windsor on 12 September: 'After breakfast, took leave of excellent Kanné, who really is an admirable man, such power of organization, so obligingly civil & thoughtful, & so gentlemanlike in his dealings. Gave him a pin with my portrait.' There is a photographic portrait of Joseph in the Royal Collection, taken in 1864. He is leaning nonchalantly against a wooden pillar, one elbow resting on a polished plinth. His hair is swept back from his face and his eyes look as if they crinkled when he smiled. He sports an impressive beard and wears a long, open frock coat with matching waistcoat and paler trousers. His watch chain loops from his pocket, indicating the importance of time management in his life.

A Travelling Wardrobe

On 24 April 1888 Joseph suffered a stroke and later died at his home in Dover Street. That day Queen Victoria wrote in her journal: 'For thirty years he had attended me on all my journeys, making all the arrangements, in a most admirable manner. He used to think of every little thing for my pleasure and comfort & had a wonderful power of organisation. I can hardly yet realise that he is gone & he will be such a loss.' The Prince of Wales attended the burial on 30 April and, along with the Queen, erected the headstone in his memory. Largely hidden from public sight Joseph may have been, but his endeavours were truly valued.

Whilst Joseph and those who performed similar roles were responsible for the transport of the Queen's travelling wardrobe and ensuring that it followed them from place to place, it was down to the dressers and wardrobe maids to prepare and pack the trunks before they could depart. Packing was an art all of its own and one that commanded pages of advice in popular travel books and periodicals. Sarah Annie Frost wrote in her 1870 publication, *The Art of Dressing Well*: 'To pack a trunk neatly, everything should be laid out in readiness, neatly folded and sorted, the light articles divided from the heavy ones and a supply of towels and soft wrapping paper at hand.' There followed detailed instructions as to the layers and distribution of the travelling wardrobe from hats to shoes, coats to petticoats. For a royal journey, likely to span many weeks, various countries and a host of engagements, packing was an art, albeit an onerous one. In 1855, Queen Victoria's dresser Frieda Arnold had written in a letter to her family a long description of the wonders of Buckingham Palace, following which she concluded: 'After this magnificence followed days full of exertion and fatigue: we had to pack and unpack continuously for fourteen full days.'

Later that same year, Frieda described preparations for Queen Victoria's state visit to Paris: 'Three days before our departure, the magnificent ship we were to travel in was already lying at anchor off Osborne . . . In the house there was endless packing and preparation.' At the same

Monsieur Joseph Kanné, Queen Victoria's courier, 1864.

time, the Queen wrote in her journal on Saturday 11 August: 'Much troubled with questions of Toilettes & other arrangements for Paris.' The dressers would liaise with the Queen to decide upon the wardrobe requirements for their trip and then spend their remaining days before travel in packing the luggage. It was not so simple as merely packing and leaving, however. Distinctions had to be made between the clothes that would be required during the journey and those which would be sent on ahead in the dressers' coach. Frieda continued: 'We left on the 17th, at five in the evening; Mary and I were travelling; Sophie was already in Paris with the luggage.' It was a process loaded with complex logistics. Dressers would take it in turns to travel with the luggage, leaving ahead of the main party in order to start unpacking before the Queen arrived at her final destination. They were issued vouchers by the courier for any expenses they might incur along the way which they could claim back. For visits that might include several relocations, the dressers would often find themselves repacking until late in the evening in order to send the luggage in advance, only to open the trunks and unpack all over again the next day.

The contents may have changed, but Frieda's experiences of preparing for Queen Victoria's travels were echoed one hundred and fifty years later by another dresser for another queen. Angela Kelly, dresser to the late Queen Elizabeth II, wrote in her memoir: 'A huge amount of preparation is involved in getting everything ready for any travelling, and especially for a Royal Tour.' Thirty outfits would ordinarily be taken on a ten-day tour so that there was a choice of two for each engagement. She would coordinate with the dressmakers to create new ensembles for the visit and then build up the list of hats, shoes and bags required to go with them. The cases would be organised with a colour-coded and numbered system, different shades of luggage tag indicating whose case belonged where, logistics that would no doubt feel familiar to Frieda Arnold and Joseph Kanné. Much like her predecessors, Angela became adept at the in-transit organisation of the Queen's clothes. Of rail travel, she wrote: 'As soon as we board the train at the station, I get straight to work unpacking. Occasionally, when we are on longer trips, I may need to press a few items. It didn't take me long to learn that ironing on a moving train is almost like surfing! You just need to find your balance as the train rocks back and forth.'

One of the changes that Angela Kelly did feel compelled to make related to the older trunks, three large leather wardrobe cases that the Queen had used for decades. The change in transport from ship to air travel meant that these familiar pieces of luggage had become impractical in the smaller hold of an aeroplane and so lighter-weight alternatives were chosen to replace them. These old and well-travelled pieces of luggage had their own tale to tell, however, one that had started in a Cambridgeshire village in the aftermath of the First World War. Tuberculosis was a disease that ravaged populations in the nineteenth century, prior to the discovery of antibiotics, which would almost eradicate the condition by the 1950s. Close monitoring was essential and in Cambridgeshire a Welsh heart surgeon, Pendrill Varrier-Jones, was the county's tuberculosis officer.

Varrier-Jones had long harboured an ambition to change attitudes towards tuberculosis sufferers and offer them a more productive way of life. Working men often hid symptoms of the disease, fearful of what would happen to their families should they be forced to give up their jobs. As men were returning from the Western Front in 1915, lungs weakened by their experiences in the trenches, so cases of TB amongst them began to rise. Varrier-Jones determined on a course of action to change the stigma surrounding those suffering from TB. He raised money at some speed to buy a Regency mansion named Papworth Hall and here he would action his ambitions for the Cambridgeshire Tuberculosis Colony. In addition to plenty of fresh air and rest, Varrier-Jones implemented a series of workshops where patients could make goods for sale and thus feel they were making a more valuable contribution to society. There was a cabinet-making workshop and a boot-repair space. He kept a piggery and a poultry farm and restocked the orchard. The success of his endeavours meant that by 1919 and after the end of the First World War, he was able to venture into more industrial spaces and so Pendragon Travel Goods was born.

A Travelling Wardrobe

It was thanks, primarily, to one of the existing Papworth residents, that this new workshop was instituted. His name was James Alexander Box. James was the eldest child of James senior, who worked as a harness maker, and his wife, Mary Jane. They lived in Southwark, close to the river and the leather tanneries of Bermondsey. By the time that James had come of age he had eight younger siblings and the family had moved to a four-roomed terrace house on Maidenstone Hill in Greenwich, a few streets to the west of Greenwich Park. Here, now aged twenty, James lived with his family and contributed to the family income through his work as a leather-bag maker alongside his father. So might he have continued, perhaps working his way up to a position indicative of greater experience, until the guns of the Great War stripped that life away. Like many young men at that time, James married his sweetheart Jane in the summer of 1915 and then signed up to join the army. He submitted his recruitment papers on 11 December 1915, joining the Royal Field Artillery where his trade as a worker of leather saw him take on the role of saddler. As I read his service record I am filled with belated dread on his behalf. His enlistment form for 'short service', expected for the 'duration of the conflict', sees him answer the routine questions – yes, he is married; no, he has never served in a branch of the forces before; yes, he is willing to be vaccinated and to be recruited into general service; yes, he has read the notice and understands what it is that he is signing up for. But how could he? I know from this record that James was five foot four inches tall with a chest of thirty-three and a half inches. He writes down the details of his marriage to Jane Charnock in 1915 and the name of his one-year-old daughter who was born in 1917. His military history notes that he took a trade test to pass as a saddler in March 1916 and I know that by January 1918 he was applying for medical discharge on the grounds of having contracted TB. Of those years in between there is a blank – no actions are listed and so I do not know if he was maintaining the harnesses of war horses at the Battle of the Somme as the guns thundered, or if he repaired saddles at Passchendaele. What I do know is that following his discharge, he was sent to Papworth, those years of war behind him but presumably never apart from him, and he decided to turn his leather-working skills towards a new product. He established a trunk-making workshop.

In a remarkably short space of time, the trunks made at Papworth gained a reputation for their quality, so much so that they were receiving orders from major retailers such as Selfridges in London. James was fearful of losing orders since, by its very nature, Papworth could not always guarantee the good health and consistent labour of its residents and so he proposed to Varrier-Jones a collaboration with his wife's family who had their own leather-working business in London. By the early 1920s, this partnership was so successful that the Charnocks moved their business out of the city and into Papworth itself, and the Pendragon Travel Goods workshop gathered increasing momentum. They received the Royal Warrant as official trunk makers to King George V in 1924, an honour that James Box lived just long enough to enjoy. He died at the age of thirty-five in 1925. There is a surviving photograph of the trunk-making workshop at Papworth, a snap of the makers taken in around 1920. Eight men are positioned in various acts of making. Three of them hold the wooden frame of the cases they are crafting, seated at a long pine table, their tools laid out in front of them. Others stand further back, frozen in the act of cutting leather or hammering rivets. The workshop is high-ceilinged and airy, windows flung wide. I wonder if one of these men is James, enjoying the peace of the countryside and the fruits of his ambitions.

After James's death, his wife Jane's family continued to run the travel goods department and received the award of further Royal Warrants in the years that followed, for King George VI and his wife Queen Elizabeth and for their two daughters, the Princesses Elizabeth and Margaret.

A Travelling Wardrobe

They retained Queen Elizabeth's official warrant from 1972 until Papworth Industries was sold in 1996. These were the cases that the Queen had been using so faithfully when Angela Kelly had taken up her post as dresser in the 1990s. These were the trunks that had undergone a revamp at the request of the Queen in 1984: 'Former trunk maker Joe French was brought out of retirement and with Roy Drury and Hugh Pattle, used their combined 150 years' experience in restoring the trunks to their former glory.' This was the story of success emerging out of sickness and the vision of a man determined to provide compassionate employment.

Much as Harriet Cave's innovative railway trunks had responded to changes in travel and dress, so too did the development of the lightweight suitcase, perfect for long-haul flights and swift onward transport plans. For many years, Queen Elizabeth had used Globe-Trotter suitcases whose pioneering, less bulky construction served her well across decades of patronage. Not averse to other practical solutions, Angela Kelly sourced additional luggage from a more familiar retailer: 'One company with a Royal Warrant is House of Fraser, so I decided to go for a browse to see if they might have anything suitable in the way of luggage. I soon found the solution: suitcases with wheels! I bought quite a few lightweight Linea cases, once again to the delight of the Buckingham Palace staff members who had risked their backs each time we went on tour.' The quest more easily to facilitate the cumbersome realities of a queen on the move remains a challenge then. The materials of the luggage might change; the modes of transport might become faster; the garments themselves might be unrecognisable from Queen Victoria to Queen Elizabeth II. But the objective remains remarkably similar. How might the complex wardrobe of the often nomadic monarch be successfully moved from A to B? Harriet Cave rose to that challenge with her entrepreneurial spirit, and so too did Joseph Kanné, coaxing royal parties on to this boat and into that carriage. Frieda Arnold accepted her role as relentless packer and unpacker, wearily folding layers of garments

Dressing the Queen

The Queen visiting Pendragon Travel Goods workshop.

between layers of tissue, only to repeat the process in reverse hours later. Angela Kelly would doubtless have recognised Frieda's exertions as she too rustled with tissue on the dressers' floor of Buckingham Palace and balanced precariously, clutching a hot iron, on board the royal train. James Box, sick and weary of war in 1919, would see how his vision of a workshop for other men like him could materialise into a luxury brand, and earn his endeavours the royal seal of approval. The world has become a smaller place since the carriage wheels of Queen Victoria's coach rumbled down European streets. She would never have imagined that her great-great-granddaughter might fly to the other side of the world many times over, but whether on plane, train or automobile, or indeed carriage, the luggage follows in her wake, a sturdy tribute to Harriet, to Joseph, to Frieda, to James, to Angela.

CHAPTER 12

Sharp Suits

Tailor-mades by Redfern and the Elusive Madame Vernon

In 1754, art historian and prolific letter writer Horace Walpole wrote to his friend Horace Mann about a horrifyingly modern turn of events he had witnessed whilst attending church the previous week. He was writing about the shocking appearance of Princess Emily, 'Coming to Chapel last Sunday in riding clothes, with a dog under her arm.' It was not the dog so much as the clothes themselves that had caused such alarm. These were clothes that were altogether too mannish in Walpole's estimation, for if women began to dress like men beyond the acceptable context of riding a horse, if they began to wear their riding habits in public – and in church of all places – then the natural order of the world was truly under threat. Sharp tailoring has long been associated with power. The early-nineteenth-century society dandy par excellence, Beau Brummell, claimed that it took him five hours a day to dress correctly in his immaculately cut garments. Tailors crafted the carapace of the powerful man.

But what of powerful women? The queens of England similarly recognised the impact of tailored clothing and wielded it successfully. They commissioned their own versions of the military uniform and the suit to signal their unusual place in a man's world. To do so, they found both established and emerging makers who could craft an entirely new facet to the feminine wardrobe, one that today we take for granted. In the world of female tailoring, businesses old and new forged a working relationship with these regal women – the decades-old manufacturer of buttons, Jennens, supplied their goods at the same time as the upstart entrepreneur John Redfern, a young draper from the Isle of Wight who would take the fashion world by storm thanks to his smart design decisions and the patronage of the world's most famous princess, the young Alexandra, Princess of Wales. Others are shadowy, little-known makers. Encased in crisp, protective tissue and tucked away in museum stores, waistcoats and jackets bear beautifully designed silk name labels for companies such as Busvine and Vernon. Their clothes remain but their stories do not. Where once they proudly displayed the royal arms on their woven business labels and their smart printed letterheads, now barely anything remains of once renowned artisans and the many families whose livelihoods depended on their success.

Housed in the Royal Collection, padded and folded carefully away from the potential ravages of light and insects, is a neat and perfectly tailored double-breasted navy blue riding habit with scarlet lapels and cuffs and two rows of glistening brass buttons. This is not the uniform of an admiral of the fleet but a young queen. Dating to 1837, this is the Windsor uniform, worn by Queen Victoria to review troops at Windsor only a few months after her accession to the throne. She was delighted with the day and her parade past the troops, writing in her journal: 'I saluted them by putting my hand to my cap like the officers do, and was much admired for my manner of doing so . . . The whole went off beautifully; and I felt for the first time like a man, as if I could fight myself at the head of my Troops.' Unusually for Victoria, who rarely wrote about her clothes, she described the uniform in her journal too: 'Dressed in a habit of dark blue with red collar and cuffs (the Windsor uniform which all my gentlemen wear), a military cap, and my Order of the Garter.'

Studying the jacket today, just a little of the workmanship of the makers might be understood. The tiny hand stitches of the fine wool cloth are barely visible and the quilted lining hidden beneath was sculpted in such a way as to mould to the Queen's body.

The garment was made by the Queen's habit maker Peter Thompson who was awarded her warrant in August 1837. Thompson, however, remains frustratingly absent from the records. I find him recorded across just a single line, in city trade directories for London in the 1840s and 1850s, his premises listed at 12 Frith Street in Soho. He is elusive. I chase traces of him through the records. I *think* he was born in 1786 and it *appears* that he married somebody called Amelia Richards in 1813. He *may* have had a son called Peter and another named Ridley. Their birth certificates attest to their father's profession as a tailor on Frith Street but I hit dead end after dead end. The name is a common one, as is the occupation. I seem to catch a glimpse of him before he dances off into the obscurity of thousands of Thompsons and tailors. I scour publications in the hope that somebody has written about his career and his associations with Queen Victoria. I feel the frustration of an evidence trail run cold and a story which, in this case, must remain untold.

Peter Thompson was not the only contributor to the riding habit, for stamped on the back of the monogrammed brass buttons are the words 'JENNENS, LONDON'. Buttons were a significant feature of uniforms, with a tradition of making that was centuries old even as the buttons for Queen Victoria's Windsor jacket were cast. The firm of Joseph Jennens & Co. originated under the original founder, Charles Jennens, in 1807 when he was described as a button and military ornament maker. By the mid-1840s, the company had a shop on Conduit Street, adjacent to Savile Row and well placed for its proximity to the increasing numbers of tailors in the area. Whilst button making, as with so many other trades, proliferated in London, another city became synonymous with their production and was home to the Jennens manufactory – Birmingham. The power of the British armed forces meant that there had been a huge demand for metal buttons in the eighteenth and nineteenth centuries. Hand-turned machines had been replaced by machinery, but it was still a labour-intensive process, one that was described by Charles Dickens in one of his columns for the magazine *Household Words* in 1852: 'We see hundreds of women, scores of children and a few men; first rows of women sit each at her machine with its handle in her right hand and a sheet of thin iron, brass or copper in the other; shifting the sheet she punches out circles many times faster than the cook cuts out shapes from a sheet of pastry.' A year later, a journalist from *Leisure Hour* visited another button factory: 'He describes the metal as being rolled into strips of about 5ft in length and as many inches in width which is cut into circular blanks by a female at a small hand press. She depresses the punch, he says, about thirty or forty times a minute and every time a blank or disc is cut from the strip it falls into a drawer beneath.' It was intensive and exhausting work, the relentless stamping of discs, the soldering of the shanks on the back and the burnishing of the finished button.

By the time that Queen Victoria's eldest son, Edward, married Princess Alexandra of Denmark in 1863, the memory of her smart navy Windsor uniform was long past. Her body had changed during the intervening years and she was not in favour of the slender silhouette displayed by her new daughter-in-law who enjoyed all of the possibilities that a new wardrobe had to offer. It was through the display of her slim figure that Alexandra, Princess of Wales, would shape not only generations of women who followed in her wake but also the fortunes of a young draper named John Redfern. Redfern was born in 1821 in Chichester. In his early twenties he had already started trading in cloth, running a drapery business first in Plymouth and then relocating to the Isle of

Wight with his wife, Harriet, and their new baby. By the late 1840s he was established at 41 High Street in Cowes. It might not have seemed an obvious move to some, but John was nothing if not canny and he realised that tying his premises to a town in close proximity to one of the official royal residences could only serve him well. It would prove to be the wisest decision of his life. The newly married Prince and Princess of Wales honeymooned at the Queen's home on the island, Osborne House, in March 1863 and Alexandra wasted no time in placing an order for 'making and fitting a muslin and silk toilette' from Redfern the high street draper. He had built a reputation for the quality of his serge fabrics and at some point in the course of their working relationship, Alexandra ordered a tailor-made. The tailor-made was a specific garment that reflected the skills of masculine tailoring but for a female clientele. These were garments that were no longer suitable only for riding horses but (and Horace Walpole would have been horrified) were also appropriate garments for the everyday.

Thanks to the Prince and Princess of Wales and their glamorous set, Cowes became a fashionable destination, the regatta was a 'must-attend' event and a yachting tailor-made by John Redfern was the most desirable of outfits. In 1851, when the business was in its infancy, John employed three assistants in his premises – John Rolls who was twenty-six and had come to the island from Dorset; Caroline Beazley who was twenty and had come from the small town of Ryde to the east of Cowes; and young Charlotte Mew, daughter of a labourer on the island. All three lived at 41 High Street, working in the shop taking orders, cutting cloth and wrapping packages for customers. By 1861, John employed six assistants and the numbers kept on growing. The vast majority of his employees were young women. Women like Grace Woolger who had grown up in her father's grocery shop in Sussex but found work with Redfern in her twenties; and young apprentice Eliza Beard who was only fourteen when she went to live on the Isle of Wight and learned to fashion the tailor-mades that would clothe the wealthiest women in the world. Redfern was able to teach his young assistants how to work from patterns, since much of his business was conducted via mail order: 'The company sent photographs of the styles available and swatches of serge. A prospective client had only to quote the style and fabric numbers, return her skirt measurements, back and front, with a well fitting dress bodice from her wardrobe and Redfern would make and return the finished garment within a week.'

Popular cartes de visite of the 1870s and 1880s capture Alexandra in her Redfern tailor-mades, exquisitely cut and trimmed, fitting her slender build in a way that Queen Victoria deeply disapproved of, and it was garments such as these that launched Redfern's name to an entirely new level. The quality of his tailor-mades and the patronage of Alexandra meant that he was able to open a branch in London and by 1884 he had opened premises on the rue de Rivoli in Paris and on Fifth Avenue in New York. Prestigious journal the *Queen* described his New York branch: 'Here as in London, at Cowes, and in Paris, Redfern's cloth gowns are *the* mode. The "sales parlour" of their Fifth-avenue establishment is daily filled with fashionable women ordering tailor-made gowns, habits, ulsters or pelisses. The assistants are all English: the workwomen, sixty in number, are from the Old World.' From three young draper's assistants on the Isle of Wight in the early 1850s, Redfern was now able to send more than sixty women across the Atlantic to stitch and sell his tailor-made gowns. I want to know what that was like for those women. How was their journey? Did they live on the premises in small lofty rooms overlooking Central Park? Did any of them ever return home or did they settle and build a life in this new world? Whilst I can find advertisements a-plenty for the various stores that Redfern opened (and others were to follow in the USA) the stories of these intrepid women remain untold.

A rare glimpse into the lives of the women crafting the Redfern brand

An advertisement for Redfern's New York salon, 1885.

came in the form of an article in the French journal *Femina* published in April 1901. In it, a young woman who has been admonished by her husband for being late for dinner, proceeds to tell him about the Parisian salon and workshops of Redfern & Sons. She described the liveried doorman escorting customers to the lift and the discreet electric bell that would alert 'a charming young girl' to welcome the client. She continues: 'Here we are in the large sale hall. In this immense room the feet sink deliciously into a soft carpet.' She visited each room, which included one corner replicating the footlights of a theatre so that customers might try on their gown in the appropriate setting. Beyond the grand salon were the workshops themselves, 'the work of the beehives' as the author described it. 'We pass through sewing workshops and more sewing workshops, all very well kept and all crowded with young and charming women.' The accompanying photographs memorialise the men and women all industriously stitching in these workshops surrounded by fabric spilling from all directions, with light flooding in from tall windows. The reporter described a delicious smell emanating from

Inside Redfern's sales salon.

somewhere and was directed to a large dining hall where some one hundred of the employees were eating their lunch. By the end of his life, John Redfern had lived long enough to see his sons take on his empire; to witness stores with his name above the door open around the world; to employ many hundreds of men and women, including seventy-three young women in his extended premises in Cowes, and to know that he was one of the most famous fashion names in the world. It is remarkable, then, that relatively few of his garments have survived. Those chic tailor-mades that brought him such fame have all but disappeared and not a single one of the garments from Queen Alexandra's wardrobe in surviving collections bears the Redfern label.

Where John Redfern's business history is present in the records but his tailor-mades are not, the opposite is true of some of Alexandra's other favoured tailors. Objects have survived in collections around the world that stand in silent tribute to the hands that fashioned them, but those makers remain obstinately invisible. There are three beautifully crafted waistcoats, now geographically separated but which once formed a part of Queen Alexandra's elegant tailored wardrobe. One, a textured hopsack weave in cream wool with a red spot, forms part of the collections at the Fashion Museum in Bath and the other two, similarly spotted in black and blue, reside in collections in the USA. All of them bear the same label – J. Busvine & Co. Neatly stitched into the cream satin linings is a waxed paper label indicating Busvine as the maker, with premises at 4 Brook Street in London. The company started by John Busvine had gained a reputation as a quality ladies' tailor by the later years of the nineteenth century. Consuelo Vanderbilt, the American heiress who, like many of her compatriots at this time, had married into the British aristocracy, wrote of her first riding experience after her marriage: 'I shall always remember the first meet with the Quorn hounds when, perfectly fitted in a Busvine habit, a tall hat and veil, I mounted "Greyling", inwardly trembling with excitement and fear . . . a host of others were eyeing me critically and so far, thanks to my tailor and a good seat, had found nothing amiss.'

John Busvine was born in 1845, living in London with his parents, Mary and Henry. Henry was a commercial traveller, working in the hat trade with no business of his own and so, when he came of age, John needed to find an apprenticeship. He became a tailor, no doubt working as a journeyman in the first instance on completing his apprenticeship but going on to found his own business as a master tailor in his own right. By the age of twenty-six, with a wife and young family, he was described as the manager of a tailoring establishment, which suggests it was not necessarily his own business, but by the early 1880s he had formed J. Busvine & Co. and in the 1890s was able to display the royal arms on his headed notepaper and employ his sons as assistants in the business. He was a skilful innovator. In 1894 he patented the Convertible Apron Skirt, a detachable component to a traditional riding habit which prevented the wearer from being dragged along with the horse in the event of a fall.

Examples of his riding habits survive in museums worldwide, yet almost nothing of his life remains in the records. Bald census records indicate the basic comings and goings of family and occupation but leave so much else to the imagination. Was John a hard taskmaster and did his journeymen tailors like him? How did his interactions with the Princess of Wales, later Queen Alexandra, take place? Did he employ female go-betweens to act as intermediaries? John died in 1909 and the reins of the business were passed to his son William but this new generational tenure was to be tragically cut short. I find William on a variety of shipping records in the early years of the twentieth century. Given the reputation of the firm with aristocratic horsewomen, there must have been a trans-atlantic trade in their sharply cut tailor-mades and William appears to have taken a number of trips back and forth to New York.

On 26 September 1914, William embarked at Liverpool on the RMS *Campania*, a passenger liner that had once been a shining light in the Cunard suite of ships. It had been considered the most luxurious liner of its day, accommodating two thousand passengers and featuring opulent Victorian interiors. William sailed on her last ever passenger crossing before she was decommissioned and so his return journey necessitated him booking on to a different vessel. It was the RMS *Lusitania*. As the ship steamed out of New York on 1 May 1915, I wonder if William was congratulating himself on work well done in the city and looking forward to returning to London and seeing his mother, Margaret, once again. Although unmarried, perhaps he had a sweetheart waiting for him, or maybe he was simply too invested in the Busvine business. The outbreak of war in 1914 had made the waters around the UK increasingly unsafe as German U-boats patrolled the area and the German Embassy in New York had published warnings in the American newspapers in April 1915, warning travellers that they crossed the Atlantic at their own risk. Did William fear an attack? On Friday 7 May, the day before the ship was due to dock in Liverpool, the *Lusitania* was sunk by a German torpedo, with the loss of 1,191 lives, among them William Busvine. He was thirty-five. The Busvine business continued to produce world-class tailored garments into the 1920s, at which point the riding habit started to disappear from the aristocratic wardrobe. It may be that one of William's brothers stepped up to fulfil the family role, but that I do not know.

Not knowing is one of the realities of research. Moments of revelation as life stories and business histories unfurl are immensely satisfying but sometimes, no matter how diligent or determined the researcher might be, those stories remain untold. Such is the case with the elusive tailor Vernon. I have studied numerous garments made by Vernon which have washed up in museums around the world. Those belonging to Queen Alexandra are invariably made from cream wool with darker decorative accents, in essence the female version of a sailor suit worn for her frequent trips abroad on the royal yacht. The cut is beautiful. The trim subtle. The lining exact. The hem weighted. They might show signs of wear or an occasional unfortunate moth hole. The woven label proclaims Vernon as the ladies' tailor responsible. And that is almost all I can find. Trade directories list the business premises at 190–192 Sloane Street, a suitably fashionable address. A journalist writing in a 1911 edition of the *Ladies Field* journal 'recommended that readers visit Vernon and reassured them that it was untrue that only the very rich could purchase clothing there'. One of their advertisements drew on their reputation for catering to customers based abroad, keeping exact patterns for clients to replicate at a future date. In the collections of the Nasjonalmuseet in Oslo, a stockman-style dressmaking dummy has the word 'Vernon' written across its base. It was known to have belonged to Queen Maud of Norway, Alexandra's daughter, who ordered regularly from the firm. I find one tantalising trade entry that describes 'Mme Vernon', challenging the assumption that like all of the other prominent ladies' tailors, Vernon was a man. Scouring records for a female Vernon yields nothing. I don't know who she was, how she came to make such a success of herself in this occupation dominated by men, how she felt when she was awarded the Royal Warrant of Appointment. I don't know who worked for her or how they came to acquire such a reputation for their exquisite work. There are crumbs of clues, including the garments themselves that lie silently in their tissue-festooned boxes, but they peter out and never arrive at the door of the mysterious Madame Vernon.

Other makers are altogether more vocal along the path of their career so that we might hear the tales of their challenges and their successes. One such brand was that of Bernard Weatherill. The tailors' trade in the UK from the nineteenth century, like countless others during this period of industrial change, was often dominated by conversations and actions around working conditions and the fair remuneration for labour. Many of the workers employed in occupations such as tailoring were beset by unstable working conditions and unequal treatment from sometimes hostile employers, as well as being paid little for their efforts. The increase in unionisation meant that there had been a number of strikes, supported by these organisations, in a bid to secure improved conditions. One of these actions took place in 1912, when fifteen hundred tailors in the West End went on strike to demand better pay and conditions. One of the strikers was a young man named Bernard Weatherill. It was probably inevitable that Bernard would become a tailor since his father James was himself a tailor in Buckinghamshire. By the age of seventeen Bernard had moved in with his brother Harry, a butcher in Kensington, and had undertaken his apprenticeship in the needle trade. By the early years of the twentieth century, however, Bernard had become disaffected with the conditions of his work and joined other qualified journeyman tailors, who worked for a master tailor, in striking. It was a decision that would alter the trajectory of Bernard's career, not for the better in the first instance. His belligerence earned him a reputation as a troublemaker and after the strikes had ended, Bernard was unable to secure a job. His only option was to strike out on his own and try to forge a success as a master tailor in his own right.

Bernard moved to Ascot and began to advertise as a maker of breeches, the knee-length style of trousers still favoured for sporting activities and court presentation. From his premises in Bridge House, Bernard employed three other makers, Herbert Henry Copsey who was an expert breeches maker; James Warron, general tailor and a young apprentice; and Bernard's nephew Victor. These three young men would turn their expertise into a world-class brand. Bernard's son Jack recalls: 'He was a hard taskmaster, who was dedicated to high quality, but I do believe that his greatest satisfaction was to seek out and buy those businesses who had refused to employ him when he was a journeyman – and to sack the bosses.' The business acquired premises on Savile Row and in 1920 was awarded its first Royal Warrant to King George V for riding clothes and livery tailoring. The very same year, Bernard's son was born, another Bernard who adopted the name of Jack. At the age of seventeen Jack himself would enter the family business and was at the helm when Queen Elizabeth awarded the company her warrant for her own riding clothes and livery. He oversaw its continued success, but Jack Weatherill was not destined to remain a tailor until retirement. In 1964, he turned his hand to a different career and was elected Conservative MP for Croydon North East, a position he would hold until 1992. In 1983, Weatherill became the Speaker of the House of Commons and was able to turn to his Savile Row roots to solve one of his immediate challenges.

The speaker's livery had become too threadbare to wear, a reality that Weatherill reported to his compatriots at the Federation of Merchant Tailors. They felt that the reputation of 'the Row' would in jeopardy if master tailor Bernard Weatherill appeared in Parliament in a rag-tag collection of garments, and so they made it their mission to create a new ensemble: 'We had to scour the earth to find black pure silk velvet and we had to gut something like five old ones to get the hand-cut steel court buttons.' The making of the distinctive breeches was handed to one of the last specialist breeches makers at Weatherill, George Roden. A photograph of George at work shows a waistcoat-clad gentleman in crisp striped shirt and dark tie, tailor's chalk in one hand and a tape measure around his neck. He stands in front of the paper bags stencilled with the names of their most prominent clients, bags that contained all of the measurements required for a perfectly tailored ensemble. When George retired, the responsibility for riding breeches synonymous with the Weatherill name was handed to Michael Smith, who would become the last bespoke breeches cutter in the world. In his seventies, he was still making his way to the Weatherill workshop on the Wednesday of each week. 'They call it rock of eye,' says Johnny Allen, a younger tailor wise to the experience of Smith. 'He has a natural instinct and a natural eye for making a coat or a pair of breeches with a really beautiful balance to it . . . Where will you ever see that again, when somebody gives the majority of his life from when he was fifteen years old to one company, to something very specialist and intricate?'

The firm would wind its way into every element of Michael Smith's life from his time as an apprentice learning felling, cross-stitching and back-stitching – 'they wouldn't let me work on anything properly for a year' – to meeting his wife, Elizabeth, who started working at the firm as a 'kipper', an apprentice finisher. Michael's reputation sealed his place as maker of the Queen's garments.

Bernard 'Jack' Weatherill never fully left his tailoring roots behind. Even during the years of his political career, and on the advice of his mother, he always kept his tailoring thimble in his pocket to remind him of his origins in trade. The establishment of Bernard Weatherill merged with another Savile Row tailor, Kilgour, in 1969, but the brand retained its name and warrant and survives to this day, although of Michael Smith and his decades-long dedication, his colleagues are sure: 'You have that feeling you'll never see the like of it again.'

The easy acquisition of a tailored trouser suit, a sharp blazer or a fitted waistcoat for any woman in the twenty-first century would have been unthinkable two centuries ago. Tailoring was the preserve of men, and women might only venture into more masculine styles in very specific sporting contexts. Horace Walpole witnessed the winds of change and shuddered at the thought of these women, striding about in their riding habits and seemingly rejecting the niceties of feminine behaviours. Royal women were already separate from social norms and so were perhaps better placed to rock the sartorial boat. Queen Victoria felt the power of her Windsor uniform and her daughter-in-law Alexandra

Mademoiselle Brésil in a Redfern tailormade, 1904.

took the tailor-mades that suited her slender form and brought them to a wider audience, making a fashion star out of John Redfern and bringing employment to hundreds of young men and women as his empire expanded.

In light of these prominent names, it seems remarkable that either the garments themselves, in the case of Redfern, or the business that created them, in the cases of Peter Thompson, Busvine and Vernon, should exist in the shadows. Companies that once sent out their bills on elaborately decorated paper and inhabited exclusive addresses – who were reported on in leading publications and patronised by wealthy clients, royal and otherwise – have all but disappeared. Madame Vernon's legacy survives in the pale wool jackets made on Sloane Street, now scattered in museum collections around the world, but of the woman herself and the makers she employed there is nothing. Bernard Weatherill suffered no such obscurity, however. Its origins were loud, born of protest and a fight for fair wages, questing for quality and a reputation built on skilled employees. The loudness carried on through the public office of Bernard's son, his political life and his visible role, in Bernard Weatherill livery, in the House of Commons. Not all stories are able to be shared and not all lives might be remembered, but in a tailored coat here and a pair of breeches there the legacy remains.

CHAPTER 13

Off-duty Tweed
The Scottish Kilts and Pringle Knits

During the Platinum Jubilee celebrations in 2022, former Royal Protection Officer to Queen Elizabeth II, Richard Griffin, shared one of his favourite anecdotes. On one of her summer trips to Balmoral, he and the Queen were walking in the countryside nearby. 'There were two hikers coming towards us and the Queen would always stop and say hello,' he recalled. The American couple failed to recognise the Queen and there followed a conversation about whether or not she lived in the area. 'She said that she lived in London but had a house over the hill.' The couple asked if she knew the region well and when she acknowledged that she had been coming to that part of Scotland for over eighty years, the tourists responded excitedly: 'Well, if you have been coming for eighty years you must have met the Queen!' She replied: 'Well, I haven't but Dick here meets her regularly.' Photographs ensued, the couple eagerly handing the Queen their camera and asking her to take a photograph of them with Richard so that they could tell their friends all about him when they got home. As an afterthought they had a picture taken with the Queen as well, the husband of the couple asking Richard what she was like. As they walked away, Richard recalled: 'Her Majesty said to me that she'd love to be a fly on the wall when he shows these photos to his American friends and somebody hopefully tells him who I am.'

Dressing the Queen

Context was everything here. In the rural spaces around Balmoral, strictly off duty, the Queen was no doubt wearing a tweed skirt and stout shoes, perhaps also a mac or a knitted twinset with her customary silk headscarf covering her distinctive hairstyle. These are not garments designed for the public royal body but rather the private individual. Informal clothes. Comfortable clothes. Practical clothes. All the same, they are clothes made in specific places whose patronage earned the makers the Royal Warrant, whether they were fashioning a waterproof coat, a pair of sturdy boots, weaving a tartan or knitting a cardigan. These are the makers at Burberry and Pringle, at Kinloch Anderson in Edinburgh and Henry Poole on Savile Row, whose fabrics might seem far from the glitter of royalty but have in fact provided garments for queens as their most authentic selves.

Scotland looms large in this narrative, not least because it has provided something of an escape for the monarch over the last almost two hundred years. Tartan became a firm favourite of Queen Victoria and Prince Albert from the 1840s, a choice replicated again and again by subsequent members of the family, but the fabric and its relationship to the monarchy is itself a complex pattern woven through with subjugation, prohibition and national identity. After the Battle of Culloden in 1746, measures were taken by the English government to suppress the Highlands and this included the identities represented through clan tartans. The 1746 Act of Proscription stated that: 'No Tartan, or Party-coloured Plaid or Stuff should be used for Great Coats or for Upper Coats.' No member of the British royal family would set foot in Scotland until 1822, when King George IV ventured across the border as part of a visit choreographed by the novelist Sir Walter Scott. His hugely popular tales of Scottish heroes had contributed to the romanticisation of the Highlands in English imaginations and so, a century after the terrible events of Culloden and against the backdrop of the Highland clearances, the British monarchy ventured forth into the heathered moorlands of the

Off-duty Tweed

Scottish hills. Twenty years after King George IV's Scottish adventure, Queen Victoria visited Scotland for the first time with Prince Albert and they both fell in love with the landscape. By 1852, Albert had purchased the Balmoral estate and his gothic vision was completed in 1856, a castle whose interiors were liberally adorned in tartan, from curtains to carpets to couches. Whilst there were tartans associated with the monarchy, specifically the Royal Stewart pattern, Albert wanted his own and so in 1857 he commissioned the Balmoral tartan. It was a pattern designed to reflect the colours the royal couple enjoyed on their Scottish journeys, the predominant grey of granite threaded through with red and black overchecks.

Traditional tartan weaving is a complicated business. Once the colours have been chosen, each individual warp thread must be arranged in the correct sequence on a contraption known as the stake warp, a wooden frame allowing the weaver to set up the pattern before the weaving has even begun, the different-coloured wefts added crosswise to build the familiar check designs. On the 1861 Scotland census alone, over a thousand people described themselves as tartan weavers – fourteen-year-old James Meldrum who lived at home with his parents; sixty-year-old Helen Collander who supported her widowed mother, Ann; and fifty-year-old Daniel McDonald who boarded with the Fisher family and contributed to their meagre income as hawkers and shop boys.

The company ultimately responsible for the Balmoral tartan, and suppliers of Highland dress to the royal family today, started out as a popular tailoring establishment in Edinburgh in the 1860s. William Anderson along with his sons Joseph and Andrew had built a reputation as military outfitters, able to supply Scottish regiments with their individual tartans. Such was their reputation as tartan suppliers that in 1903 they received their first royal commission from King Edward VII. From their George Street premises in Edinburgh, twenty-four employees contributed to their reputation as one of the most successful makers of Highland dress. Six of these employees worked in the shop whilst the rest worked in the basement workshop. 'Only one machinist was a woman (Miss Reid) and all the rest were men,' writes Deirdre Kinloch-Anderson in her family history of the firm and I immediately feel some sympathy for Miss Reid. Did she enjoy being the sole female employee amongst all of the male tailors and makers, or did she dread each day as she took up her place in the workshop? Their days were long, beginning at 6.00 a.m. and extending to 7.00 p.m., but it appears to have been a company that inspired loyal service. The company records include a letter from 1925 signed by ten employees of long standing who had all been rewarded with a presentation for their work. Two photographs mark the passing of time. The first, taken in 1890, features three rows of whiskered and sober-suited men, all the employees of the firm at that time. The second, taken forty-five years later in 1925, pictures similarly whiskered and suited older men, the hair now silver and the suits a little old-fashioned. This photograph was taken to celebrate their long service, the very same employees whose younger faces were captured in 1890.

William Kinloch seemed to inspire devotion amongst these men who would retain their employment with the firm for so long. His reserved demeanour was both strict but fair. Every employee was issued with a booklet – *Rules and Instructions for Staff* – a set of directives to ensure the smooth running of the business. It instructed amongst other things that: '**1.** Everyone must be in his or her place and business in full swing by 9 a.m. **2.** All fixtures, table and warehouse dressing must be completed by 9.30 a.m. **3.** Wrappers and Covers must not be put on until ten minutes before closing time.' It was a straightforward list of the dos and don'ts to ensure both the efficiency of the business and the contentment of the staff. Beyond the instructions, however, there lay a philanthropic ideal. When William heard the news that one of his tailors had been killed during the First World War, he purchased a small flat for the man's widow and young children and charged them a minimal rent as well as employing the young woman in his household to boost her income. Without a national welfare scheme to support her, the outcome might have been very different for this now unknown young family. By the 1930s, the company had received the Royal Warrant of Appointment from King George V, a title they would continue to hold through the reigns of his son King George VI, his granddaughter Queen Elizabeth II and now King Charles III, specialising in a range of different weights of tartan woven in the distinctive Balmoral pattern and sported by royal women for over a hundred and fifty years.

Whilst Kinloch-Anderson provided the Balmoral tartan kilt that the Queen might wear during her Scottish sojourns, the fine-gauge knitted sweaters and cardigans that would complete her country ensemble were sourced from another Scottish stalwart – Pringle of Scotland. The story of Pringle knitwear centres around the town of Hawick, fifteen miles north of the England–Scotland border, an industry that grew from its close association with the raw material of the local landscape – sheep and wool. The availability of high-quality wool in this part of Scotland, favoured by sheep farmers, made it the perfect location in the late eighteenth century for framework knitters specialising in hosiery. On 26 June 1794, the master hosier William Beck recorded the addition of a new apprentice, sixteen-year-old John Pringle, whose name would come to represent the height of quality knitwear for generations of customers. In the first half of the nineteenth century, production changed from solely hosiery to include the manufacture of underwear, garments which would serve them well for almost a century. By the early years of the twentieth century, however, fashions were changing and the new vogue for ladies' sportswear saw the firm venture into outer garments. They opened a knitted coat department in 1910 and by the 1930s their cashmere knits were gaining a following. 'They were bought by the patrons of Harrods and Marshall & Snelgrove and were worn to point-to-points and on the moors with pearls and "sensible" shoes.' This was the British aristocracy at play and these were the perfect understated pieces. In 1948 Pringle were awarded their first Royal Warrant by Queen Elizabeth, consort to King George VI, and again in January 1956 when they were appointed knitwear manufacturers to Her Majesty Queen Elizabeth.

Much like Kinloch-Anderson, this was a family-orientated firm, one that valued and rewarded loyal service. Gerry Graham started to work for Pringle in 1967 at the age of fifteen: 'When we started we either went in as an apprentice to learn a certain trade or else you went to a department "through the mill", working in every single department to see what area you wanted to work in,' he recalled. Gerry started in the order office, processing orders from clients and transferring them to the production line, but then moved to the sample room where initial designs were made up. 'We did the sampling to see if it was going to be a success,' he told me, sharing the range with buyers from large London stores. In the course of our conversation, Gerry told me about the rest of his family and their role within the Pringle mills. 'My mother and my father both worked in Pringle's. My mother was a final examiner, she checked garments for quality before they were dispatched. My father was a security man, he checked people who were coming and going. My sister she worked in the invoice office and my other sister she was known as a body linker, she joined the front, back and sleeves. My brother he worked for just a short spell and he was called a bar filler. Cuffs had to be transferred to a knitting frame so the bar was transferred to the knitting frame.'

I love listening to his memories of a world now lost to mill closures and changing technologies. The town had its own ecosystem of textile manufacture. Gerry explained: 'When you were a trainee in the factory we had a textile college in the town, a technical college where we sent all the youngsters to learn the basics of the knitwear industry. You were actually taught all the different jobs of making a jumper.'

The final exam was to make a complete jumper from start to finish. I asked Gerry if he knew when royal orders had been received, thinking of the note that has survived on Clarence House headed paper, the official residence of the Queen Mother. It is short but to the point – typed text reads: 'WITH THE COMPLIMENTS OF THE DRESSER TO HER MAJESTY QUEEN ELIZABETH THE QUEEN MOTHER' and handwritten underneath in blue ballpoint pen, simply: 'NEW CARDIGAN PLEASE'. Gerry was certainly aware of the nature of the royal patronage. 'You were always told if there was anything special to be made, it was given a bit more priority. More quality checks and such. You were aware. You had an idea who it was for.'

Pringle oversaw the welfare of their workers with a variety of initiatives. There was a nursery at Glebe Mill, run by matron Agnes Dobbs. 'My sister's daughter was one of the first ones to go there,' Gerry remembers. He has fond memories of the other activities provided by his employer outside of working hours: 'They would arrange apprentice trips to see shows. My first trip was to Newcastle in 1967. It was the *New Musical Express* tour and we saw Engelbert Humperdinck, Cat Stevens, the Walker Brothers and Jimi Hendrix too. This is what Pringle did for youngsters.' He described the sports, each mill having its own football and hockey teams. There were dances and picnics and competitions. It was work but it was community too. And then it changed. The first inkling of disquiet came as early as the late 1960s, he told me. 'The railway closed in 1969 and it started to change then, it went into decline because there was no way in or out.' Where once there had been as many as five thousand people employed in the mills of Hawick, today only a few remain. Pringle survives but its production in Hawick does not and whilst the brand might be found in stores worldwide, the family firm and the community it supported lives only in the memories of people like Gerry.

A rural activity that has been universally enjoyed by royal women

Dressing the Queen

Spread from the *Pringle Annual* published for Pringle employees, 1962.

from Queens Victoria to Elizabeth is horse-riding. By the mid-twentieth century the nature of equestrian wear was more egalitarian, jodhpurs being worn by both men and women alike, but in the nineteenth century it was a more gendered affair. Women were expected to ride side-saddle and so the riding habit ruled. They are complicated garments, on the one hand tailored to fit, glove-like, around the torso but with a skirt expansive enough to cover the legs of the wearer on horseback, one knee hooked around the pommel of the side-saddle. There are loops to carry the skirt whilst walking and sometimes a matching pair of stirruped trousers for added security beneath it all. To study a surviving nineteenth-century riding habit in a museum collection is to bear witness to all the skill of the tailor – the padding, the precision stitching, the shaping, the lining and the fastenings. The firm that took on this challenge of crafting riding habits for royal women is one that has arguably earned the distinction of being the oldest brand on Savile Row with a heritage stretching back to the early 1800s – Henry Poole & Co.

Henry Poole was born on 8 September 1814, the son of a draper, James

Poole, who had made his name as a maker of military tunics, a skill much in demand during the campaigns of Wellington's army in the Peninsular Wars. The family lived on Old Burlington Street within sight of Savile Row where one or two tailors had already established themselves. In 1846 James Poole died and Henry took up the reins of the family business with an ambition that would take it to new heights, with new premises, impressive showrooms and a growing clientele. His success, according to one contemporary memoirist, was in part thanks to canny employment choices, describing 'the firm's well known trio of high priests, Mr Cundy (General Supervisor), Mr Dent (Coats) and Mr Allen (Trousers)'.

For many years, Garwood Dent was 'Coats' at Henry Poole. Garwood was born in Norfolk in 1835 and, like Henry Poole himself, had grown up in a tailoring family, his father, William, working in the trade. By the age of twenty-five, Garwood had travelled to London and was working as a shop man in a woollen draper's, perhaps hopeful of a role in the same trade as his father. He lodged with Alfred Culley and his family on Argyle Street. Alfred was a police constable and I wonder if this gave Garwood's mother, Sarah, some comfort when she thought of her son in the city. He was not to be a shop man for long, however, and climbed the ranks at Poole's so that by the early 1870s he was able to describe himself as a tailor. Garwood was well established, sharing a half-stuccoed, yellow-brick terraced house on Albert Street with his wife, Sarah, and their three small children. In spite of the potential turmoils of the journeyman tailor's experience, Garwood maintained a steady trajectory at Poole's. By 1901, more than forty years after leaving his family home in Norfolk and chancing his luck in London, he was describing himself as a tailor's foreman. By 1911 he had finally retired and lived to the grand old age of ninety. Such a long association with Henry Poole's doubtless brought Garwood Dent into the orbit of the royal clients who had begun to make the firm a name synonymous with tailoring expertise.

It was thanks to some royal theatricals that Henry Poole (and Garwood

Dent) would become the tailor to the monarch. The Prince of Wales, future King Edward VII, had watched a performance by the French actor Charles Fechter playing the role of an adventurer in a tattered coat, 'but the acute royal eye quickly noticed that the garment was well cut, and at the end of the play he [Prince Edward] sent for the actor and asked him for the name of his tailor. The answer was Poole.' The Prince placed his first order with Poole's in 1860 according to their ledgers and was married in a scarlet tunic made by the tailor for his wedding on 10 March 1863. A week to the day after this celebrated marriage, new measurements were recorded in the pages of the Henry Poole ledgers, those for the glamorous new Princess of Wales, Alexandra.

I spent some happy hours amongst the unique archive at Poole's leafing through these enormous ledgers. Many other tailors lost their historic records in the Blitz during the Second World War but Henry Poole's survived; what remains are a series of beautiful brown leather volumes with the name of each customer recorded in curling cursive at the top of the page. A single line of measurements in the tailor's shorthand gave the makers all they needed for the creation of Alexandra's riding habit, which was ordered on 25 March: 'A fine black habit lined silk bound braid – £12/12s. A pair of black elastic trousers lined silk. 2 sets collars and cuffs.' What the neatly recorded order cannot reveal was the nature of the interactions between a male-dominated tailoring establishment and the very real contemporary issues around propriety and the female body in such surroundings. It would have been inconceivable for any woman, not just the Princess of Wales, to have had her body measured or her riding habit fitted by a man. This was a challenge that Henry Poole had met some years earlier, however, as it became apparent that the vogue for riding habits was a market worth cornering. The first-recorded habits made for female customers were made in 1847 when Miss E. Waite was measured and a year later in July 1848 the two daughters of the Earl of Mountcashell each ordered 'a silk-lined habit in superfine rifle-green cloth at a price of ten guineas each'. The complexity of the fit for a side-saddle riding habit inspired an innovative installation within the showroom at Poole's. A dummy horse, named Bucephalus – the famous steed of antiquity, belonging to Alexander the Great – was positioned in the premises so that the riding habits could be fitted in situ, ensuring that the garment would function successfully.

To further meet the needs of these female clients, Henry installed six small silk-lined cubicles in his showroom and hired a dozen young female fitters to ensure that there could be no accusations of immodesty at Henry Poole. It was a decision that would change the course of Henry's own life, when Emma Walker entered his employment. Emma was born in 1818 in Deptford, Kent. Her father was a draper and so it seems that she had grown up with a knowledge of the properties of cloth. At some point in the 1850s, whilst living with her sister Elizabeth and their widowed mother, Emma secured a job at Henry Poole's as one of his female fitters, charged with the measuring, smoothing and tweaking of the tailored sportswear. It appears, quite simply, that they fell in love. Neither had been married before but in 1859, when Emma was forty and Henry forty-two, they became husband and wife. Emma moved into Henry's Thames-side house, Dorset Cottage, and for a time they shared a life together.

Henry was a complicated man, however, and his ambitions and desire to maintain friendly relations with his most celebrated clients would not serve him well. The wealthy did not pay. The bill for the two green riding habits, ordered on account by the Earl of Mountcashell in 1848, was still outstanding a full fifteen years later. In July 1863, interest to the amount of £43 had accrued, taking the debt to £118. In 1871, the bill still remained unpaid. This was far from unusual and the long, long periods of credit that Henry extended to these clients left him in serious debt. On 8 October 1875, as a very sick man, Henry wrote to his executor Charles Bingley: 'The trouble will not be what you thought – There will be nothing much to leave behind me. I have worked for a prince and for the public

& must die a poor man.' Henry died in 1876, leaving his cousin Samuel Cundy and his sister Mary Ann to sort out the muddle left behind. Emma died less than a year later. It was not the end of Henry Poole, tailoring establishment to the rich and famous, but it did signal an end to the creation of riding habits. As Samuel and Mary Ann sought to streamline the company and recoup some of the debts, it was a branch of the business deemed superfluous to requirements. By the end of the 1870s, the female fitting rooms were gone and the mighty Bucephalus sold.

If Henry Poole had acquired a reputation as a legendary British tailor, another manufacturer who began his operations in the mid-nineteenth century would also go on to become one of the most recognisable of British heritage brands. His name was Thomas Burberry. Burberry began his career further away from the luxury retail hub of London. In 1856, he opened a draper's shop in the Hampshire town of Basingstoke. At this time a draper's shop was an important local retailer, offering a diverse range of goods from everyday garments to accessories, to cloth and haberdashery. Living as he did in an area dominated by agriculture, one of the garments that Thomas sold in the largest quantity was the labourer's smock. Smocks were functional coveralls that protected the wearer from their environment, sturdy pale cotton gowns that pulled on over the head, worn by men working on the land in all weathers. Waterproof clothing was very much in its infancy in the mid-1800s. Whilst John Emary of Aquascutum had patented a waterproof cloth some years earlier and Scottish chemist Charles Macintosh had given his name to the rubberised coat, these were fabrics that were laminated in order to offer protection from the rain. They were unwieldy and not altogether practical. Thomas decided to take a different approach and, alongside a local mill owner, worked on the idea of waterproofing the yarn before it was woven. The experiments proved successful. He had created a fabric that was, itself, waterproof. He called it gabardine. Whilst agricultural workers benefited from the new fabric and the smocks that Burberry produced, he was determined to find a new market for his material and began to target the aristocracy on their country estates. It was a canny move and by the early 1890s, Burberry had opened an exclusive store in London's Haymarket. For the first time he began to supply the military with his gabardine outerwear, designing a double-breasted knee-length coat that would make a practical addition to the officer's kit. He called it the Tielocken, but it would become the famous Burberry trench coat.

In addition to soldiers, the Burberry brand allied itself to tales of derring-do. They kitted out aviators and motor racers. They supplied polar adventurers and mountaineers and advertised their superior garments being worn to the furthest extremes of the globe. At the same time as excelling in these spaces, Burberry found himself at the centre of less edifying publicity. In 1916, the company was subject to an inquiry about the treatment of its employees. The MP for Leeds East, James O'Grady, asked the President of the Board of Trade, 'whether he is aware that the method of manufacture adopted some years ago by this firm involves the employment of women, in place of skilled men, at piece rates much less than those paid in fair houses'. Women would often take work home after hours, contravening the Factory Act, in order to boost their terrible wage. Burberry himself actually tried to discourage union membership by offering to pay an extra couple of pence a week to non-unionists.

Two women who worked for Burberry at this time and may have been living on the sharp end of his poor wages were Ada and Annie Atwood. Ada was born in 1876 and Annie was her younger sister by six years. Both unmarried, they had jointly entered the needle trades, living together in a small brick terrace on George Street in Basingstoke and working together at the Burberry factory. As with so many working families, children followed parents into trades. Their father, George, had been a tailor as was their brother Harry. Between the wars, both sisters continued working for Burberry, working their way up to teaching the new seamstresses. Burberry coats were made from start to finish by a single maker, rather than components stitched by different hands, and their role was to introduce apprentices to the fashioning of the luxury garment. By the outbreak of the Second World War, Ada in her mid-fifties was described as an unemployed tailoress and Annie was working as a packer of medicinal supplies.

In the 1930s, the Great Depression forced the company to lay off many of its female workers and in spite of their long service and invaluable knowledge, Ada and Annie were not indispensable. Here, the tale of Ellen White brings a particularly twenty-first-century flavour of fakery to the Burberry legacy. Ellen was born in Basingstoke in July 1912. Her father James was a blacksmith and so when Ellen left school in 1926, it was expected that she would contribute to the family's income as soon as possible. She found work as an apprentice seamstress with Burberry, perhaps trained by Ada or Annie Atwood, but the economic depression cost her the job. Having been unemployed for some weeks, the story goes that Ellen answered the door one day to find her former Burberry supervisor, making her an offer she could not afford to refuse. According to a local newsletter, the supervisor had been covertly copying the patterns for the men's and women's raincoats and had decided to open a workshop making fake Burberrys. As one child in a family of eight, Ellen needed the money and so she accepted, travelling each day to the small premises on Alexandra Road. For eighteen months, Ellen and her friends stitched their fake Burberry coats, which were sold with great success to department stores along the south coast and into London.

I don't know what happened to the fake Burberry racket. Given the company's poor treatment of its female employees during the First World War and the fate of poor Ada and Annie, I admire the spirit of Ellen but the trail runs cold. It was not until the post-war period that Burberry was awarded the Royal Warrant to supply raincoats to Her Majesty Queen Elizabeth II, by which time it was in something of a style rut. Even so, its manufacturing processes relied on the skill of its female workforce, with three hundred seamstresses working at their Reading factory. Brian Kitson, newly employed by the company after his National Service in the 1950s, recalled his first visit to the factory: 'The cut and trimmed garment would be handed to a seamstress who made the entire garment individually, including the hand-drawn collars to ensure a perfect fit.' It would have been a process recognisable to Ada and Annie and to Ellen too, when she stitched the fake raincoats in the little Basingstoke workshop. Today Burberry is a juggernaut of heritage style, one of the big names in British luxury goods Following the death of Queen Elizabeth in 2022, it retained its Royal Warrant under the new household of King Charles III. Beyond the catwalk and the glossy magazine features, though, I think

The Henry Poole workshop, 1944.

of those women whose relentlessly stitching fingers fashioned the trench coats that would make Burberry the household name it is today.

I wonder at what point the American tourists, sharing their holiday snaps with friends back at home, realised they had met the Queen? What was she wearing that day? Possibly a slightly battered Burberry over a sensible Kinloch-Anderson tartan skirt? Perhaps the coat was fastened over the top of a cashmere sweater from Pringle. These are not necessarily the garments that make the headlines. There are no glistening silks or fluttering feathers here. This is an altogether more discreet wardrobe worn by women who are not in that moment subject to the flash of the paparazzi lens and the inevitable newspaper columns that follow. In another sense, as far as the makers are concerned, there is as much skill here as there is in a court gown or an embroidered robe. The tailors at Henry Poole, under the strict eye of Mr Garwood Dent (Coats) made some of the finest, most functional tailored garments in the world. Thomas Burberry, in spite of his questionable record as an employer, had developed a pioneering textile technology and then successfully marketed it to the most celebrated adventurers of his day, creating what would become a world-renowned luxury brand. William Anderson founded a manufacturer of Highland dress that would thrive into the twenty-first century and remain in the hands of his descendants. Quite the legacy. Pringle might not be the community firm it once was, but there are hundreds of families in the Hawick locale who must remember the impact it had on their lives, from childcare to concert tickets. Gerry Graham's reminiscences recapture a way of life and work that may have disappeared but lives on in his stories. The longevity of the garments too, remains to tell its own tales. The ancestry of these objects and their former makers survives in the DNA of a modern Henry Poole suit, a new Burberry coat, a Kinloch-Anderson kilt or a Pringle intarsia knit. They live on to tell the tale of some of the most iconic British success stories and the men and women behind the brands.

CHAPTER 14

The Secrets of Stockings
The Lost Arts of Ann Birkin and John Meakin

Monday 11 March 1946 was an important day in the annals of the Kayser Bondor stocking factory. Situated in the small town of Baldock in Hertfordshire, the manufacturer, like countless others in early post-war Britain, was trying to reinstate its production of goods in peacetime, its work having been turned over to the war effort for six long years. Queen Mary was keen that the young Princess Elizabeth should be well versed in the challenges of British manufacture and liaised with a number of businesses to arrange a series of royal visits. Owing to their proximity to London, the Kayser Bondor works were chosen for one of these visits. Caroline Haslett, in her role as chair of the Board of Trade's Hosiery Industry Working Party, corresponded with the managing director of the company, John Goodenday, in a series of letters, described by archivist Asha Gage. Caroline wrote that the princess 'would like to see some of the war work that is still carried on, but in particular she wants to see the stockings being produced'. Photographs of the visit show Princess Elizabeth in a dark wool skirt suit with broad lapels and a felt hat perched on her trademark curls, decorated with a silk flower. A crowd of employees and their families lined the roadway as she walked towards the factory, and once inside she was pictured alongside workers at their machines, spools of thread ranged in front of them. She was given a pair of the company's stockings, for which she ensured she exchanged two clothing coupons, the requisite number for a pair since rationing was still in force.

Like every woman in the country at the time, the Princess was of course wearing stockings, a staple of any wardrobe, and yet, visible though they were, the origins of Elizabeth's stockings are far harder to track down compared to so many other garments in her wardrobe. Obvious, but intimate, stockings and later on tights were worn daily for the entirety of her royal career. She never wore trousers and so they performed an important part in the propriety of her particular wardrobe. According to reports, a lady-in-waiting would always carry a spare pair in her handbag in case of a laddering emergency, but beyond snippets such as this details are scarce. Ironically, it is far easier to track down not only the makers, but the stockings themselves, of royal women a century earlier. The fine gauge of the knit and unique embellishments made Queen Victoria's stockings more collectible than the modern nylons of more recent years. Queen Victoria's hosiery has survived in a whole host of private and public collections. Her penchant for gifting the more ubiquitous of her garments to ladies-in-waiting and other members of the royal household means that auction houses and museums frequently encounter a royal stocking or two. Stockings equated to respectability in the nineteenth century and well into the twentieth so their manufacture employed thousands of people in Britain, initially at single-operator knitting frames and later on in more mechanised spaces. Roles varied from knitting to cutting to seaming and even embroidering, with royal production centring around the East Midlands, Derbyshire and South Wales. Stockings and tights might not have the impact of other royal garments. They were either hidden under long skirts or, in more recent decades, designed to be unobtrusive, invisibility their main object – and yet for so many people in Britain, their manufacture was a way of life. The making of stockings paid the rent and put food on the table.

The Secrets of Stockings

The manufacture of stockings is a story both of very early innovation stretching way back to the early seventeenth century and of a traditional way of life that remained unchanged for far longer than other textile processes. The invention of the stocking frame machine was prompted, according to legend, by an all too common patriarchal complaint – that of a man feeling neglected by his partner and the amount of time she spent on her domestic duties rather than tending to his entertainment. William Lee came up with the idea of creating a contraption consisting of multiple knitting needles rather than just one, in order that his wife might fashion garments more quickly. Whether this impetus is apocryphal or not, the outcome was revolutionary. In a letter dated 6 June 1610 written to a potential investor, Lee described his machine: 'a certain invention or artificiality being a very speedy manner of working and making in a loom or frame all manner of works usually wrought by knitting needles as stockings, waistcoats and suchlike . . .'

By the late 1600s, adaptations to William Lee's original idea saw hundreds of knitting frames operating in England, the chattering of multiple needles fashioning countless loops serving the nation's stocking requirements. The old manner of making stockings saw them created in the round by a single maker with one pair of needles, but Lee's machine meant that the shape of the stocking was knitted in a flat panel which then required making up with a gored panel at the ankle and a seam running up the back of the leg. William Lee came from Nottingham and this was one of the areas which, by the middle of the eighteenth century, would become a centre for the stocking-making industry. In a working pattern that was so familiar, most of the workers were operating on frames within their own homes, the wooden machines taking up precious room in small cottages. Within these confined spaces, the operation of the frame itself was no mean feat: 'Working the stocking frame required considerable physical effort, both from the hands and arms in moving the carriage and from the feet and legs in working the treadles. Good sight was also needed as the frame required frequent adjustment.' It was an industry that involved all of the family in the home. Whilst the men undertook the knitting, their wives would take care of the seaming and children could wind the yarn in preparation. It was also an industry riven with corrupt masters and poverty. Frames were expensive and so the only way that the framework knitters could work was to rent one from a master hosier at an exorbitant rate, which had to be paid regardless of circumstances. One knitter was asked in 1844 by a government commissioner if he regularly paid his two shillings rent for his frame. He replied: 'Yes, and always have paid it whether I have been on full work, or half work, or quarter work, whether sick or well, whether one day little work or no work or whether there are any circumstances, as there are sometimes, that you cannot do any; the charges have to be paid all the same.' Compared to other textile manufacturing processes, framework knitting did not move into larger, steam-powered factory spaces until the 1870s, a relatively late

The stocking-frame machine, a line drawing, 1763.

change in industrial practice, and so the cottage industry retained its importance in the fashioning of stockings.

It was within the walls of two such small and ordinary cottages that stockings were made and decorated to be worn in the most lavish palaces of the country. Amongst the many thousands of portraits in the Royal Collection featuring aristocratic and regal subjects, there are two photographs that belonged to Queen Victoria herself of two very different subjects. One shows an elderly lady, sitting on a high-backed chair. She wears a dark dress buttoned to the throat with a heavy woollen shawl about her shoulders. A small bonnet is perched on the back of her head. In her hands she holds aloft a needle and thread, in the very act of stitching, it seems, and on her lap sits a snowy white stocking. The second photograph is a head and shoulders portrait of a similarly elderly sitter, a man facing the camera in a dark wool suit, jacket and waistcoat buttoned, and a soft black tie knotted at the neck. His hair has been carefully combed with a side parting and his clipped white beard circles beneath his chin. They are Ann Birkin and John Meakin. They both worked for the company I. & R. Morley, then the world's largest stocking manufacturer, and they had both worked on fashioning Queen Victoria's stockings for six decades.

Ann Birkin was born in Nottingham in 1816, eldest daughter to George, a rate collector, and Ann. Whilst her immediate family did not appear to have connections with the city's hosiery industry, it would have offered one of the most likely employment opportunities for thousands of girls like Ann in the early nineteenth century. Whilst the work of the frame smith was considered suitable for men, Ann would have had the option to become a seamer or later, a cutter, but she chose a slightly different route. She became a chevener. Her job was solely to embroider stockings, stitching patterns in a panel from the ankle to calf. Once the stockings had been completed, sewn into shape by the seamer, the chevener would stitch their designs. Chevening patterns would be drawn on to slim pieces of paper or card and marked up with instructions for the stocking embroiderer to follow.

By the second half of the nineteenth century, the chevener's work had become highly fashionable as stocking colours and designs were created to match the shoes with which they were worn. In 1875 the publication *The Milliner and Dressmaker* described 'slippers of pearl grey rep, embroidered with rosebuds with grey stockings, also embroidered with the same'. And by 1890 the *Young Ladies' Journal* was reporting: 'Thus with a dress of dark navy-blue with a red pattern, the stockings are identically alike; with a coffee-coloured dress, trimmed with blue, they are coffee-coloured, embroidered with blue silk spots and so on.' The royal compliance with this popular trend remains in the collections of the Met Museum in New York, where they hold several pairs of shoes that once belonged to Queen Alexandra, along with their corresponding, matching stockings. The makers are absent. The chevener who was perhaps given the design to follow in accordance with the colour of the shoe goes unrecorded, her work on the stocking unsigned, unremarked. A pair of rosebud-painted slippers from the 1870s are paired with a cream pair of openwork stockings, and some low-heeled lilac pumps come with decorated stockings in matching shades. Their connection remains intact but their maker will never be known.

The firm of I. & R. Morley, Ann Birkin's eventual employer, had four hundred and fifty makers-up, completing the seaming, and five hundred cheveners, all working in the villages around Nottingham from their own homes. Ann Birkin was the only one amongst that five hundred who could call herself chevener to the Queen. It is Ann's silk embroidery discernible on the white stockings worn by the Queen for her coronation in 1837 which survives still in the Royal Collection. She stitched, too, the embroidery that graced the stockings worn by the Queen for her Golden Jubilee and her Diamond Jubilee as well as countless others in between. For most of her adult life she lived in

The Secrets of Stockings

Ann Birkin, Queen Victoria's chevener, c. 1900.

the village of Ruddington, south of Nottingham itself, and undertook her embroidery as an outworker, gaining something of a reputation both for the celebrity status of her stockings and the longevity of her employment. A newspaper article described Miss Birkin in 1901, 'who lives in a neat cottage in the little village of Ruddington, where she is a notable personage on account of her occupation'. She never married, but lived with her niece Jane who was employed in the same endeavours as her aunt and shared a house with her in Ruddington. Some years later Ann appeared in the press once again, this time in relation to her length of service which, at seventy-two years, was believed to be a world record for continuous employment in modern industry. On the 1881 census, she described herself as 'Stocking Embroideress (HM)' and I wonder with what pride she informed the census clerk that she worked for the Queen. Her work survives in the stockings that are still in museum collections today and in the photographic portrait stored in the Royal Archive.

Fourteen miles west of Nottingham, in the town of Derby, another expert outworker was employed by I. & R. Morley for specialist stocking orders. John Meakin was destined to become a frame smith, following in his father's footsteps straight to the treadles of the wooden stocking frame. He was born in 1816 and after his early years of education he was apprenticed into the same industry as his father. Like Ann Birkin, he too worked for I. & R. Morley from his own house which, by the middle of the nineteenth century, was a terraced cottage on Talbot Street in Derby. There he would work with the fine silk yarn, operating the frame with such skill that he became the most sought-after frame smith for important commissions. Surviving pieces indicate the quality of his work. One pair of Queen Victoria's pink silk stockings in a collection are described as being 'as sheer as a modern nylon stocking', comprising forty-eight stitches per horizontal inch and eighty rows per vertical inch. These were gossamer threads looping row upon row upon the frame of John Meakin. John married Ann Lancaster in 1839 and the couple went on to have a large family, at least two of their sons taking on the job of framework knitting like father and grandfather before them. Where so many objects in the Queen's wardrobe remained anonymous, the stockings made by John Meakin do bear the slightest acknowledgement of his labour. Inside the welt of the stocking, the initials JM appear alongside an M for the firm of Morley. It is a small credit to the man who spent six decades of his life knitting stockings for the wealthiest of women. At some point in 1898, Queen Victoria gave a personal recognition to John

The Secrets of Stockings

Meakin for his services rendered, when they exchanged photographs, his joining Ann Birkin's in the Queen's collection of portraiture, and hers standing perhaps on a mantelpiece or leaning near to the frame at which John had spent most of his adult life.

If you draw a straight line in a westerly direction on a map of the UK from Birmingham, you will cross the Welsh border and arrive at Newtown. On the Old Kerry Road, a large red-brick building curves along the path of the highway within a stone's throw of the railway station. It is grandly porticoed, arched windows filling the three storeys of space, and above the main entrance a coat of arms heralds its significance. It is the royal arms and the business within was, for many decades in the town, one of significant international innovation. At the very top of the building, its name is inscribed in huge letters for allcomers to see: 'PRYCE-JONES. THE ROYAL WELSH WAREHOUSE'. From this enormous space and via the railway next to which it was deliberately positioned, the textile goods produced by Pryce-Jones travelled to all corners of the globe and into the wardrobes of the royal palaces thanks to the canny strategies of one man, Pryce Pryce-Jones. Pryce was born near Newtown in 1834. His father was an agricultural labourer and so it would have been absolutely necessary and completely ordinary for a boy in Pryce's position to undertake the basics of schooling before venturing out in search of a trade. At the age of twelve he had joined a local draper, John Davies, as an apprentice and by the age of twenty-two he had forged a life there to such an extent that he took over the business himself. He married the very same year that he became proprietor of the draper's, in 1856, and by 1861 he and his wife and their young children were living in Newtown with their three employees, Pryce's brother John and two other assistants, Thomas Jones and Mary Powell. Drapery businesses were ten a penny in the mid-nineteenth century but Pryce had a quite different vision for the Welsh wool flannel in which he dealt. Having grown up in rural Wales, Pryce was all too aware of the difficulties that many people had in acquiring goods if they happened not to live in urban centres. Using the new and efficient railways to his advantage, Pryce produced one of the world's first mail-order catalogues, illustrated with his flannel undergarments, and he began to transport them further and further afield.

It would prove to be a revolutionary business model that would generate more than a quarter of a million customers for the Welsh firm and make Pryce-Jones a multi-millionaire. On the 1871 census, Pryce described himself as a flannel merchant now employing eighteen persons, some of whom found their accommodation with the Pryce-Jones family on Severn Street in Newtown. They included twenty-one-year-old John Shaw, John Jones who was fifteen and Frederick Jones who was nineteen. The eldest live-in employee was fifty-five-year-old Thomas Davies, working as a draper's porter and presumably responsible for the logistics of manoeuvring bundles of orders from warehouse to railway. By the later years of the nineteenth century, these eighteen employees had expanded to over four thousand as the mail-order business grew and grew. Royal Warrants followed, not only from Queen Victoria but her daughter-in-law Alexandra, Princess of Wales, and European royalty who could rely on the efficient transport model – Pryce-Jones offered next-day delivery for his UK customers. Queens Victoria and Alexandra were warmed for decades by the Welsh flannel supplied by Pryce-Jones in the form of underskirts and possibly stockings, although the origins of these are always harder to determine. The great success of his strategy was such that in 1887 Queen Victoria knighted Pryce-Jones in recognition of his services to industry. He moved to Plas Dolerw, a late Regency mansion above a meadowed bend of the River Severn but almost within hailing distance of his grand Royal Welsh Warehouse. It was far from his origins in a farming community on the Welsh borders.

When Pryce-Jones died in 1920, he left a business which, despite struggles that would follow with the Great Depression in the 1920s, would

The Secrets of Stockings

Women working in the Pryce-Jones factory, 1953.

continue to manufacture woollen goods well into the 1950s. They were not the only Welsh firm, however, that would enjoy royal patronage, for at the same time as Pryce-Jones, a Rhys Jones, formerly a travelling salesman, also became a woollen merchant, this time seventy-two miles to the south of the country in the small town of Ammanford. Rather than specialising in stockings, the firm that Rhys Jones founded in 1892 became best known for its socks. In its early years, the small factory in Ammanford met the needs of its local population in a most functional and necessary way, knitting socks for the thousands of miners in the region. The coal-mining industry dominated the valleys of South Wales and serviceable woollen socks for a life underground were the mainstay of the company's output. Those same qualities were put to the test with the outbreak of war in 1939 when the colour of the wool became standard khaki and the business knitted for victory.

By the 1960s, the company was employing dozens of mostly young women; a photograph from the period taken outside its single-storey brick factory captures them in a uniform of white coats, the company name attached to the wall above their heads. It was a name that, oddly enough, would come to pre-empt the royal custom that would follow. The company was, and still is, called Corgi Socks. Princess Elizabeth was given her first Pembroke corgi as a gift in 1944 but did not start to order from the company until later and so the name is a coincidence, given the patronage and subsequent Royal Warrant. The company received the warrant of the Prince of Wales in 1989, one that has been renewed under his new reign as King Charles III. Where stockings and later tights were the preference of the late Queen for the entirety of her life, the rare occasions when she did wear socks saw the order placed with Corgi. It is a company that has been passed on to the descendants of Rhys Jones, each generation taking on the factory and the responsibility of keeping the knitting machines working. At its peak in the 1960s, Corgi employed a hundred and sixty local men and women but today, as more of the machinery has become automated, that number has reduced to thirty-eight, many of them long-serving employees of more than twenty years.

Lisa Woods, the great-great-granddaughter of Rhys Jones, explains that, in spite of the new machinery, 'we still make our handmade socks for the specialist market'. They occupy the same premises, the rhythmic back and forth of the knitting machines generating a wave of sound. Around the walls, shelves house myriad cones of coloured wool. The hands of workers snip and link and check the patterned socks that the circular machines spiral into creation, traditional methods and mechanisms running alongside the automatic and the digital. Like so many other of these small, niche, garment manufacturers, it is an unlikely setting for a pair of socks made for Ralph Lauren or Burberry, or indeed for kings and queens. Yet here they remain, their Royal Warrant placed above the company name. In the face of mass production and millions and millions of cheap, disposable pairs of socks, they have survived to carry on knitting.

From amongst the more than two thousand five hundred gifts that Princess Elizabeth received on the occasion of her wedding in 1947, there were one hundred and thirty-one pairs of nylons and seventeen pairs of silk stockings given to the young bride. In 1953, she was again the recipient of another pair of stockings, this time from the then US Ambassador to the UK, Lewis Douglas, and his wife. The newly crowned Elizabeth wrote to Douglas: 'I was so very delighted to receive the wonderful surprise of the stockings from yourself and Mrs Douglas and I am so very grateful to you both for your kind thoughts of me.' At this point in British history, with rationing still a controlling force in the population's access to textile goods, stockings had acquired a previously unimagined currency. We learn about them precisely because, in this unusual wartime context, they had come to represent the ordinary made rare. Stockings were democratising, worn by almost all women. For this very reason of ordinariness, Queen Victoria could afford to dispose of her stockings via the women in her household, strangely personal gifts that have subsequently found their way on to the open market. These unassuming pieces, identifiable only because of the royal cypher stitched at the stocking top, go on to command a price that far exceeds their original cost.

The association with the royal foot has brought them a notoriety beyond the threads from which they are knitted. Unlike those more obvious symbols of royalty – the hats or the gloves – the stockings, the tights, the socks are rooted to the ground. They are generally invisible, intended to be ignored, but for that very reason they command a strange fascination. They are the unknown made known. Ann Birkin was celebrated for her almost proximity to the royal foot during her lifetime and John Meakin marked his contribution to the gossamer garment when each pair left his frame. Pryce Pryce-Jones made his fortune and changed the face of retailing through his own relationship with garments never designed to be seen in public, and today Corgi socks maintain a tradition of Welsh woollen knitwear, selling to big brands and big names from their small factory in the South Wales valleys. Perhaps it is the total recognisability that makes royal hosiery so fascinating, an everyday sartorial act familiar to us all.

CHAPTER 15

Silk and Structure

Corset Making from Madame Roxey Caplin to Rigby & Peller

Royal corsets are invisible. They do not exist anywhere in real life, not in museums or private collections. They do not appear in auctions and there are no photographs. Where almost all of the other garments from a queen's wardrobe have some public profile, there is next to nothing documented about corsets. Never gifted. Never sold. Never discussed. This is for good reason, of course. So much about the clothed royal body has been widely disseminated for so long but the corset is different. It maps out the shape of the wearer, a piece of private armour not for public consumption.

The warrant holders for the queens' corsets are, as with all other suppliers, carefully recorded. Elaborate-sounding establishments that fit the exclusive nature of their wares – Madame Drion-Regnier; Madame Lambert; Mrs Addley Bourne; Madame Marcyle and more recently Rigby & Peller. Yet they too are, for the most part, discreetly absent. Apart from some elaborate stationery and finely drawn advertisements, I can find almost nothing – not a lace or a whalebone in sight. Yet corsets themselves are one of the most widely discussed and controversial of objects in popular dress history. They have become the visual shorthand for female oppression, period screen adaptations often adopting the corset trope as a convenient means of conveying the strictures of femininity through the tight lacing of a vicious corset. Scholars and makers have begun to unravel this trope in more recent years. All women wore corsets. Not all women tight-laced them. It was a ubiquitous garment, worn for centuries. As such, the corset-making industry employed many thousands of men and women and prompted innovators and entrepreneurs to make their mark. So where to find the elusive corsetière?

Visual records of corsets, especially relating to the stay maker in the eighteenth century, were widely available. From Hogarth caricatures to the more scientific engravings by Diderot, the industry of stay making was frequently illustrated, a trade that employed predominantly men owing to the sturdiness of the materials used and the efforts required to fashion them into a robust garment. By the nineteenth century, the workforce had changed. Lord William Barry, writing about the corset trade in 1868, indicated that there was one male to every twenty-five females employed in the making of corsets. Its value to the economy was enormous: 'The total value of stays made for British consumption annually cannot be less than £1,000,000 sterling to produce which about 36,000,000 yards of material are required. The stay trade of London employs more than 10,000 in town and country, whilst the provincial firms employ about 25,000 more.' As the sewing machine became more widely available, so it was easier for women to manipulate the materials required although even then it could be difficult. A Mrs Turner, recounting her days making corsets in a small workshop in Yorkshire, remembered of a certain fabric: 'It had such a rough surface that it made their fingers sore when they pushed it through the machines.'

Mrs Turner's descriptions of corset making in the 1940s are almost identical to those of makers nearly a century earlier. First, the pieces were cut from a pattern. Mrs Turner's business had five sets of patterns from which a number of different sizes might be made. The outer fabric and lining fabric would be cut into the various panels which would be pressed. These would be sent to the machinist and then the boning channels would be added. For much of the nineteenth century boning consisted of the thin strips of baleen that were still available via the whaling industry but by the twentieth century these were replaced with steels or metal spirals. Eyelets would be punched through stiffened buckram at the centre front with an awl, care being taken not to cut the fabric and potentially weaken its structure. Finally the laces would be threaded and decorative stitching added. It is a process mirrored in the expert reconstructions of present-day makers such as Bernadette Banner who has gained a remarkable following on YouTube and other digital platforms with her accurate recreations of historic dress. Watching her video that followed the making of an 1890s corset from an original pattern is to gain great insight into the skill of the corset maker. From the placement of the pattern pieces on the cloth – some following the grain of the fabric and some cut crossways to enhance the curve around the body – to the stitching and insertion of the boning and the formation of the eyelets, it offers a window on to the world of the corset maker who would be doing this not just once but thousands of times to produce the kinds of numbers suggested by William Barry.

    The industry was ripe for innovation. A corset favoured by countless women and also, it is suggested, by Queen Victoria herself, was William Sparks Thomson's 'glove-fitting corset'. Thomson was an American who had started his career in the 1840s in his father's grocery store in New Haven. By the 1850s, he had opened his own dry-goods store in New York and was beginning to venture into the world of women's undergarments, first patenting a hook for the new cage crinoline that made it easier to stitch, and then designing the glove-fitting corset. Such was the demand for his designs that he ran two large factories in New York which operated night and day and employed more than a thousand women. He brought his wares to Europe. His glove-fitting corset revolutionised construction and wear of the garment, taking it from a two-piece pattern with multiple boning sections to an eight-piece pattern that more closely followed the contours of the body. By the early 1860s he had a manufacturing presence in London and by the 1870s he himself lived in the city. Queen Victoria was apparently a customer but the evidence is scant and certainly there are no glove-fitting corsets that bear her name.

Another possible candidate for the title of corset maker to Queen Victoria might be the wonderfully named Madame Roxey Caplin. Caplin was born in 1793 in Canada but by the 1830s was working as a corset maker out of 53 Berners Street in London. Like Thomson, she brought huge innovation to her designs, so much so that at the Great Exhibition of 1851, she won the prize medal for 'Manufacturer, Designer and Inventor' for her innovative corsets. She wrote her own book on the subject, published in 1856, in which she outlined the various anatomical benefits of her inventions, emphasising to the reader that: 'In our corset, the wearer can breathe freely, and the pulsation of the heart is not the least interfered with, whilst the various motions of the body can be performed without any extra exertion or fatigue.' The medal-winning corset that was displayed at the Great Exhibition survives still, as part of the collections at the Museum of London. It is a vibrant electric blue silk with white contrast stitching, impossible to miss, it would seem – I wonder if it caught Queen Victoria's eye on her visits to the Crystal Palace? Maybe she ordered a Roxey Caplin corset, though if that were the case it does not survive.

The size and success of these large undergarment businesses make it hard to believe that, in most cases, they have simply disappeared almost without trace. Advertisements by the dozen still survive for the company of Mrs Addley Bourne. Her name appears in Queen Alexandra's wardrobe accounts although she was not an official warrant holder. Her grand letterheads proudly proclaim that they were a 'Family Draper, Jupon and

Silk and Structure

An illustration from Roxey Caplin's book *Health and Beauty*, 1854.

Corset Manufacturer to the Court and Royal Family'. The scale of their business was staggering and yet I have been unable to find a single petticoat, camisole, bustle, crinoline or indeed corset that bears the Addley Bourne label. Mrs Addley Bourne was in fact called Ann. Ann Philpot was born in Dover in 1839 and her earliest memories must have involved the tactility of cloth. Her father, Edward, was a draper in the town and so the selling of fabric sat at the heart of her childhood. She married Benjamin Bourne who was ten years her senior and together they set up in business as linen drapers in London.

By 1861 they were living at 37 Piccadilly, an address that placed them in the centre of the city's retail district. Ann was only twenty-two years old but already their household included numerous employees. In addition to her sister Mary who was working for them, there were five more apprentices and draper's assistants: nineteen-year-old Emma Lucker from Hampshire; Marius Heath and Charles Bayer, both fifteen and already apprenticed to the draper; Thomas Taylor, a twenty-year-old assistant; and Hudson Carter aged eighteen. Ann was barely older than those that she employed and was, besides, already mother to a one-year-old baby girl. Whilst the census records consistently describe her as an 'outfitter's wife', the copious advertisements that filled newspapers and periodicals over the next two decades tell a different story. Unusually, it appears that Ann was the driving force behind the expanding enterprise. As her family grew, so too did the business with some smart marketing strategies.

By the late 1860s, the name Mrs Addley Bourne had become synonymous with a whole host of undergarments. Valued customers would receive a *Book of Illustrations*, an early product catalogue, in which would be featured the full range of their garments. Royal associations were hinted at through the choice of names given to their wares. Customers might choose an 'Alice' nightdress or a 'Beatrice' petticoat, the daughters of Queen Victoria unwittingly lending their support to the burgeoning underwear empire. The scale of the enterprise is revealed in an advertisement that featured in an 1866 issue of the *Illustrated London News*: 'A thousand crinolines at half price . . . beautiful shapes but a little dusty – offered for a short time during stock taking.' It is a staggering figure. Crinolines were bulky objects and yet Mrs Addley Bourne had the capacity to store a thousand of them, besides the countless other garments they kept in stock, not least the corset. Many of the surviving illustrations that advertised their wares featured the swanbill corset, which came in a variety of options. There was a swanbill for 'tall figures' and one for medium and short. There was an 'elegant swanbill' with additional stitching and lace trim, and there was a nursing swanbill with lacings at the side. There was even a handmade swanbill that cost a little extra. The enterprising Ann Bourne embraced the possibilities of mail order, advertising that customers could simply 'send size of waist with Postal Order to prevent delay and inconvenience'. She simultaneously catered to the affordable mass market and to royalty, sending swanbill corsets to suburban housewives and princesses. Tracing the manufacture of these corsets is more difficult, however. Whilst we might follow the trail of Ann herself and of Benjamin, both of whom retired to Surrey in 1885, the women who constructed their famous corsets prove more elusive.

Silk and Structure

What did their world consist of, as they sat cutting, pressing, stitching or lacing the prolific undergarment?

A glimpse at such a life is possible through another major corset-making enterprise, located in the town of Market Harborough, which employed hundreds of women. In 1830, William Symington had moved from Scotland to Leicestershire to set up in business as a draper. There he married the daughter of a local stay maker, Sarah Gold, and by the early 1850s they were advertising 'stay making' as one of the services they offered in their shop. By 1861 and with the advent of the sewing machine, the small drapery business had moved all of its production into corset making. It would become a global enterprise, Symington's corsets being purchased by fashionable women around the world and made in the company's Market Harborough factory where they employed sixteen hundred women running five hundred machines. The visual record attached to Symington's, which includes hundreds of photographs, illuminates the working life of corset makers in the late-nineteenth and early-twentieth century and the census records for the town are filled with the names of the workers who thronged through the factory doors every day. In 1901, these factory doors were featured in striking detail when the film-makers Mitchell and Kenyon made one of their 'factory gate' reels catching the Symington's workers as they left for the day. Through the wooden double doors flood the men and women finishing their shift, the men buttoned into waistcoats and working jackets, flat cloth caps on their heads, and the women almost all wearing dark or pale straw boater hats, some clad in tailored coats buttoned to the neck or open to reveal a soft necktie and blouse beneath. They pour out, chattering and smiling, linking arms with their friends as they head home for the day. Amongst them may have been sisters Lily and Carrie Potter who lived at 7 Coventry Road, both of whom worked as corset makers like their widowed mother. Perhaps Amelia Penn is one of the young women, heading home to Heygate Street where she lived with her mother and aunt. Maybe the shyly smiling figures included Sarah Elizabeth and Mary Ann Branston, sisters who lived together in three rooms at 2 Bowden Lane and were both corset-box makers.

A later film titled *A Trip Through Libertyland* made in 1929 took the cameras into the factory itself and followed the workers through the varied processes. There are men feeding seventy-two layers of sturdy cotton through a band saw, cutting hundreds of panels an hour to be sent to the machinists. The silent footage then leads the viewer through each stage. White-smock-clad women check for quality at long scrubbed tables. The camera pans around the 'White Room' – a vast workroom with high ceilings and light walls, criss-crossed with wooden workbenches and long pendant lights suspended above – filled with women industriously marking the panels of cloth that tower in identically cut piles. One of the captions interspersed throughout quips: 'They work so fast in this department we thought of putting this on in slow motion,' before cutting to row upon row of women at their machines, the pattern pieces to one side of them ready to be stitched together.

Symington's had a reputation for its excellent pastoral care. The company arranged for social and sporting events to take place amongst the workforce, overseeing dances and trips to the cinema. This was not the case for all corset makers, and many women worked under very different conditions. It was, as so often the case in any number of the needle trades, poorly paid. A pamphlet published in Portsmouth in 1974 that collected the reminiscences of corset workers in the city noted: 'Wages were miserably low and hours long. There would be fines for arriving late. Learners paid a deposit of 10% and received no wages for some months.' A seamer, Gwyneth Daly, who worked in the industry for seven years from the late 1940s, recalled the noise: 'It made my head bad the first couple of days I was there. But my mum said, "Don't tell the managers that's what it was, tell him you had a bad cough," so I wasn't allowed to say the noise of the machines made my head bad in case I got the sack.'

Where the warrant holders Madame Marcyle and Madame Lambert may have left little trace in the historical record, one royal corsetière has left a more indelible mark in the world of royal corsetry and that is Rigby & Peller. Like Madame Roxey Caplin and Mrs Addley Bourne, this too is an establishment born of female enterprise and entrepreneurial spirit, founded first through an escape from fascism. Alongside other makers, craftspeople such as Cornelia James with her suitcase of glove leather or Aage Thaarup and his head full of hats, a young Hungarian refugee named Margit Peller found herself in London in 1939, adrift and alone in the unfamiliar city. A typed docket dated 30 November 1939 noted that her application for exemption from the Female Enemy Alien internment programme had been approved and so she was free to find accommodation and work. She listed her occupation as corset maker but her current employment was 'Nil'. Fate would take an unexpected turn in the fortunes of Margit, or Gita. Her search for lodgings took her, somehow, to the door of Bertha Rigby where she became a boarder in the early years of the war. Remarkably, Bertha too was a corset maker and within a matter of weeks they had decided to open their own establishment on South Molton Street.

Perceptions of the corset as a garment relegated to the nineteenth century are not accurate, given the number of corseted undergarments that were still being produced well into the post-war years in Britain. Symington's continued trading until 1967 and Mrs Turner, as proprietor of the rather unglamorous-sounding 'Scientific Corsetry' in Yorkshire, was still making corsets until the early 1970s, mostly for older women for whom it had been a regular garment in their wardrobe. She explained to an interviewer in 1977: 'There comes a time in the life of many women when they cannot get satisfactory corsets from Marks & Spencer and that is where Scientific comes in.' Rigby & Peller would come to provide a similar, but more expensive, bespoke service for women in London. Whilst commercial manufacturing of cheaper, ready-to-wear bras and girdles had become the norm in the post-war period, those who could afford it might still opt to have custom-made underwear. Rigby & Peller's reputation for such a successful and discreet service meant that by the early 1950s, they were making the corseted undergarments for the young Queen Elizabeth. The details of their work were never revealed but their name was listed amongst the dozens of suppliers to the royal wardrobe. In 1956, both Gita and Bertha wished to retire and so the business was taken on by Gita's niece Tessa Seidon. Tessa continued to meet the requirements of royal patronage, to the extent that, in 1960, she was awarded warrant holder and the golden royal arms were displayed above the black paintwork of the Rigby & Peller shopfront. The royal seal of approval was not enough on its own, however, to ensure the continued success of a business whose customers were older and less in need of the same undergarments they had once favoured.

In 1982, Tessa decided to approach somebody else to take on the responsibilities of the shop and made contact with June Kenton. Like so many corsetières before her, June had grown up with textiles as the backdrop to her youth. Her parents owned a number of clothing shops and her first job was behind the counter, her interest being especially in the lingerie they sold. 'My parents decided that I should be a proper corsetry fitter. They sent me off to do an intensive course at the Berlei Corset School in Oxford Street. I loved it.' By the mid-1960s, June and her husband, Harold, had opened two wholesale clothing shops of their own and in 1970 opened their first shop specialising in lingerie and swimwear: 'There was nothing like the choice of bras we have today, what we did was fit the front and alter the back. We did not have our own workroom but we had brilliant outworkers who could keep up with the demand.' Their continued success meant that they were the obvious choice to take over at Rigby & Peller. June recalled her first visit to Buckingham Palace when the potential new warrant holder must be approved: 'We had to be outside the Queen's bedroom at one minute to nine – not five minutes before or two minutes after.' The Queen approved and June was the proud new royal corsetière.

Under June and Harold's stewardship, the shop went from strength to strength. They inherited four experienced seamstresses, some of whom would end up remaining with the company for over thirty years. Like so many other bespoke trades, corsetry is work that offers longevity of employment for those who wish to stay. Press and publicity followed. There were television appearances and June became famous for her ability to fit customers by eye. It became her mantra that 85 per cent of women were wearing the wrong-sized bra and the name of Rigby & Peller became synonymous with a luxury experience that need not be exclusive to only the very wealthy. She took care never to talk about the underpinnings ordered by the Queen and so the public face of Rigby & Peller existed happily alongside its more discreet responsibilities. That is until 2017 and the publication of June Kenton's autobiography. June wrote at length about her life in the rag trade, her career, her experiences. She did not write about the Queen other than those brief recollections of her first visit to the palace. She certainly did not write about the Queen's corsets. There were one or two short references to her interactions with the Queen Mother and Princess Margaret but that was enough. A few short months after the book's publication, the Royal Warrant, held by the company for over fifty years, was revoked. No details are ever given by the royal household for decisions relating to individual warrant holders, but June later admitted that she regretted 'not being wise enough' to have avoided any revelations, however small, about her interactions with the Queen.

June Kenton learned the hard way what those royal corset makers before her had established. You do not discuss the royal corset. The warrant may be publicised but the wares are most certainly not. Madame

Drion-Regnier and Madame Lambert, corset makers to Queen Alexandra, did not make a public noise about their royal patron and so traces of them in the historical record are almost non-existent. The equally glamorous-sounding Madame Marcyle, listed for many years as corsetière to the Queen Mother, is just as obscure, but somewhere their workshops employed nimble-fingered women who would have pieced together the panels of cotton and silk, inserted the slim bones into fabric channels and passed the laces of the corset criss-cross fashion through the sturdy metal eyelets. If they knew that the corset they had machined was destined to fasten around the body of the Queen then they never spoke or wrote of it.

The woman responsible for the uniquely shaped corset made to fit the changing physicality of Queen Alexandra may have secretly wondered at its proportions but would never have revealed those personal realities to another soul. Unlike so many of the other pieces of clothing worn by a queen, there is at least some frame of reference in our own lives. We generally all wear shoes and coats, dresses and occasionally a hat. Very few of us ever wear a corset and so they too have become almost mythical objects. To watch the silent film of the employees streaming out of the gates at Symington's or glancing at the camera from their sewing machine is to witness an entirely lost world. It was a world that has been populated with female innovators and businesswomen. It allowed Madame Roxey Caplin to win the coveted Great Exhibition medal in 1851 for her brilliant blue corset and it saw Mrs Addley Bourne (Ann) Bourne, build an underwear empire. The royal corsets themselves may be invisible, but in film and photograph and stitch, we can find the makers still.

CHAPTER 16

What Lies Beneath
Of Linen Maids and Laundrywomen

When my children were small, I remember reading to them the picture book by Nicholas Allan titled *The Queen's Knickers*. 'The Queen likes to dress smartly,' it begins. 'So she has an enormous wardrobe for her clothes . . . and a slightly smaller chest of drawers for all her knickers.' There follows the irreverent journey of the special pairs that the Queen might wear for all occasions, since it is never not funny to say 'knickers' to a three-year-old. The quiet genius behind the picture book is the very unknowable nature of its subject. The author's imagination, and that of his readers, can run wild, because who will ever really know anything about the Queen's knickers? Royal linen forms the final layer between skin and the rest of the royal wardrobe, a liminal space between the utterly private and the public body. In older traditions, the royal bedlinen served as evidence of consummation, as bedchamber women would inspect the sheets of the newlyweds on the morning after the wedding, a practice which is unthinkable by modern standards but which formed part of the more protracted bedding ceremonies carried out to ensure dynastic continuity. The satirist Isaac Cruikshank envisaged the moment of retiring in his 1797 cartoon entitled 'The Wedding Night', which depicted King George III and Queen Charlotte leading a merry bunch towards a bedchamber following the marriage of their daughter

Princess Charlotte to Prince Frederick of Württemberg. The bedding ceremony was a crowded affair, up to the very moment when the royal couple were undressed and the groom drew the curtains firmly around the bed.

These were ceremonies that had lapsed by the middle of the nineteenth century, although questions of succession forced a different kind of scrutiny. Queen Victoria was endlessly interfering when it came to questions of her eldest daughter-in-law's fertility. Princess Alexandra had married Victoria's eldest son, Bertie, in 1863 and from that moment the Queen ensured that she was well informed as to the potential arrival of an heir to the throne. She hired a Dr Sieveking as the Princess's personal physician. He wrote in his diary after an interview with the Queen: 'I thought her most gracious, her voice as clear as a bell and her smile more winning than that of any woman.' Her charm offensive was deliberate. What she required of Sieveking were regular updates as to the Princess's health, including her menstrual cycle. When the young Princess Alexandra gave birth to her son two months prematurely, Sieveking was unable to make it in time to assist and it was one of the Princess of Wales's ladies-in-waiting, Lady Macclesfield, herself a mother of thirteen, who took care of the immediate needs: 'She made the bed with clean linen, cleared away the bloodied sheets and wrapped the baby in cotton wool.' Between menstrual cloths and the realities of childbirth, the discretion required of laundering royal linen was a very real concern, not to mention a logistical nightmare.

The supply, organisation, maintenance and laundering of the royal linens, both body and bed, became part of a complex chain that began with the draper, men such as Walter Capper whose firm supplied royal linens with increasing frequency from the 1850s, and continued into the royal residences and the domain of the linen maid. Women like Jane Reeve, Eleanor Simons and Emily Baalum spent their days accounting for the fabric in their care, directing it to their owners who were identified on shirts and shifts and petticoats via stitched royal cyphers. From the linen cupboards of palaces to the boiling vats at Richmond and a huge laundry tasked solely with the cleanliness of linen from all of the royal households. Here, professional launderers like Sarah Sparks and Catherine Fleming scrubbed and starched, hidden by high walls and a screen of trees, ensuring that prying eyes were kept at bay. Where shoemakers and milliners might proudly advertise their royal connections, those that might air the dirty linen most definitely could not. More than any of the other suppliers to a queen's wardrobe, this was a workforce truly in the shadows.

The world of a linen draper might conjure up visions of a wood-panelled shop. The contents of countless drawers might be labelled underneath shining brass handles, and rolls of cloth would hang temptingly to be perused by the discerning customer. Compared to many other textile trades in the nineteenth century, a linen draper would seem to have chosen wisely – not for him the battle of looms or the noxiousness of dyes. It was, however, a trade that demanded long hours and active participation, heaving the weighty goods about the shop, loading and unloading stock. It was, too, a business that found itself often on the sharp end of the satirist's pen. In Charles Dickens's *Sketches by Boz* written in 1836, he wrote that linen drapers are 'elegant young men behind the counter, each in a clean collar and white neckcloth like the lover in a farce'. His preoccupation with fine clothes and shop work made him far less of a man, according to Dickens. The accompanying illustration of a fictional draper named Horatio Sparkins by cartoonist George Cruikshank depicted an effeminate man holding forth across his counter, encircled by keen female customers. The writer H. G. Wells offered a slightly different version of life as an apprentice draper which began in 1880 at the Windsor drapery of Messrs Rodger & Denyer. He lived in a dormitory with ten other

Dressing the Queen

Horatio Sparkins by George Cruikshank from *Sketches by Boz*, 1836.

men and boys, sharing 'four miserable wash-hand stands'. There was a 'dismal little sitting room' where they might spend their brief hours of freedom and a dark underground dining room where all of the employees would eat. Each morning at 7.30, he had to 'without fail, dust, clean windows, eat a bread and butter breakfast at half past eight, prepare my cash sheet and so to the routine of the day'. He dealt with the cash and the receipts during opening hours, then on completing his cashing-up at the end of the day he would 'help to wrapper-up and sweep out the shop and so to escape at half past seven or eight o'clock to drink the delights of freedom until ten'.

Wells wrote of the prison-like restrictions and his feeling of being trapped in this profession he despised. It was a profession that could reap rewards, however. In 2010, during a trip to the magical National Archives in Kew, I was leafing through the enormous volumes relating to the supply of Queen Victoria's household. These volumes of Extraordinary

Accounts are filled with countless invoices and handwritten notes recording the flow of goods into the royal residences. In one of these volumes I came across an invoice from a linen draper, charging the household for a number of sheets and pillowcases. What made his invoice memorable and his name stay with me, was the exquisite little pencil sketch that accompanied the bald figures of the bill. The initials V R were drawn in a curled cursive and above the letters was a crown. It was the royal cypher of Queen Victoria, the monogram that would be stitched to all of her linen, and Walter Capper was seeking approval for his design. It was a beautiful little inclusion, linking the supplier to the household, the Queen to her clothes.

Walter Capper was born in 1815 to a Quaker family in Middlesex. Both his paternal grandfather, Jasper, and his father, John, were drapers, established in premises on Gracechurch Street, so Walter's career was assured should he follow the family business across the threshold of the linen draper's shop. It was a successful enterprise and one that was beginning to grow by the time that Walter joined the family firm, acquiring a Royal Warrant of Appointment along the way. In June 1839 he married Eliza Mills and only a month later he was awarded the Freedom of the City of London. One of the oldest ceremonies in London, first awarded in the thirteenth century, it gave greater freedoms to guild members in the City but by the nineteenth century was given in recognition of somebody's contribution to their trade and community. Walter and his family would continue to benefit from the success of the business and its royal patronage. The 1881 census finds them living in a comfortable villa on Shooters Hill Road in leafy Greenwich. Walter describes himself as a linen draper 'employing 200 people', a significant business indeed and one which had made him a millionaire several times over by the time of his death in August 1890.

Once the orders had been made and the goods delivered from drapers and general outfitters such as Walter Capper, the responsibility for the avalanche of linen in the royal household fell to the linen-room maids in each of the royal residences, from Sandringham to Osborne House, Windsor Castle to Buckingham Palace. Each property employed two or three linen-room maids, women whose role in the royal household often appears to be of long duration but might vary over the course of their careers. Eleanor Simons appears on the 1911 Buckingham Palace census as a linen maid but her employment in the household stretched further back and into other residences. She was born Eleanor Elizabeth Hancock in 1861 in Northamptonshire where she grew up with her mother, Jane, her father, John, who was a chairmaker, and her siblings. She went into domestic service at an early age and found her way to London where she was eventually employed in Marlborough House, the busy London residence of Edward and Alexandra, the Prince and Princess of Wales. Here she worked as a housemaid and met Harry Simons, a footman. Their marriage took place in April 1889, in the leafy quiet of Hanover Square. Harry continued to work in the royal household whilst Eleanor left service and remained at home with their daughter Welyn, in a small golden-bricked terraced house on Kilburn Lane. Their house looked towards the railway track across to the green space of Queen's Park. It was to be a short-lived domestic interlude, however. In 1894, Harry died and Eleanor had to rebuild her life. Royal connections served her well and by 1901, she had returned to Marlborough House where she resumed the role of housemaid. Ten years later, now aged fifty, she had relocated to the grandeur of Buckingham Palace where she had taken up the post of linen maid. Accounting for the constant tide of linen into and out of Buckingham Palace would have been a relentless task. Every single day, hundreds of items of linen, both bed and body, had to be counted, folded, stored. They had to be sent out for laundering and then sorted on their return. Named and numbered, each piece was itemised, ticked off, accounted for. It required an organised mind and presumably Eleanor was chosen not just for her experience in the royal household but

What Lies Beneath

Wash house at the Wolverhampton Steam Laundry, late nineteenth century.

also for her quick head for figures. The palace was in a constant state of change as members of the family arrived and departed, visitors required towels and clean beds, snowy tablecloths had to be laid out and whisked away after every meal. The linen maids worked to the rhythm of palace life but always out of sight.

Eleanor worked alongside Emily Balaam in the palace. Linen maids together, I wonder how they shared the load and how they allocated the different tasks allotted to them. Both aged fifty, I hope that they found friendship as they toiled away in the linen room. Emily had been born in, of all places, Pentonville Prison in London in 1861. Her father was a warder in the convict service and so Emily's childhood must have been an unusual one as each posting took them to a different correctional facility. By the age of eleven Emily had left Pentonville and was living on the Isle of Wight in Parkhurst Prison where her father had been promoted to Principal Warder. Her mother had died, leaving Emily and her sister May to grow up in these less-than-conventional surroundings. She left home and worked as a nurse in private houses, residing in 1891 in the household of stock and share dealer Arthur Balance. She disappears from sight in the records for a time; her name is frequently misspelt and so following her path is circuitous, but she appears along with Eleanor in Buckingham Palace, a single woman in her fifties, folding the King and Queen's most intimate garments.

Sometimes the women occupying these positions moved with the occupant of the house – Eleanor started at Marlborough House and moved with Edward and Alexandra to Buckingham Palace – whereas some seemed to stay in the residence for the duration of their working lives. Anne Mackay was born in Inverness-shire in 1845. By her mid-twenties, she had left Scotland and was working in service as a housemaid for Sir George Howland Beaumont. Young women often started their domestic service further down the aristocratic ranks before finding employment with a member of the royal family. At some point in the course of the next decade she moved from Sir George's Leicestershire country estate to within the castle walls at Windsor, working as one of thirty-four housemaids in the royal residence. By 1891, she had become one of the two linen-room maids to work at Windsor, a role that she was still carrying out ten years later. Anne remained in Windsor following her retirement – her more than quarter of a century of employment in the castle difficult to leave behind, perhaps. The walls that dominate the town were only a short walk away from the house on Beaumont Road that Anne shared with her niece Helen, a regular reminder of its place in her life.

Whilst we can easily bring to mind the facades of these royal buildings and in some cases might even have ventured inside those with public access, the linen rooms have been, and will for ever remain, an unknown. Behind the immediate splendour, somewhere in labyrinthine passageways, Eleanor and Emily and Anne counted, checked, smoothed and allocated mountains of linen, sending it forth upstairs to bedrooms or downstairs to dining rooms. But what of the other end of their operation? As they gathered in the equally large, less snowy heaps of dirty linen, where was it sent to restore it to gleaming white?

The path to laundering the royal linens was actually a railway track, one that carried over a ton and a half of dirty laundry every single day on a steam train from the capital out to the suburbs of Richmond. Prince Albert had spent the early years of his marriage rationalising the often chaotic structures within the royal household, bringing order and logic to systems that had been failing for generations. Over the course of these years he had dealt frequently with Thomas Cubitt, the builder and architect behind alterations to Buckingham Palace and the creation of Victoria and Albert's island retreat, Osborne House on the Isle of Wight. Albert had identified a need to deal more efficiently with the mountain of washing produced by the royal family every day and so turned to Cubitt for collaboration on a custom-built, state-of-the-art steam laundry. The newly opened railway line from the city out to Richmond with its already established royal connections as part of the Crown Estate made it an obvious choice for Albert. The more rural location offered discretion, along with the eventual high walls and screen of trees that hid the laundry from view. Only the Italianate tower, not dissimilar to Cubitt's design at Osborne, hinted at the buildings beneath.

Opening in 1846, the laundry operated for over eighty years, processing tons of linen every single week. Yet today, its existence is little known. I first stumbled across a brief reference to the establishment in 2009 during research for my doctoral studies but could find almost nothing relating to its operations, hitting frustrating dead ends in the records. Were it not for the efforts of one woman, it would most probably have disappeared from view altogether. Lucinda Ganderton is a textile artist and writer who lives on Kew Road and learned by chance that the royal laundry had once been located at the bottom of her street. Keen to find

Dressing the Queen

Royal laundry basket label, *c.* 1880.

out more, she discovered that nobody had ever investigated or written about this remarkable place. She set out herself to uncover more and was able to piece together a picture of the establishment. One late October morning, I met Lucinda via Zoom for an illuminating chat that was completely inspiring. She told me just some of the many stories she had uncovered about the laundry and generously shared the rest of her research with me, keen for it to find a broader audience. I loved it. Writing can be an isolating process and so these moments of connection are golden, discovering a common spark of wonder.

Every day, wicker baskets of linen would arrive at Richmond train station from the various royal residences. Reversible brass labels on the baskets indicated the destination of the contents, with 'ROYAL LAUNDRY' on one side, and on the other the palace to which they would return, ensuring that the right linen landed in the right place. From the goods yard in Richmond, a horse-drawn van would collect the baskets and take them to the walled premises, hidden away from curious eyes. Once these vans had passed beyond the gates of the royal laundry, the operations within were almost impossible to discover. One contemporary writer noted that: 'There are very few of the private establishments of Royalty more difficult to obtain permission to see over than this.'

What Lies Beneath

One singular visitor gained entrance to the laundry as part of a bold adventure. In 1864, a young American diplomat named Elihu Burritt decided to walk the length and breadth of the UK and during this odyssey his perambulations took him to Richmond. Somehow he persuaded the then superintendent, John Thomson, to give him a tour of the laundry, a place that Burritt subsequently described as the 'great lavatory of royal linen'. He later wrote about his experience that day, describing the gardens and the working conditions, which were far better than he had imagined they might be. He lauded the progress of science providing the labour-saving devices, marvelling at the Chedgey box mangle, a pressing and folding device that he described as 'undoubtedly the most perfect and expensive machine of the kind ever made'. Perhaps more remarkably still, he was able to offer some statistics relating to the quantities of royal laundry handled: 'When the Queen is at Windsor, twenty-four baskets, averaging 150 lbs each, are sent daily, or 3,000 lbs, equal to a ton and a half of soiled linen or 700,000 individual pieces each year.' The numbers were staggering and it required a considerable workforce to service the endless flow of cloth through multiple stages of cleaning and finishing.

On arrival the washing would be sorted and inspected. Minor repairs might be carried out before the various objects were sent on their way to the next room. Large industrial laundries such as this contained enormous metal vats for the first clean, the linens within pummelled with rods to remove stains. The next part of the process was the spinning. Unlike smaller domestic spaces where a hand-turned mangle was sufficient to deal with a family's washing, in the royal laundry there was a spinning room filled with belt-driven machines. After that the drying would take place, either in a large room with multiple drying racks or, if the weather permitted, on the large drying ground that ran almost the entire width of the buildings at the back of the laundry. Sheets and tablecloths would be laid out on the grass where a combination of daylight and the photosynthesis of the grass beneath worked as a natural whitener. Finally the piles of sheets, towels, chemises, drawers, shirts, handkerchiefs and nightgowns would find their way to the ironers, women who were highly skilled having been taught from a young age how best to gauge temperature and manage different fabric types and construction styles. Scorching the linen of the royal household must be avoided at all costs.

Evidence of the lives of the laundresses themselves, hundreds of whom would have passed through the gated entrance to the royal laundry every day during its eight decades of industry, is scarce. One surprisingly candid interview with an anonymous employee, named only as 'A Chat with the Queen's Laundress', was published in *Lady* magazine in 1894. She begins by acknowledging that 'the ivy-clad building is almost as jealously guarded as the entrance to Buckingham Palace' before describing the intricate arrangements for the laundry that arrives. The table and bed-linen arrived in baskets. 'The personal linen, on the other hand, arrives in wooden boxes and is sorted in a special room. Each box has a brass plate bearing the owner's name as well as a number.' Regular monitoring and cross-checking of laundry marks was essential to ensure that no mistakes were made once the clean washing was ready to be distributed back to its respective residences.

Much like their linen-maid counterparts who handled the same garments at the palace end of the operation, there were laundresses who remained in the employ of the royal laundry for long periods of their lives. One of these women, for whom the laundry provided a consistent income at different times in her life, was Sarah Sparks. Sarah was born in Exeter in 1826. Her mother, Mary Ann, was a laundress and so from an early age Sarah must have been aware of the skills required for such a role. She herself worked towards becoming a dressmaker but in 1848 she fell pregnant and gave birth to her daughter Elizabeth. The difficulties of raising a child as an unmarried woman at the time meant that Sarah's parents took on Elizabeth and described her as their own daughter on the 1851 census. Leaving her child in the care of her parents, Sarah had left Devon and travelled to Richmond to live with her older sister Maria and husband, Alfred. The young couple both worked in the royal laundry and so the connection was forged.

For a time Sarah returned to Devon and lived once more with her parents and her daughter Elizabeth, now aged twelve. She worked as a dressmaker and along with her sister Mary, a milliner, was able to support the family with her wages. When her father, Robert, died in 1869, it was time for a new chapter in their shared family lives. Sarah, along with her mother and her daughter, relocated to Richmond, three generations of women beginning afresh. No longer a dressmaker, Sarah became, like her mother before her, a laundress, walking through the gates of the teardrop-shaped grounds every morning, past the entrance lodge and along the wall leading to the main laundry building. She walked the same path for the next thirty years until her death in 1903 at the age of seventy-seven.

When Sarah started working at the laundry, she would probably have encountered Catherine Fleming who was already a laundress of long standing at the establishment. Widowed in her mid-thirties, Catherine had to support her young son George and so found lodgings with other employees of the laundry on Clarence Street, just half a mile from the laundry gates. Catherine never remarried but spent the next three decades living at different addresses within a short distance of the laundry, to cross its threshold each day. Her presumably careful industriousness meant that she was able to retire and aged seventy-seven she was listed as the head of her household at number 20 Shaftesbury Road in Richmond, 'living on her own means' with George who had become an accountant, and with a lodger to subsidise their household income.

To scroll through the pages of the Richmond census records in the second half of the nineteenth century is to witness the evidence of hundreds of laundresses or people otherwise finding their employment there. It was a vast enterprise, not only a feat of mechanical and logistical endeavour but also one that provided an income for so many in a single community. Yet it is a feat that is almost entirely unrecognised today. In 1920, the laundry was deemed too expensive to remain in operation and so it was closed. The premises were eventually leased to a motor company and the brick building was renamed the Tower Garage, Cubitt's grand edifice offering a landmark for the motor mechanics who worked there until the later 1960s when the garage closed and the distinctive building was demolished. Now, barely anything remains, either in bricks or print, to recall the complex and essential service that operated out of Kew Foot Road.

Given the secrecy that traditionally surrounded the laundering of royal linen, it comes as no surprise that this is an area of the royal wardrobe which, in the twenty-first century, is still kept entirely hidden. Those responsible for the making, the maintaining and the laundering of the monarchy's bedlinen and body garments remain, rightly so, even more tight-lipped about their services than their Victorian predecessors. One day, public census records might reveal the later counterpart to linen maid Emily Balaam or to laundress Sarah Sparks, each working at either end of a system connected entirely by miles and miles of white linen, one in the relative hush of a palace store room and the other amongst the hot, damp din of a steam laundry. Perhaps, after all, we will have to rely on Nicholas Allan and *The Queen's Knickers*. As the picture book draws to a close, the Queen visits a primary school in her 'everyday knickers', feeling awkward not to have something more special on, when a little girl whispers in her ear: 'Don't worry about your knickers, Your Majesty . . . You see, no one can see them anyway.'

CHAPTER 17

Hidden Women
The Dressers and Their Domain

There is a portrait in the Royal Collection that I have long admired. In muted chalks, sketched out on buff-coloured paper, it is the portrait of a lady. The head-and-shoulders composition has captured her dark-coloured dress pleated in a style that was fashionable some decades earlier than the 1880 date of the drawing. On her head sits a fine white cap frilled at the edge with black lace and there is an oval, amber-coloured brooch at her throat pinning a plain white collar. Of the many thousands of royal subjects that reside in the art collections of the monarchy, this is somebody quite different. Her name was Marianne Skerrett and for almost half a century she was head dresser to Queen Victoria. Where the makers and warrant holders providing goods to the royal wardrobe are scattered around the United Kingdom, some regional and some rooted in the streets of London, the domain of the dressers lay within the palace walls. They held the threads that connected all of the suppliers in complex networks back to the body of the Queen herself. Through them, the variety of garments made elsewhere arrived in the wardrobes of the royal residences to be documented, stored and maintained.

Unlike the Queen's ladies-in-waiting, aristocratic women who served in a more public capacity, the role of the dresser was to facilitate the appearance of the Queen whilst remaining almost entirely invisible.

Dressing the Queen

These are the women at the very centre of royal dress and often they were the women most closely associated with the Queen. They were there when she woke and they remained at their post until she went to bed. Their presence was one of comfort and familiarity, and the length of time that these women often remained in post was indicative of the closeness of their connection to the Queen. Whilst they may have remained hidden behind the doors of the palace, closeted in the dressing rooms of royal residences, the meticulous record-keeping of the royal household means that they are easier to find than many of the suppliers with whom they dealt on a daily basis. Marianne Skerrett, Frieda Arnold, Bessie and Nettie Temple, Ada Sibley, Margaret 'Bobo' MacDonald and Angela Kelly – these are just some of the women who, from dawn till dusk, dressed and undressed the Queen.

As with most areas of the British class system, there was a hierarchy in the wardrobe. The principal dresser oversaw the duties of second dressers and below them were two or three wardrobe maids. Their work encompassed everything from attending to the Queen herself and the various changes of dress that would punctuate each day, to the mending of garments in their care. It was detailed work that took some time to memorise. Amongst the many papers relating to the dressers in the Royal Archive, there is one informal scrap that illustrates the complexity of their job. Scribbled in pencil on a piece of paper, an unnamed dresser, new to her role, had written down the detailed instructions she was to follow when attending Queen Victoria: 'After the Queen comes in the dressing room the morning I am on duty give the water tepid for the face and eyes with a little camomile tea in it,' she wrote, reminding herself of the exact order that she needed to prepare for the morning. After the Queen had bathed, she continued: 'Fasten the stays – put the petticoat over the head – then give the watches to be wound up & put the little chain with the locket & the velvet with the other locket over the head – then give the drawers – then hold the box with the rings then the crinoline & the body petticoat & the tray with the brooches – then the skirt, then the body & the keys with the thinnest chain over the neck, tie the string of the body round the waist, put the brooch in & give the watch.' It is a breathless stream of instructions, perhaps written in haste as a more experienced dresser told her what to do. I imagine the piece of paper tucked into a pocket and perhaps discreetly consulted as she waited for the Queen to emerge from her bath.

The spaces that the dressers inhabited varied from custom-designed wardrobe and dressing rooms in the newly built residences of Osborne House and Balmoral to the modified arrangements in older buildings such as Buckingham Palace or Windsor Castle. In these spaces were the areas for the garments to be stored. At Osborne House the largest wardrobe was thirteen feet long and five feet wide with six doors, five large lower drawers and wings that pulled out, incorporating more drawers and additional hanging space. There were mirrors and a table and chairs where the dressers might sit and undertake any running repairs on garments that had been identified as in need of attention.

The appointment of dressers was often an informal affair, enquiries being made of existing members of the royal household to find suitable young women. Marianne Skerrett was a niece of the former treasurer to Queen Charlotte; and Mary Ann Andrews, one of Queen Victoria's wardrobe maids, was the daughter of Charles Andrews who served the Queen's uncle, King Leopold, in Belgium. Frieda Arnold was the friend of one of the Queen's serving dressers Sophie Weiss, born in the same town of Karlsruhe in Germany. They were not aristocratic women but were from trusted families, known to the Queen in some capacity. Alexandra, Princess of Wales, employed two sisters as her dressers whose father was head carpenter at their Sandringham estate. Bessie and Nettie Temple both grew up on the estate. Jeanette or Nettie was born in 1869 and her sister Bessie only a year later in 1870. They were the same age as Alexandra's own children. When Alexandra employed the sisters, she did so on a rota basis to ensure that one of the daughters was always on hand to be with their widowed father William. She clearly grew fond of the two young women. An account of one trip to Scotland accompanied by Bessie, hints at the value of their company for the Princess. Bessie's room was further away from Alexandra than she liked: 'In the middle of the night the Princess summoned her and for some reason or other desired her to stay in the room til morning. Bessie prepared to lie down on the sofa; the Princess, however, insisted that Bessie must sleep in her bed whilst she herself took the sofa, and it was only with the greatest difficulty that she could be persuaded of the incongruity of such an arrangement.' After some years of service and at the age of twenty-five, Bessie left Alexandra's household to form her own. She married Harry Sinclair in the parish church on the Sandringham Estate on 25 February 1895 and moved with her husband to Gosport in Hampshire, bringing up her three children in the town. The royal connection was never lost, however. Ten years later, Alexandra was in Portsmouth, waiting to board the royal yacht for a European tour, and whilst she was there she took one of the yacht's small dinghies over to Gosport. A local newspaper reported: 'From first to last hardly anyone was aware that the Queen was in the town.' This newspaper clipping was kept by Alexandra herself and pasted into her travel album, underneath which she wrote: 'We paid a visit to Bessie Sinclair!'

These bonds of real friendship do seem to exist often in the records of the Queen and her dressers, but there were occasional, if rare, instances of discord. An intriguing set of correspondence between the Office of Robes in Queen Victoria's household and a dresser named Marie Downing in 1885 hinted at some unfortunate circumstances. Marie Downing left her post in May 1885 and in June she wrote to Sir Henry Ponsonby to confirm that she had received payment for her 'Board Wages'. She continued: 'She begs also to thank him for the trouble he has had in obtaining for her a satisfactory return for her "peculiar" dismissal.' The Queen had awarded Marie a pension of £50 a year 'in consequence of the difficulty she has experienced in obtaining a position'. As I read the memos passing back and forth between officials – one half-written in black ink and the reply noted in red – I wrote in my own notes: 'WHAT IS IT???' What had happened to Marie to bring about this particular course of events?

I found that historian Helen Rappaport had had the same experience when she had encountered these records in the archives, and she undertook some spectacular sleuthing. Marie moved to North Dakota with her husband, Harry Williams, a marriage she had kept hidden from her employers. When she arrived in New York, she 'discovered' to her delighted amazement that the Queen had sent several trunks of gifts for her 'favourite attendant' on board the same ship. This was the story that Marie told a reporter for the *Winnipeg Free Press* in 1930. Inside the trunks were an unprecedented selection of objects – an embellished court train, a satin parasol, jewels, a watch, a signet ring, dresses and a semi-precious stone paperweight. Queens were certainly generous in giving gifts to their staff, especially dressers, but not on this scale. It was completely contrary to the tone of the memos in the archive. Rappaport concluded: 'Like it or not, one has to ask the question: did Marie slowly and systematically purloin some of those "gifts" from Victoria?' It seems likely and is all the more remarkable for its rarity. Almost universally, the dressers were loyal and remained in their jobs either until they married or came to the role after they had been widowed.

One of these widowed women who found meaningful employment after the death of her husband was Harriet Giltrap. Harriet entered Alexandra's service in 1886 and would remain with her until Alexandra herself died in 1925. Born in Staffordshire in 1856, she would become one of the longest serving of Alexandra's dressers, a role that was both busy and demanding since Alexandra, as Princess of Wales and later Queen, had to keep up with regular civic duties as well as court events. It meant that Harriet presided over one of the most expansive and public wardrobes in the world. A document in the Royal Archive, 'Relative to Household Appointments', outlined exactly what Harriet and others like her were expected to do: 'In the first place scrupulous tidiness and exactness in looking over everything that Her Majesty takes off, never omitting to mend things which require it at once – to look over the bonnets, gloves, caps, cloaks etc before Her Majesty puts them on.' The list continues: '2ndly to see that everything is right and in its place before Her Majesty gets up, goes to bed or dresses so that there can be no confusion or anything missing. 3rdly to take note when anything is getting torn or dirty and to have others got. 4th to think over well everything that is wanted or may be wanted when Her Majesty goes to London to hold a Court etc to be certain that everything is in its right place.' For the fulfilment of these duties, Harriet was paid £15 a quarter, her salary listed amongst the many other expenses in Alexandra's

Harriet Giltrap, Queen Alexandra's dresser, c. 1890.

Wardrobe Accounts. The 'scrupulous tidiness and exactness' expected of the dresser was demonstrated until the very last, when she wrote an orderly description of her mistress's remaining clothing over two pages of text following Alexandra's death. Neat descriptions of each gown were given, indicative of the knowledge that she held over the provenance and wear of each garment. The list was submitted to the new queen, Queen Mary. It was Harriet's final duty as dresser.

Taking up the mantle as dresser to the new Queen Mary in 1911 was Ada Gertrude Sibley whose route into royal service seems to have been different to her predecessors. Ada was born in Wimborne, Dorset, in 1882 and grew up in the middle of a host of siblings that consisted of five brothers and two sisters. Her father, Edward, was a local blacksmith. The size of the family and their modest means meant that Ada had to find work as soon as practicable and by the age of eighteen she was recorded as working as a housemaid in Bournemouth for Richard Elwes, a man of private means who could afford the seven servants with whom Ada shared her days, and his wife. Perhaps Ada showed promise early on, expressing an interest in the duties of the lady's maid who cared for Richard's wife, Kathleen. Emma Froud was listed high in the ranks of the household's domestic servants, second only to the cook, so it is likely that Ada would have learned something of the role observing Emma at work. Somehow and in a shift of fortunes now lost to us, Ada came to the notice of the Queen. What sparked the royal attention is hard to guess at – there were no connections that appeared to warrant the appointment but by 1911, twenty-eight-year-old Ada appears on the Buckingham Palace census listed amongst the dozens and dozens of other servants as a lady's maid. In common with all of those women who had filled the role of dresser before her, Ada would have familiarised herself not just with the personal needs of the Queen herself but with the myriad contents of the wardrobe. She would have undertaken the mending and cleaning of garments in her care. She would have folded and pressed, replenished the wardrobe with sundries that needed frequently to be purchased. She would have hung up one garment and taken down another as the duties of the day required, dusting hats, polishing shoes and laying out stockings.

In addition to these functions, Queen Mary's dressers performed another daily task relating to the public attention of the Queen and her sartorial choices. The Royal Archive contains six slim red leather volumes, embossed with a gold crown, each alike. Inside, written carefully on the title page, are the details of what lies within: 'Gowns & Jewels Worn by H.M. the Queen at Principal Functions'. These are the dressers' diaries, documenting each ensemble worn in public by Queen Mary from the beginning of her reign in 1911 to the 1930s. More than merely serving as a description of a dress, they performed an important function. For half a century or more, the court circular had offered descriptions of the appearance of prominent royal women in *The Times* and this interest only grew. These diaries acted as an aide-memoire to the dressers and to the Queen to ensure that she did not wear the same garments in the same company, generating a circulation of outfits and embellishments. The entries are short and informative: 'Gown of Indian pink and gold material, emeralds and diamonds, the Garter star,' reads one entry for an evening event in 1913.

Details of the event helped the dressers to place the gowns and those who may have attended. On 12 May 1911 for the opening of the Festival of Empire exhibition, the entry read: 'Gown of pale mauve charmeuse silk, feather hat to match. Pearl and diamond necklace & rows of crown pearls.' The next evening for a visit to the opera, the dresser wrote: 'White satin, lilac flowered gown. Pearl and diamond comb, pearl collar, 2 rows of crown pearls, pearl and diamond brooch with chain and drop.' As the entries continue, it is possible to spot when the same dress was worn to different events. There was a 'mauve stamped velvet gown' with amethysts that Queen Mary wore on 15 May for dinner. She wore it again on 2 June at Lady Derby's with diamonds and at another dinner on 12 June with amethysts and diamonds. Literally dripping with jewels, these were important details for the dressers to keep in order to make decisions about which gown could be worn with which jewellery depending on the type of occasion and the people who were attending.

Occasionally a maker is mentioned, perhaps to help different dressers distinguish one garment from another. In May 1913, the description read: 'Harrods beige charmeuse and georgette gown,' serving as a quick means of identifying this dress from any other. The handwriting changes across these volumes and so one of the hands must be Ada's. An article in the *Evening Standard* from August 1930 bears the headline: 'Leaving the Palace to Get Married'. In a long column all about Ada Sibley, her knowledge of the wardrobe and particularly of the Queen's jewels is highly praised by the journalist: 'Miss Sibley's service for the Queen calls not only for a profound knowledge of dresses and their appurtenances, but also for an expert knowledge of furs and laces and a collector's appreciation of such trifles as fans and jewellery.' The news correspondent writes that Miss Sibley will be missed most by the Queen and quotes her as saying that 'Miss Sibley has personality'. It is a fond tribute to twenty years of service which concludes: 'In spite of her important duties she remains as ever incorrigibly youthful and light-hearted.' On 27 August 1930, Ada married widower James Tyler, a horticulturalist from Norfolk. He was forty-eight and she was forty-two. I hope that they had a happy marriage after her unusual career. They disappear from view after their marriage and I find Ada at the end of her life as a widow. She died on 17 January 1954 at the age of seventy-two, less than a year after her former mistress Queen Mary.

Queen Mary knew the woman who would go on to become dresser and close confidante to her granddaughter the future Queen Elizabeth II. Margaret MacDonald was born in the Black Isle in Scotland in 1904,

Dressing the Queen

Margaret 'Bobo' MacDonald, with young Princess Elizabeth and her mother, *c.* 1929.

growing up in a tied cottage next to the railway that provided her father's income. Her first job took her to a modest hotel where she was employed as an apprentice chambermaid but, like Ada Sibley before her, the trajectory of her life would take an unexpected turn. In 1926, at the age of twenty-two, she was employed by the Duchess of York as nursemaid to her six-week-old baby, the Princess Elizabeth. In the 1920s, nursery staff still provided a continuity of care to little aristocratic children, especially those of royal birth whose parents were often attending functions elsewhere. As a toddler the Princess would play hide-and-seek in the garden with Miss MacDonald, who would seek her charge out, calling: 'Boo!' Young Elizabeth would clap her hands and cry: 'Boo, boo!' in reply and the nickname stuck. Miss MacDonald was referred to as Bobo for the entirety of their life together. And what a life it was. When Miss

MacDonald was employed by the Duchess of York there was no inkling that the Princess Elizabeth would one day become Queen, but the abdication of King Edward VIII in 1936 altered the path of their lives. As Elizabeth's role changed, so too did Miss MacDonald's. From nursemaid, she became the future Queen's dresser and would remain in the role until 1990, serving the Queen for over sixty years.

She attended every major event of the Queen's life, rarely seen but ever present. She was there for the coronation of the Princess's father when he was crowned King George VI; she was there when Elizabeth married, and she accompanied the young couple on their honeymoon. She supported her mistress in Kenya when the Princess learned of the death of her father in 1952 and she oversaw the preparations for the young Queen's coronation wardrobe. She became a force to be reckoned with amongst the rest of the royal household. 'Aboard the royal yacht, nervous crew referred to her as the "QE3" and woe betide anybody who crossed Miss MacDonald.' Unusually for somebody whose primary function was the smooth management of the Queen's wardrobe, Miss MacDonald maintained long-running feuds with her principal couturiers: 'The dressmakers hated Bobo even as they sought to placate her, making presents of fine shoes and beautiful handbags not only to the Queen but to her dresser.' Legend has it that she reserved an especial enmity for Hardy Amies, the fact of which the Queen was all too aware: 'About to knight Hardy Amies, in 1989, the Queen reached for the sword, caught his eye and murmured, deadpan, "Bobo will give me hell for this." ' It was a position of enormous power. Miss MacDonald was there every morning with the Queen's tray and the day's news, overseeing a network of communication from all of the royal residences. There was nothing that she did not know about the Queen and her staff and as such she acted as a formidable guardian to her beloved mistress. In 1990, she was relieved of her duties but continued to live in a suite of rooms in Buckingham Palace where she died in 1993. She had been the Queen's constant companion for all of those years.

Dressing the Queen

Miss MacDonald was not the only woman to have served the Queen as dresser; as ever it was a job that demanded more than one person's attention and Peggy Hoath would serve as a senior dresser for thirty-four years. She had entered royal service in 1959 and so had attended the Queen through all of those momentous years, working as ever in the shadows, to ensure that the logistics of the wardrobe ran smoothly. It was not always plain sailing, however, and at Peggy's funeral in 2018, friends recalled one of her more tumultuous moments at work. Peggy had, apparently, a friendly but robust rivalry with another of the dressers, May Prentice. During a royal visit to Holyroodhouse, Peggy and May entered into a dispute one evening that, unbeknown to them, had disturbed the Queen. It was to the amazement of other staff that the Queen appeared in the pages' quarters wearing her nightgown and clutching a blanket, unable to sleep for the noise of the row: 'She was very fond of Peggy and obviously couldn't bring herself to criticise her. Everyone just looked at each other and shuffled out of the room to let the Queen sleep.' It is a story that echoes down the years, recalling Queen Alexandra's determination to sleep on the sofa so Bessie Temple could have the bed, the closeness of the dresser and her place in the Queen's world a recurring thread.

It was through Peggy Hoath that the Queen communicated with the woman who would become the kind of companion in later life that Miss MacDonald had been at the beginning. In 1992, Angela Kelly was working as housekeeper to the British Ambassador in Berlin when the Queen and Duke of Edinburgh stayed at the residence. She met the various members of the royal household on their arrival, including Peggy Hoath: 'I was so impressed by their professionalism,' she would recall. 'Everything was executed with efficiency and precision, from the delivery of the luggage to the unpacking of the cases.' The royal entourage were installed in the ambassadorial residence for four days. 'I spent quite a bit of time with Peggy, who was a lovely lady. She told me she had been the

Queen's Dresser for the last thirty-four years and was now considering her retirement. We agreed to keep in touch.' A few weeks later, Angela received the most unexpected telephone call from Peggy: 'She said that Her Majesty had requested she get in touch to ask would I consider coming to work at Buckingham Palace?' It was a call that would change Angela's life, and an indication of the handing over of duties from one dresser to another. Peggy had obviously recognised something in Angela that fitted into the blueprint of life in the royal wardrobe, seeing in her a safe pair of hands.

Angela was born in Liverpool in 1957 and grew up in a two-up two-down terraced house between the football grounds of Everton and Liverpool. Her mother sewed and had a flair for designing clothes, the back room of their house frequently being turned into a temporary sewing room. Local women would come to her for their wedding and bridesmaid dresses, such was her reputation as a dressmaker. Angela was taught the skills that would serve her so well, from a tender age, watching her mother at the trusty Singer sewing machine: 'In fact, aged eight, maintaining that precious machine was my first task as an assistant dressmaker.' She was employed in a sewing factory at the age of fifteen and as a young mother made clothes for her family.

In 1994, those skills would come into their own. Following an interview at Buckingham Palace, Angela was appointed to the post of assistant dresser, reporting to Peggy Hoath on the Dressers' Floor as the domain of the wardrobe was known. It was here on the Dressers' Floor that the complex choreography relating to the Queen's appearance would unfold. As well as designing garments herself, Angela oversaw the work of a deputy dresser and three assistant dressers in a structure that would have been familiar to Queen Victoria one hundred and fifty years earlier. In volumes recognisable to Queen Mary's dressers, Angela and her colleagues kept diaries that outlined the frequency of wear for different garments. Angela records that: 'Typically,

Angela Kelly.

the lifespan of an outfit can be up to around twenty-five years,' and so the careful rotation of her clothes and their public outings formed part of the daily record-keeping. Like the many dressers whose role it had been to manage the Queen's wardrobe before her, Angela liaised with the suppliers, arranged dates for fittings and placed orders for new items. She advised on colour and style and controlled the many moving parts of so complex an endeavour. She also drank tea and watched television with the Queen, twenty-five years of companionship contributing to a friendship ending only when the Queen died in September 2022 and the Dressers' Floor fell silent.

In April 1855, the state visit of the Emperor and Empress of France had caused Queen Victoria some anxiety around her appearance. She wrote in her journal that she had had 'such trouble with my toilette, dresses, bonnets, caps, mantillas etc of every sort and kind'. At the receiving end of this turbulent turning over of her wardrobe were Frieda Arnold and the other dressers, all working tirelessly to ensure that the visit ran smoothly and that each element of the Queen's appearance passed muster. The visit was a diplomatic success and a logistical one for the dressers. Having described the visit to her friends in a letter home, Frieda concluded: 'I shall end this letter for now, and send you a thousand greetings and many kisses my dear friends. The illustrious guests have left, the Palace seems dead. You cannot imagine the throngs of people and the bustle of servants running about that there have been these last days.' It was a moment to breathe and take stock of the events in which they had taken part, there but not there.

Marianne Skerrett would have recognised the role undertaken by Miss MacDonald or Angela Kelly. Bessie Temple would have shared similar tales, perhaps, with Ada Sibley or Peggy Hoath or Frieda Arnold. The clothes might change, along with modes of transport and methods of communication, but at its heart the role of the dresser has remained unchanged. It is a role that seemingly occupies a liminal space, the in-between world of public and private. The fruits of their labour are observed by millions but they themselves are often unknown. They might become the close confidantes of the queens they serve and yet they are staff. They spend their entire working lives amongst royalty and the aristocratic families of the UK but most usually they hail from backgrounds that would be recognisably more normal for the vast majority of the British population. They have stitched, pressed, folded, planned, diarised and liaised over every aspect of the Queen's appearance but they have also kept confidences and protected privacy. As monarch followed monarch so each succeeding generation of dresser followed in their wake, picking up the pieces of her wardrobe ready to do it all again the next day, dressing and undressing the Queen.

CHAPTER 18

Public Grief
Whitby Jet and Courtaulds Crape

'London Bridge is down.'

Every British prime minister from the 1960s onwards knew the meaning of these words. If they should receive a phone call containing that specific phrase, it meant the Queen had died, and from that very moment a complex chain of events would swing into motion. Code names had been chosen to communicate the death of the monarch for much of the twentieth century, dating to the period when telephone switchboard operators might hear the news before an official announcement had been made. The Queen's father, King George VI, had been 'Hyde Park Corner', Queen Elizabeth the Queen Mother was 'Operation Tay Bridge', and Prince Philip the Duke of Edinburgh was 'Operation Forth Bridge'. Several times a year as the decades passed, Operation London Bridge was reviewed and revised by the government and relevant organisations who would need to start the domino-like implementation of the meticulous plan. The longevity of Queen Elizabeth II's reign meant that the process had been discussed dozens of times, often with the Queen herself who had oversight of some of the arrangements. That reign came to an end when Operation London Bridge was activated on 9 September 2022 with the news that Queen Elizabeth II had died at Balmoral, the monarch's Scottish home.

Dressing the Queen

Loss is a personal experience but one that queens as public figures have had to share. Often lacking public voices or the opportunity to be candid, royal women have traditionally expressed their grief through dress, the fabric of mourning shrouding the royal body. The most famous widow in the world during the second half of the nineteenth century was Queen Victoria herself, the loss of her beloved Albert aged only forty-two in December 1861 plunging the Queen into a grief that appeared unending and overwhelming. Whilst black had long been the colour associated with mourning, the nineteenth century had begun to codify loss into an increasingly complicated form of etiquette. Rules had to be observed around the outward expression of grief, reinforced by those who were successfully marketing the mourning process. There was money to be made and goods to be sold to those who wanted to observe the appropriate prescribed processes. An entire industry was founded on this evolving etiquette, one that included black crape weavers in Essex, jet carvers in Whitby and the specialist hair workers who fashioned sentimental jewellery from the locks of loved ones. Few, if any, of those industries survive today, only the mementos of mourning themselves, those outward signifiers of love and loss expressed through sentimental jewellery and black cloth.

It was a particular type of jewellery whose origins sprang from ancient woodlands that would fuel the prosperity of a single town far from London, the seaside settlement of Whitby. One of the first things I learned, working with a collection of historic dress in Devon as a teenager, was how to distinguish jet from other black jewellery. There were many pieces in the collection, acquired over decades as well as the garments that they once adorned. I held a black brooch in my hand. It was warm and lightweight, far from the cold hard facets of other types of jewellery. 'French jet,' I was told, was a cheaper mourning jewellery made from glass, and would always be cold to the touch, unlike the softer, warmer contours of jet itself. More than 180 million years ago during the Jurassic period, a tree not dissimilar to the monkey puzzle was part of the native flora of the land that would eventually form part of the north-east coast of England. The fossilisation of this wood produced the dark-coloured but lightweight material which would become one of the first gems to be mined. For thousands of years, jewellery made from the material that we now call jet was prized for its depth of colour and shine. Seams of the fossilised wood could be found in the landscape around this coastline, miners digging into the hillsides in search of the inky gemstone.

A change in sartorial tastes, as well as increasingly complex and commodity-driven mourning etiquettes, would briefly take Whitby to new heights of fame. As garments became broader and weightier in the middle of the nineteenth century, so jewellery followed suit. Chunky necklaces and bracelets and elaborate brooches replaced the finer styles of the previous decades. Some examples of Whitby jet were displayed at the Great Exhibition in 1851 and when, less than a decade later, Albert the Prince Consort died, so the orders came rolling in. Where previously, in the 1830s, there had been two shops selling jet in the town, employing twenty-five people, forty years later there were twenty shops supporting an industry of fifteen hundred workers.

As early as 1850, it was one Thomas Andrew who was advertising his business as the 'jet ornament manufacturer to HM the Queen'. At this time Thomas was living at 85 Haggersgate in Whitby, a road running parallel with the broad banks of the River Esk. He was married to Rachel and they lived there with their six children. Thomas had been born in Whitby in 1804 and would become first a plumber and glazier. On both his marital paperwork and the 1841 census he is described as such and so it seems that Mr Andrew had something of the entrepreneur about him. Perhaps he began to witness the growing popularity of jet and decided that here was an opportunity to take his life in another direction. Within a decade he had made his name in the industry. He employed four men and one apprentice, each of them following the traditions of jet working.

Turning jet from a brown-hued, roughly mined rock into a highly polished black gemstone took the skill of different workers carrying out different processes. Once mined, the freshly hewn lumps of jet were sold by the miners to the rough jet merchant who in turn would sell to the jet manufacturer. The rocks would then be handed from the foreman of the works to the workers whose first job was to remove the brownish outer coating with a chisel. At this stage the jet was ready to undergo the process of 'chopping out', reducing the roughly cut jet into the various sizes required. The worker would begin the shaping of the jet, wetting it before passing it over a sandstone grit wheel, after which it came into the hands of the craftsman whose job it was to carve, engrave and polish the jet into its finished form. The tools of the trade were hand-fashioned to suit the person working the material, no high-tech machinery or custom-made pieces but instead old pieces of a hacksaw blade with a handle made out of a clothes peg. 'They looked very crude but they were treasured, sometimes being handed down from father to son.'

Contemporary photographs capture moments of making in Whitby. Armed with their home-made tools, we catch them during a moment of concentration. Mr J. W. Barker, his sleeves rolled up, peers through his round spectacles, 'chopping out' a piece of jet with his chisel, his workbench strewn with the industry of jet. Another photograph sees Mr Barker this time in a cap, his chopping-out block and lathe in front of him, carefully carving a piece of jet in his hand, strips of emery cloth lining the workbench ready to rub down the edges of his design. A third image sees Mr Barker working at one of the later stages of the process known as 'leading', the polishing of the jet ornament on a lead wheel to remove any unwanted carving marks. He stands in front of this wheel alongside another man, a younger version of Mr Barker, clad in waistcoat and cloth cap, similarly engaged at the lead wheel. His name was Joe Lyth and he was the last man in Whitby to be formally indentured as an apprentice. He served his seven years under the tutelage of Mr Barker. Joe grew up in Whitby under the care of his mother, Mary, and stepfather, Henry, who was a mariner, the occupation of many a Whitby man. Joe was taken on by Mr Barker, learning the many steps to creating a finished jet ornament. One of his apprentice pieces survives, an engraved plaque with the motto 'Prepare To Meet Thy God' carved into it amongst trailing roses and a cross. I imagine him following the instructions of the bespectacled, moustachioed Mr Barker, finessing his

Whitby jet workers.

chopping out, his carving and engraving and one day his leading, captured by the photographer, their movements at the wheel a mirror of one another. Joe continued to work long after the death of his master, Mr Barker, and even when the industry went into decline in the 1890s as fashions changed once again. His legacy would live on, however. Following his death in 1952, his workshop including all of his well-loved tools, his pattern books and pieces of his work were acquired by the York Castle Museum to become a part of their permanent display. Through Joe Lyth, the history of Whitby jet would carry on, his workshop offering a window into a lost world.

Jet was not the only jewellery prized for its sentimental qualities. Jewellery that incorporated, or was made entirely from, human hair was a common and fashionable addition to the mourning apparatus, maintaining a material connection to loved ones. Decorative objects fashioned from hair can often produce a squeamish reaction from the modern observer. It feels a little macabre to retain something of the corporeal self when, in the twenty-first century, we have more access to memorialising our loved ones. Via photographs, videos and voice notes, we might visualise and listen to people we love even after they are gone. The nineteenth century had no such facility. If they were lucky, a family might have had a photograph to recall the likeness of a face but they would not be great in number. Hair was unchanging. In colour and texture, it was a part of a person preserved. It might be curled or plaited. It could be woven into net-like braids and fashioned into a necklace or a bracelet. This was a job that required patience and dexterity to weave the finest of filaments into a wearable object.

Hair workers proliferated in the second half of the nineteenth century, and the sourcing of a reputable maker was the first, most important, decision according to Alexanna Speight – herself a hair worker – whose name was given as the author of a book on the subject published in 1871. 'When we think of the imperishable nature of human hair we can easily understand the anxiety with which a tress or lock cut from the forehead of a friend who is perhaps long amongst the dead, or separated from us, not only by miles and miles of ocean, but by new ties and new cares, is preserved.' With these anxieties in mind, the author cautioned against the hasty choice of a maker. The book describes the unscrupulous jeweller who might have no regard for the treasured lock of hair. If the hair was discovered to be too short or not plentiful enough for the design they had in mind, then rather than suggesting an alternative design, such a maker 'dishonestly matches the hair with other hair, perhaps already worked up, and the unhappy dupe lives on in the delusion that he possesses the hair of a friend whose memory he cherishes, whilst he in fact has that of some person he has never either seen or heard of.' The solution, according to Speight, was to learn the art of hair work yourself and weave tokens of love in the security of your own home. The book acted as an extended tutorial for the beginner as well as, in entrepreneurial spirit, offering not only a personal home visit to teach hair work but also a starter kit contained in a cedar-wood box, providing all the tools required.

The unusual name, Alexanna Speight, is the researcher's friend and she was easily traceable through nineteenth-century census records. She was born Alexanna Harper in Clerkenwell in 1826, never straying far from her birthplace as she grew up. She married Alfred Speight in May 1854, a confectioner who also lived in Clerkenwell, and they set up home together in Goswell Street. By the time that the 1861 census was taken, Alfred and Alexanna had three small children. Alfred was described as a dressmaker whilst Alexanna entered 'hair worker' as her occupation. It was a job that lent itself to homeworking, the hair worker needing nothing more than a small braiding stool, a palette and a range of small hand tools to complete the hairwork ornaments.

The book takes the reader, step by step, through the various processes necessary to complete the jewellery. First, the hair itself required cleaning: 'All you have to do is take, say about half a teacup full of hot water and dissolve in it two small pieces of borax and soda, each about the size of a nut.' The hair needed to be left in the solution for about a minute before being taken out and left to dry on a wooden palette, drawing a flat palette knife across it to remove any particles of dirt or oil. After another rinse in borax-infused water, the hair would be ready to work. Speight included myriad designs to follow. It might be woven in a trellis-like pattern and mounted on to card to be turned into a brooch. It could be carefully curled into the shape of a feather for inclusion in a locket. Most delicate of all, it could be woven into a fine mesh and sewn into a cylindrical braid and, with metal fittings, become a larger piece

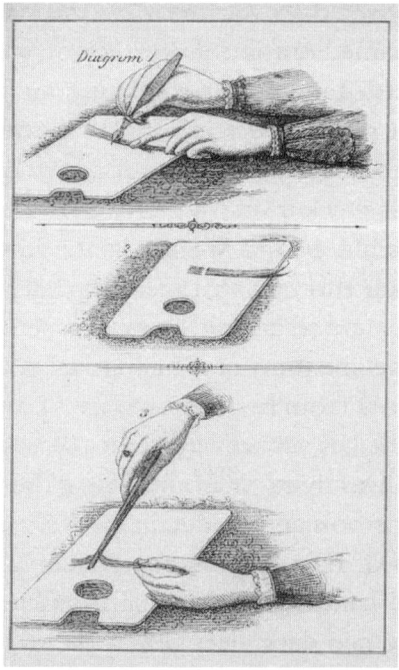

An illustration from *The Lock of Hair* by Alexanna Speight, 1871.

of jewellery. This part of the process was undertaken in much the same way as lacemaking, a three-legged stool supporting longer lengths of hair which were attached to a series of wooden bobbins and woven into a net.

The book naming Alexanna as the author was published in 1871, but the census tells a different story. By 1871, Alfred was living with his children and his second wife, Ann, along with the children from her first marriage. Alexanna had died in 1864. Alfred took on the role of hair worker in her place, describing himself as a 'hair net maker', and published his book under his first wife's name, perhaps thinking that it was more appealing than his own. It was his innovative spirit that promoted the tutorials and the mail-order kit for the budding amateur.

Queen Victoria had her own examples of jewellery containing locks of hair from various loved ones, and the man tasked with their preservation was a hair artist named Antoine Forrer. Forrer was from Winterthur in Switzerland but settled in London to open a studio dedicated to the most intricate of hair work, operating from exclusive premises on 136 Regent Street. The scrolling paper labels attached to his cases proclaimed that he was an 'Artist in Hair and Jewellery, By Appointment to the Queen'. He employed fifty people in his quest to provide the finest hair-work pieces. His census entry for 1851 records twenty young women all living on Regent Street and all hailing, like Forrer himself, from Switzerland. Aged from between twenty-seven and sixteen, each was described as a 'worker in hair', but from here the trail runs cold. None of them is recorded as living in the UK subsequently and so perhaps they spent this brief period of their lives living and working in the bustle of London, busy at their braiding stools and wooden palettes, plaiting and weaving the many-hued locks of hair delivered by Forrer's illustrious clients. I wonder how they felt, handling the locks of the faceless departed, curly and straight hair, grey, fair, dark, fiery red. Did they weave the hair and think of home? Did they explore the city during the brief hours beyond the workshop and write to their families in Switzerland of London, its sights, sounds and smells? I wonder, too, if they ever knew of the origin of the locks of hair that they handled, if Ann Steinegger, Margaretta Hanhart or Christina Meier or any other of the twenty named young women were aware that a particular commission had belonged to the beloved husband of Queen Victoria? As with countless other makers all over the city, their artisanship survives still in the Royal Collection, their artistry caught beneath the glass of a brooch or a locket that survives in the context of the celebrated wearer but not the hands that made them.

Both the polished jet of Whitby and the woven braids of hair workers in London would have found themselves worn against the other most ubiquitous signifier of mourning in nineteenth-century Britain, the crinkled cloth that was Courtaulds crape. The arc of its popularity mirrored that of both jet and hair jewellery, the second half of the nineteenth century briefly generating a boom in the accoutrements of grief that was on the decline by the 1890s. For the few decades that such strict mourning practices were in force, though, fortunes could be made. So it was for the family of Samuel Courtauld and the fabric that would make them a household name. The fabric itself was not an innovation specific to the 1800s. According to Lou Taylor, author of the definitive volume on mourning dress: 'The first mention of mourning crape in royal British funeral accounts was in 1694 at the funeral of Queen Mary II.' Ceremonial attendees at the funeral – trumpeters, drummers and foot guards – were decked out in bands of black crape as a mark of respect for the monarch. The earliest patent for the fabric in England was taken out at the end of the seventeenth century but it would need the Industrial Revolution to bring quantity to the market and make black crape the choice of fashionable widows, queens included.

Crape was not an easy fabric to produce, not least because it required all vestiges of shine to be removed from its silken surface. Hailing from Greek mythology and the tale of Narcissus obsessing over his own image through the reflected surface of water, the rejection of shiny surfaces became a part of the mourning rituals. Thus crape was required to exhibit an entirely matte surface. It was also distinctive for its crimped finish, a lengthy process described by the biographer of Courtaulds as the 'most mysterious pillar of the enterprise'. The Courtaulds factories were located in Essex across three mills that focused on different aspects of crape production. First the silk crape yarn was spun with a high degree of twist at the mill in Halstead to generate the first part of the wrinkled effect. After weaving, the undyed fabric would be subjected to steaming and stretching in order to disrupt the laying of the warp and weft threads before it was passed through a heated crimping machine. Then, after it had been steeped in a hot liquid, the crinkling of the cloth would increase before it was dyed and finally underwent the process of 'dressing'. Since the dyed crape resulted in a softly sheened fabric, this stage required the removal of any suggestion of shine: 'The crape was passed through various combinations of boiled up starch, glue and treacle. The final result was a triumph of engineering and technical skill.'

This complex act of 'finishing' was undertaken by workers at the Bocking mill in Essex by women including Caroline Gentry. Caroline was born in Braintree in 1829. Her father was in the army and stationed in the area, her mother Ann a silk winder. Given the size of the Courtaulds enterprise – which, by the time Caroline was of an age to work, was employing two thousand local men, women and children – it was probably inevitable that she would find a job at one of the Courtaulds mills. By her early twenties she had become a silk weaver, living at home in Crown Yard, Braintree, with her mother and father, who was now an agricultural labourer but also a Chelsea Pensioner. Caroline's wage would have made a welcome addition to the household's small income.

Within the next ten years, both of Caroline's parents had died and at

Dressing the Queen

Crape finishers at Bocking Mill, Braintree, 1859.

the age of thirty-one she was living alone in the town of Bocking where she now worked as a crape finisher. Amongst the pages of the official biography of the company, *Courtaulds: An Economic and Social History*, is a photograph taken in 1859 of women who were crape finishers at the Bocking factory. One row standing and one row sitting, the women are pictured in front of the brick wall of their workplace, shawls crossed over the bodices of their dresses. Is one of these women Caroline Gentry? Did she enjoy a level of camaraderie in spite of their long hours before she walked home to a more solitary existence? It was certainly taxing work. The increased governmental interest in the working conditions of women in the early 1840s found much to criticise: 'In 1842 a *Report on the Employment of Women* recorded case after case of women whose eyesight had been damaged by sewing mourning fabric for long hours in poor light.' But it was work and it was an employment that Caroline had spent more than a decade refining when choices were not prolific. Through her hands would pass the yards of crinkled silk whose shine she would gradually strip away, to be left with the lustreless and lightweight fabric of grief. The resultant rolls of crape would find themselves unfurled in mourning warehouses and dressmaking establishments to be fashioned into the bodices and skirts of black dresses, indicative of the very first stage of formal mourning.

I well remember my own first encounter with crape and its association with the unending grief of Queen Victoria. When I worked as a volunteer at Killerton House in the early 1990s, preparations were under way for the opening of an exhibition which included one of the black 1890s dresses belonging to Victoria herself. Strips of crape had been incorporated into the fabric of the dress, symbolic of the raw emotion she still felt all those years after Albert's death. Those closest to her in her lifetime were not immune to the realities of her strict adherence to mourning etiquette. In one of her frequent letters home, Marie Mallet, a lady-in-waiting, informed her husband: 'I am sending for my mourning trappings . . . we never escape jet for long.' In another missive home in August 1900, she wrote: 'We have a funeral service here tomorrow and are draping our clothes in crape.' Crape had become the official uniform of the grieving widow and in that sense mourning attire became a democratising aesthetic. The middle-class widow and the Queen alike were bedecked in Courtaulds crape.

Although Queen Victoria was not unaware of the importance of a positive relationship with the press, she could not have predicted the intense scrutiny and enhanced access to the material culture of monarchy that her descendants would experience.

During the days following the death of Queen Elizabeth II on 8 September 2022 and her state funeral on 19 September, the media examination of every element of the preparations and the format of the day itself was forensic. In spite of a more relaxed attitude to mourning attire in the twenty-first century, Debrett's, the publication and keeper of British etiquette over more than two centuries, established that black was still the official dress code for the monarch's funeral. Whilst crape had been dispensed with decades earlier, attendees should wear either a black morning suit for men, or for women a black skirt or coat of below knee length, with a hat. For milliner Stephen Jones, this meant that in his central London store in the days leading up to the funeral he sold only black hats. 'Everyone wanted to be appropriately dressed, not fashionably dressed,' said Jones. 'Hats were a symbol of Queen Elizabeth's reign, because she herself always wore them.' Designer makers were the order of the day for the royal women attending the Queen's funeral. Catherine, Princess of Wales, wore a black Alexander McQueen coat and a Philip Treacy hat with a birdcage veil. Sophie, the Countess of Wessex, wore a custom-made dress by Suzannah London that featured intricate lily-of-the-valley embroidery, a tribute to the Queen's favourite flower. Jewellery was carefully chosen in the knowledge that an observant worldwide audience would analyse every choice of brooch, necklace and earring.

This role of the jewellery and the fabric of mourning in 2022 would have been recognisable components of funereal aesthetics to Queen Victoria. The wearing of black; the choice of pearls, which Queen Victoria had established as a symbol of mourning in the aftermath of Prince Albert's death from 1861; the veiled face. These have remained constants in the formal expression of loss. As ever the fashioning of that aesthetic, then and now, belongs to other, unseen figures. It relied on the jet miners of Whitby seeking out seams of the gem and the artisans to shape it. It required the talents of Antoine Forrer's young hair workers, dozens of young women no doubt homesick for their Swiss families as they wove the finest of threads. It called on the skills of countless women like Caroline Gentry, compromising their eyesight in the quest to produce the inky sea of black crape that shrouded the nineteenth-century woman in her grief. Queen Victoria might have been the most famous widow in the world but Queen Elizabeth became the longest reigning monarch.

Public Grief

Her funeral was beamed around the globe, ensuring that the sartorial expressions of those attending would come under the closest scrutiny. The details of floral embroidery, designer millinery and sentimental jewellery demonstrated that the ability to convey meaning through dress and its accoutrements is as powerful now as ever it has been in the past.

EPILOGUE

New Beginnings

Did the elderly lady whom I had met back in 2017 in the Anglican church of Tewantin, Queensland, watch the coronation of King Charles III? I wondered this often in the weeks leading up to the coronation when the volume of detail emerging across news outlets and social media channels was so extensive. The appetite of the twenty-four-hour news machine requires constant feeding and so the minutiae of the preparations were pored over as the date of the ceremony drew near. Did she reflect on that last coronation and her own proximity to it?

Those people who had witnessed both coronations would have been able to draw on that thread of similarity that traced back a thousand years of tradition. Words, music, vestments, garments, symbols combined into a ceremony that was both ancient and modern as the twenty-first-century monarchy endeavoured to represent a very different world from that of 1953. It is a world more ambivalent about the role of royalty during a cost-of-living crisis – a family beset by scandals, a privileged few who could not possibly comprehend what life looks like for the vast majority of the nations they represent. And yet I felt moved by the ceremony. I found the symbolism and the tradition compelling, history repeating itself in front of our very eyes, the material objects loaded with stories of the past and of those who played a part in their creation. Here, still, were the unseen hands of the many. Nimble, skilled fingers darting, needles flashing.

For each of the queens and queen consorts whose complex wardrobes have filled these pages, their own or their spouse's coronation inevitably formed a pivotal space in their lives. There was always the before and the after. Their anointing as queen or consort marked a shift in identity, a new set of responsibilities, a different home even. Following the death of Queen Victoria in January 1901, her daughter-in-law Alexandra began to prepare for the ceremony of their lifetimes, almost forty years after their marriage. Members of the household did their best to advise her on protocol, since the last coronation of a queen consort had taken place in 1831, beyond the living memory of almost everybody. Alexandra, however, who had spent more than four decades honing her public facade, was in total control. She commissioned Lady Curzon, the Vicereine of India, to undertake the creation of her gold overdress, handed to the most skilled embroiderers in India. The dress itself was fashioned by her favoured couture seamstresses at Morin Blossier. On 9 August 1902, eighteen months after the death of Queen Victoria, she appeared in a blaze of gold under the first electric lights to be installed in Westminster Abbey; a moment of pure theatre of her own devising.

The planning of her mother-in-law's coronation in 1838 must have acted as a cautionary tale. The contemporary diarist Charles Greville wrote of Queen Victoria's coronation: 'There was a continual difficulty and embarrassment, and the Queen never knew what to do next.' The garments made for Queen Victoria followed all of the prescribed components but the lack of choreography made the ceremony appear slightly shambolic in spite of the gorgeousness of the vestments themselves. Alexandra would not make that mistake. Less than a decade later, her own daughter-in-law Mary would, in turn, enact those same ceremonies in a dress of British origin. The cream satin gown was created by the firm Reville & Rossiter and the women at the Royal School of Needlework set to their frames once again to work their magic in gold thread for the coronation of King George V and Queen Mary in 1911. Some of those women would repeat their endeavours in 1937 when Queen Elizabeth, consort of King George VI, would wear a satin dress by Madame Handley-Seymour – who could surely never have imagined as a child in Liverpool that one day she would be responsible for a coronation gown. Knowing that her dress would be embroidered at the RSN, she created a cotton toile of the dress over which the floral design was painted in gold, a three-dimensional aide-memoire from which the embroiderers could work. This toile survives today, a rarity of the art of the dressmaker and the embroiderer, never designed to last but acting as a kind of shadow image of the final piece. Such was the intricacy woven into each ceremony, driven at the behest of the queen or consort in question, but wrought into being by the hands of the many.

Much was made of the sustainability embedded into the choices made for the coronation in 2023 of Charles III, a public figure who has championed the environment and the human cost of consumption. It was entirely in keeping with the world view of King Charles and Queen Camilla. And yet those garments that were so visible to a global HD television audience had undergone transformations that required all of those traditional skills and a multitude of participants to realise them. The very order in which the various garments are added to and removed from the monarch was set out in the fourteenth-century volume, the *Liber Regalis*, published for the coronation of King Richard II in 1377; a thread of continuity that connected Charles with his mother, his grandparents, his great-grandparents and beyond. If the service and order of symbolic ceremonials were the same, so were many of the actual garments themselves. The two robes that bookended the ceremony on arrival to and exit from Westminster Abbey had been worn by the King's grandparents King George VI and Queen Elizabeth for their 1937 coronation. Careful conservation of the crimson velvet robes of state and the purple velvet robes of estate were undertaken by the Royal School of Needlework, whilst the linings and gold lace were rejuvenated by Ede & Ravenscroft, their contribution to British ceremonial dress still significant long after the redoubtable Rosa Ede.

One of the few completely new pieces for the ceremony was the silk overshirt made from English spun silk by the firm of Turnbull & Asser. Founded in 1885 and since 1903 located on Jermyn Street, Turnbull & Asser received their Royal Warrant in 1980 from Charles, then Prince of Wales. The commission of the coronation shirt represented a long-held association and a continuation of patronage worn for the entirety of the coronation. Much of it was unseen, hidden beneath the glitter of other tunics and robes, donned and divested at different points, but the shirt was a constant. The only visible details were the embroidered collar and cuffs, stitched with oak leaves and acorns.

The robes that followed varied in their biographical tales, all having appeared at one or more previous coronations, thus maintaining the connection between the body of the monarch and consort and their glittering carapace with moments and ancestors past. The Colobium Sindonis, a simple white linen tunic worn after the anointing, had belonged to King George VI whilst the long-sleeved silk Supertunica had been worn by both King Charles's grandfather and mother, respectively in 1937 and 1953.

The oldest garment to feature in the ceremony was the Imperial Mantle, first worn in 1821 for the coronation of King George IV. This was an event that combined opulence with scandal, the crowning of an unpopular Prince Regent whose spending on his coronation ran to more than twenty times that of his father's in 1761, coming in at almost £240,000 (£21 million by today's reckoning). That the mantle survives at all is surprising, given the fate of much of King George IV's wardrobe. Following his death in 1830, much of his sumptuous sartorial collection was put up for public auction by a Mr Phillips at his rooms on New Bond

New Beginnings

Street, possibly an attempt by the new King William IV to recoup some of the costs. The *Caledonian Mercury* gave an account of the sale: 'There was very slight competition for any of the articles, and we did not observe that they were knocked down to persons of distinction. The proceeds of the sale could not have amounted to any considerable sum.' One of the most significant lots was his crimson coronation robes which had originally cost in excess of £24,000 to make but which were purchased at a knock-down price by Madame Tussaud, where they would remain on public display in their Baker Street premises for almost thirty years.

Throughout each traditional twist and turn of the coronation ceremony, the King was flanked by his consort, Queen Camilla, whose own coronation gown had been designed for the occasion by Bruce Oldfield. The ivory peau de soie (or paduasoy) was woven by Stephen Walters in Suffolk, a company specialising in jacquard fabrics since the early eighteenth century. The silk was embroidered in silver and gold, the gown twined with silver florals to represent the couple's love of the countryside. Two golden embroidered terriers made their way on to the hem, personal mementos of a life lived beyond the public sphere. It was a gown that had to appear as a traditional symbol amidst a whole host of coronation conventions, at the same time as being stamped with her own personality in a twenty-first-century context.

During the months after the coronation ceremony itself, various garments and regalia from the day went on display in Buckingham Palace. The velvet robes, the coronation dress worn by Queen Camilla, the beautifully embroidered anointing screen. Just some of the textiles at the heart of the service, woven and stitched by makers past and present, were temporarily visible at close quarters for members of the public to enjoy, their makers' labour evident even if they were not.

There was a sense that the death of Queen Elizabeth II represented the end of an era. For most of the British population, she was the only monarch to have reigned through the course of their lives, a public figure whose consistency formed the backdrop to parts of our national identity. Now there are signs of change. A modern monarchy seems entirely contradictory for by its very nature it is about the old, the established, the traditional. But change it must in the face of new global challenges and economic realities. A whisper of that change was visible in the sartorial choices of Catherine, Princess of Wales, during the 2023 coronation. Like many of the royal women who have preceded her, Catherine chose a trusted design house for her gown of white crepe. It was created by the team at Alexander McQueen, featuring silver motifs of the British nations – the rose, the thistle, the daffodil and the shamrock – stitched in silver bullion. Rather than don one of the many tiaras in the Royal Collection, Catherine wore a silver-and-crystal headpiece with embroidered leaves. It was designed by milliner Jess Collett, a far cry from the diamonds of old and said to be a statement of intent, a demonstration of a new monarchy that may dispense with some of the old trappings.

Whatever such changes might look like in the future, there are those for whom the monarchy continues to contribute to their livelihood. As technology prioritises the machine, in the face of mass consumption the work of the hand becomes an act of resistance. For those makers by hand of gloves, of hats, of shoes. For embroiderers and knitters. For stitchers and weavers. For the countless makers past who barely scraped an existence, at the same time as fashioning clothes for a queen. And for the makers present who endeavour to celebrate the art of slowness in a fast-paced world, may your needles fly and your worth be recognised. These are your stories.

Acknowledgements

In a book that is a celebration of the many unknown hands that contributed to royal wardrobes past, I feel incredibly fortunate to have had the support of those who have made their own contributions and were willing to share their insights with me. Julie Crocker at the Royal Archive provided the records of numerous dressers. Lucinda Ganderton's personal research into the history of the royal laundry is unsurpassed and she shared her work with me with such generosity. Gerry Graham spoke to me about life in the Pringle factory, recreating an approach to industry that has largely disappeared. Jane Hattrick generously shared her wonderful research that charted the employees at Norman Hartnell. Genevieve James not only recounted the memories of her mother, Cornelia, but also described what it is like to work with a Royal Warrant. Stella Maclaren was a joy to speak to and I will always treasure the stories she told of life in the palace. Stewart Parvin allowed me to ask all the questions to get an insight into the life of a queen's dress designer – thank you. Brian Turner spoke with such passion about his life making passementerie on the very day that his business was closing its doors for the last time – I will always remain grateful for the time he spent chatting to me.

I was a lucky recipient of one of the Hosking Houses Trust's residencies in 2024, thanks to the vision of the wonderful Sarah Hosking. Sarah recognised, many years ago, that women who are trying to write whilst holding down a job and possibly raising a family at the same time rarely get the space to think. I spent a month writing in the trust's cottage, 'a room of one's own', where I wrote more than I would have imagined possible. It felt like a truly special gift. Thank you, Sarah.

Acknowledgements

My luck continues with the support of my wonderful editor at Chatto & Windus, Clara Farmer, and her team, including Rosanna Hildyard, Leah Boulton, Rowena Skelton-Wallace and copy-editor Mary Chamberlain; and of course Victoria Murray-Browne and all at Vintage, thank you. From designers to PR, there is so much work behind the scenes at a publishing house that I will never see but I do not take for granted. My thanks to you all. I will for ever count my blessings that my path crossed with that of Clare Alexander. She is the best of agents in all ways.

My friends and family have witnessed the ups and downs of this project and I thank you all for the coffees, the wine and the listening ears. Mum and Dad, your unwavering faith in me has always seen me through wobbly days. Iwan and Elis, Imogen and Summer, I am a fortunate mum indeed. Stuart . . . just everything. Always.

List of Illustrations

Every effort has been made to trace copyright holders and obtain permission for use of copyright material. The author and publishers apologise for any omissions and would be grateful to be notified of any corrections that should be incorporated in future editions of this book.

PLATES

1: Queen Elizabeth II in her coronation robes leaving Westminster Abbey, London, after being crowned, 1953 © World History Archive / Alamy

2: Court presentation ensemble, 1896. Brooklyn Museum Costume Collection at the Metropolitan Museum of Art, gift of the Brooklyn Museum, 2009; Anonymous gift, in memory of Mrs John Roebling, 1970 © public domain, courtesy of the Metropolitan Museum of Art

3: Woman's court presentation ensemble, *c.* 1928 (silk and lamé with net, sequins, rhinestones and ostrich feathers) © Philadelphia Museum of Art / Gift of Mrs Charles T. Porter, 1963 / Bridgeman Images

4: Bonnets worn by Queen Victoria, 1845–55 © London Museum

5: 'Passementerie Workshop' by Karl Meunier, *c.* 1884, oil on canvas © Grohmann Museum Collection at Milwaukee School of Engineering, Milwaukee, WI

List of Illustrations

6: Coat manufactured by Dieulafait & E. Bouclier, *c.* late nineteenth–early twentieth century. Gift of Miss Irene Lewisohn, 1937 © public domain, courtesy of the Metropolitan Museum of Art

7: Boots probably worn by Queen Victoria, J. Sparkes Hall & Son, 1880–99 © Historic Royal Palaces, United Kingdom

8: Accessory set, 1870s. Gift of Miss Irene Lewisohn, 1937 © public domain, courtesy of the Metropolitan Museum of Art

9: Close-up of the wedding shoes of Princess Elizabeth, 'Ivory Duchess' satin self-lined sandals designed by Rayne © Central Press / Stringer / Hulton Royals Collection via Getty Images

10: 'Two Women Looking at Fabric in a Shop', Anonymous, British, nineteenth century © public domain, courtesy of the Metropolitan Museum of Art

11: Riding ensemble by Morin Blossier, *c.* 1902 © public domain, courtesy of the Metropolitan Museum of Art

12: Genevieve James, courtesy of Genevieve James

13: Riding habit jacket, made *c.* 1885–6, John Redfern & Sons. Given by the Hon. Mrs S. F. Tyser © Victoria & Albert Museum

14: Expanding travelling basket by Harriet J. Cave & Sons, registered design 4822, 1866 © National Archives, ref. BT45/25 (4822)

15: 'Cinq Heures Chez Paquin' – 'Five Hours at Paquin', Henri Gervex © Carlo Bollo / Alamy

16: Blue silk and cotton corset by Madame Roxey Caplin, 1851 © London Museum

List of Illustrations

17: Detail of a pair of cream patterned cotton stockings, initials 'VR' and crown worked at the top of the leg, said to have belonged to Queen Victoria, late nineteenth century © public domain, courtesy of Auckland War Memorial Museum, Tāmaki Paenga Hira

18: 'Queen Victoria's dresser Marianne Skerrett' by Rosa Koberwein, 1880, chalk on paper © Royal Collection Trust 2025 | Royal Collection Trust

19: Queen Elizabeth II is pictured during a walkabout to commemorate her Silver Jubilee, June 1977 © Popperfoto via Getty Images

20: Diamond Jubilee, Thames River Pageant © Chris Furlong / DP via Getty Images

21: Mourning dress belonging to Queen Victoria, *c.* 1894. Brooklyn Museum Costume Collection at the Metropolitan Museum of Art, gift of the Brooklyn Museum, 2009; Gift of C. W. Howard, 1950 © public domain, courtesy of the Metropolitan Museum of Art

22: 'Queen Victoria's dressing room at Balmoral' by James Roberts, 1857, watercolour © Painters / Alamy

TEXT ILLUSTRATIONS

p.19: Photograph of Lily Lee. Reproduced by permission of the Warner Textile Archive, Braintree District Museum Trust; **p.26:** Ede & Ravenscroft tailor Ji Hae An Sykes © Ji Hae An Sykes; **p.27:** George Doré, silk weaver, at his loom, late nineteenth century © private collection courtesy of Tracey Offord; **p.39:** Embroiderers in Hartnell's workshop, 1944, Ministry of Information Photo Division Photographer © Imperial War Museum; **p.40:** Embroidery sample for Queen Elizabeth's coronation dress © private collection, courtesy of Claire Williams; **p.57:**

List of Illustrations

From 'Process of feather making . . .' Miriam and Ira D. Wallach Division of Art, Prints and Photographs: Photography Collection, the New York Public Library © The New York Public Library Digital Collections; **p.69:** The Coronation: Re-Modelling the Imperial State Crown, 1953 © SuperStock / Alamy; **p.77:** James Churchyard, Norwich silk shawl weaver, c. 1910, courtesy of Norfolk County Council Library and Information Service; **p.79:** Detail of a jacket by Dieulafait & E. Bouclier, 1865–70 © public domain, courtesy of the Metropolitan Museum of Art; **p.91:** Photograph of two girls plaiting straw for bonnets etc. at Wilston, Hertfordshire, by Godfrey Bingley, 1890 © Victoria and Albert Museum, London; **p.94:** Plait stall in Luton © The History Collection / Alamy; **p.100:** Milliner Aage Thaarup at work, 1940 © Tim Gidal / Stringer / Picture Post via Getty Images; **p.107:** Evening slipper, Gundry & Son, 1840–9 © public domain, courtesy of the Metropolitan Museum of Art; **p.109:** Line drawing from *Shoemaking, old and new* by Fred A. Gannon, 1911 © public domain; **p.117:** A still from the British Pathé film *Jewelled Shoes*, Jean Matthew working at Rayne shoes, 1953 © image courtesy of British Pathé; **p.122:** 'Pose of trimmings in Worth's studio, great Parisian couturier', 1907 © Boyer / Roger Viollet via Getty Images; **p.132:** Madame Clapham, provenance unknown, courtesy of Kingston Theatre Hotel, Hull; **p.135:** Avis Ford, designer at Madame Handley-Seymour, from 'The Mysterious Miss Ford', *Sunday Herald*, Sydney, Sunday 13 Feb 1949, provenance unknown, courtesy of National Library of Australia; **p.140:** 'Glove makers: interior view with various tools of the trade', etching by Defehrt after Lucotte © public domain, courtesy of Wellcome Collection; **p.143:** A Dents gloveress at work, 1890s © Dents Glove Museum, Warminster; **p.147:** Cornelia James at work, courtesy of Genevieve James; **p.155:** A Hartnell sketch © Hardy Amies Ltd / Mary Evans Picture Library; **p.164:** Stewart Parvin at his work table © David Burke, courtesy of Stewart Parvin;

List of Illustrations

p.172: Monsieur Joseph Kanné, Queen Victoria's courier, 1864 © Royal Collection Trust 2025 | Royal Collection Trust; **p.178:** Queen at Papworth Travel Goods from *On the Road: A Papworth Story* by Rowland Parker (Pendragon Press), photographer unknown; **p.185:** An advertisement for Redfern's New York salon, 1885, public domain; **p.186:** 'Salon de Lingerie, Redfern', *c.* 1910, from *Les créateurs de la mode* by Alfred Jungbluth, p. 42 © public domain; **p.193:** Mlle Brésil in a Redfern tailormade, from *Les Modes: Revue mensuelle illustrée des arts décoratifs appliqués à la femme*, August 1904 © public domain; **p.202:** Spread from *Pringle Annual* published for Pringle employees, volume I, Dec 1962 © Pringle of Scotland Ltd; **p.209:** Savile Row – Tailoring at Henry Poole and Co., London, England, UK, 1944 © Ministry of Information Photo Division Photographer / Imperial War Museum; **p.214:** 'The Stocking-Frame and Other Apparatus Used in the Manufactory' from *A New and Complete Dictionary of Arts and Sciences*, The Society of Gentlemen, 1763 © public domain; **p.217:** Ann Birkin, Queen Victoria's chevener, *Carte de visite*, *c.* 1900, private collection, courtesy of Brad Purington; **p.221:** Women working in the Pryce-Jones factory, 1953 © public domain, courtesy of the National Library of Wales; **p.229:** Illustration from *Health and Beauty* by Madame Roxey A. Caplin, 1854 © public domain; **p.240:** Horatio Sparkins by George Cruikshank from *Sketches by Boz*, 1890 © public domain; **p.243:** Wash House, Wolverhampton Steam Laundry, Wolverhampton, late nineteenth century © Wolverhampton City Council – Arts and Heritage / Alamy; **p.246:** Royal laundry basket label, *c.* 1880, courtesy of the Armoury of St James's; **p.256:** Harriet Giltrap, Queen Alexandra's dresser, *c.* 1890 © Royal Collection Trust 2025 | Royal Collection Trust; **p.260:** 'T.R.H. The Duchess of York & Princess Elizabeth with Nurse', published by J. Beagles & Co., *c.* 1929 © National Portrait Gallery; **p.264:** Angela Kelly at the Investitures at Buckingham Palace, November 2012 © John Stillwell – WPA

List of Illustrations

Pool via Getty Images News; **p.271:** 'A scene from the Whitby Jet Industry' © Universal History Archive / Universal Images Group via Getty Images; **p.274:** Illustration from *The Lock of Hair* by Alexanna Speight, 1871 © public domain; **p.278:** Crape finishers at Bocking Mill, Braintree, 1859 © Warner Textile Archive

Notes on Sources

Introduction: Many Hands . . .
2   Hartnell, Norman, *Silver and Gold*, Evans Brothers Ltd, London, 1955, p.121
3   Ibid., p.122
3   Ibid.
9   Stoney, Benita and Weltzien, Heinrich C. (eds), *My Mistress the Queen: The Letters of Frieda Arnold, Dresser to Queen Victoria*, Weidenfeld & Nicolson, London, 1994, p.147
10 Office of Robes ledgers, National Archive, LC13/5, p.31

1. Ceremonial Splendour
14 Goodale, Sir Ernest, *Weaving and the Warners 1870–1970*, F. Lewis Publishers Ltd, Leigh-on-Sea, 1971, p.48
16 Dickens, C., *Household Words*, 5 April, 1851
17 Ibid.
18 Goodale, Sir Ernest, op. cit., p.20
20 Hansard, Vol.322, 28 February, 1888, column 1600
20 Cited in Howarth, Stephen, *Henry Poole: Founders of Savile Row*, Bene Factum Publishing, Honiton, 2003, p.79
21 Robertson, W. B. (ed), *Encyclopaedia of Retail Trading*, Harmsworth Business Library, Vol.VII, 1911, p.265, cited in Breward, C., *The Hidden Consumer: Masculinities, Fashion and City Life 1860–1914*, Manchester University Press, Manchester, 1999, p.105
23 Walpole, Horace, *The Letters of Horace Walpole*, Vol.3, Richard Bentley, London, 1840, p.145

Notes on Sources

25 Cited in Campbell, U., *Robes of the Realm: 300 Years of Ceremonial Dress*, Michael O'Mara Books Ltd, London, 1989, p.38

26 Ibid., p.42

26 Ibid.

27 Magsino, I., 'Savile Row Tailor Ji Hae An: This is what being British looks like', *W Magazine*, April, 2021

2. Little Hands

31 *The Times*, Friday, 7 December, 1900, p.4

34 Kay-Williams, S., *An Unbroken Thread: Celebrating 150 Years of the Royal School of Needlework*, ACC Art Books, Woodbridge, 2022, p.47. This is the definitive history of the RSN and includes names of other embroiderers who trained and worked at the school as well as detailing its continued work over the decades.

36 Ibid.

38 Hartnell, Norman, op. cit., p.128

39 See Reynolds, H., *Couture or Trade: An Early Pictorial Record of the London College of Fashion*, Phillimore, Chichester, 1997

39 Hattrick, J., *A Life in the Archive: The Dress, Design and Identity of London Couturier Norman Hartnell, 1921–1979*, University of Brighton, unpublished doctoral thesis, 2011, p.226

40 Ibid., p.225

3. Presented at Court

45 MacCarthy, Fiona, *Last Curtsey: The End of the Debutantes*, Faber & Faber, London, 2006, p.4

47 Duff Gordon, Lucile, *Discretions and Indiscretions*, Frederick A. Stokes, New York, 1932, p.60

47 Ibid., p.90

48 Ibid., p.113

48 Ibid., p.114

Notes on Sources

48 Ibid., p.82
48 Ibid., p.46
49 Ibid., p.47
49 MacCarthy, Fiona, op. cit., p.57
51 Mayhew, Henry, *The Shops and Companies of London*, Strand Publishing, London, 1865
52 Ewing, Elizabeth, *History of 20th Century Fashion*, Batsford, London, 1974, pp.39–40. The whole account is given but there is no information about how and when the interview was given. Presumably to the author at some point.
53 Ibid.
53 Ibid.
54 Ibid.
55 Abrevaya Stein, Sarah, *Plumes: Ostrich Feathers, Jews and a Lost-World of Global Commerce*, Yale University Press, New Haven, 2008, p.54
55 Ibid., see ch. 2 for details of the London feather trade.
58 https://www.youtube.com/watch?v=hgEeHvzJ2Bw
58 Both of these quotes are cited from Arch, Nigel and Marschner, Joanna, *Splendour at Court: Dressing for Royal Occasions since 1700*, Unwin Hyman Ltd, London, 1987, p.123
58 MacCarthy, Fiona, op. cit., p.11

4. All That Glisters . . .

60 Menkes, Suzy, *The Royal Jewels*, Guild Publishing, London, 1985, p.157
61 Field, Leslie, *The Queen's Jewels*, Harry N. Abrams Inc, New York, 1987, p.27
61 Ibid., p.28
62 Cited here: https://www.rct.uk/collection/stories/the-crown-jewels/the-cullinan-diamond
63 Lovett, Robert W., 'Rundell, Bridge & Rundell – An Early Company History' in *Bulletin of the Business Historical Society*, Vol.23 No.3, Sept 1949, p.154
63 Cited in ibid., p.157

64 Cited here: https://regencyredingote.wordpress.com/2019/08/02/rundell-bridge-and-company-by-george-fox/
64 Field, Leslie, op. cit., p.186
67 Cited here: https://hancockslondon.com/makers/wolfe-co-e?srsltid=AfmBOoo_ZA_Jwo9P1UrvCTtTmveZ5z7CvRqdNKLjfX0_wL1goQJi1Krl
69 Cited here: https://layersoflondon.humap.site/map/records/east-hill-estate-1941

5. Coats of Many Colours

74 http://www.queenvictoriasjournals.org/search/displayItemFromId.do?FormatType=fulltextimgsrc&QueryType=articles&ItemID=18510614
74 Cited in Clabburn, Pamela, *The Norwich Shawl*, Norfolk Museums Service, Norfolk, 1995, p.16
76 Cited here: http://www.norwich-heritage.co.uk/publications/Norwich_Yards_Book_web_sample.pdf
77 Cited here: http://www.staugustinesnorwich.org.uk/uploaded_files/Living%20Down%20the%20Yard%20-%20Wyer.pdf
78 Westman, Annabel, *Fringe, Frog and Tassel*, Philip Wilson Publishers, London, 2019, p.x
83 Trump, Margaret, 'When I was at Marshall & Snelgrove' in *Costume*, Vol.22, 1988, pp.85–93
84 Amies, Hardy, *Hardy Amies: Still Here – An Autobiography*, Weidenfeld & Nicolson, London, 1984, p.85
84 Ibid.
84 Ibid., p.39
85 Ibid., p.61
85 Ibid., p.58
87 Walker, Catherine, *Catherine Walker: An Autobiography*, HarperCollins, London, 1998, p.25
87 Ibid.

Notes on Sources

88 Ibid.
88 Ibid., p.71

6. If You Want to Get Ahead . . .

89 Ellis, S. M. (ed), *A Mid-Victorian Pepys: The Letters and Memoirs of Sir William Hardman*, Cecil Palmer, London, 1923, p.280
89 McDowell, Colin, *Hats: Status, Style and Glamour*, Thames & Hudson, London, 1992, p.25
90 Jones, Stephen, *Hats – An Anthology*, V&A Publications, London, 2009, p.51
91 *The Queen: The Lady's Newspaper*, 9 November, 1861
92 Davis, Jean, *Straw Plait*, Shire Publications, London, 1981, p.22
92 Ibid., p.15
95 Burney, Fanny, *The Wanderer or Female Difficulties*, Longman, London, 1814, p.426
95 Thaarup, Aage, *Heads and Tales*, Cassel & Co., London, 1956, p.84
97 Matthews David, Alison, *Fashion Victims*, Bloomsbury, London, 2015, p.44
98 Ibid., p.76
98 Thaarup, Aage, op. cit., p.45
98 Ibid.
99 Ibid., p.80
99 Ibid., p.83
100 https://www.britishpathe.com/asset/187043/
102 Kelly, Angela, *The Other Side of the Coin*, HarperCollins, London, 2019, p.89

7. Best Foot Forward

109 See Cox, Pamela and Hobley, Annabel, *Shopgirls*, Arrow Books, London, 2014
110 Sparkes Hall, Joseph, *The Book of the Feet*, Simpkin, Marshall and Co., London, 1847, p.84
110 Ibid., p.131

Notes on Sources

111   Ibid., p.133
111   Defoe, Daniel, *The Complete English Tradesman*, Charles Rivington, London, 1725, p.330
113   See Pick, Michael, *Rayne: Shoes for Stars*, AAC Editions, Woodbridge, 2015, p.22
114   Cousins, Angela, *Kids from over the Water – An Edwardian Working Class Childhood in South East London*, Mereo Books, Cirencester, p.6
115   Ibid., p.86
115   Ibid., p.87
116   Ibid., p.89
117   Cited in Pick, Michael, op. cit., p.93
118   Kelly, Angela, op. cit., p.80
118   Ibid., p.80

8. Fashioning a Silhouette

121   Royal Archive letter, RA/AA/33/7
121   Cited in Pope-Hennessy, James, *Queen Mary*, George Allen & Unwin Ltd, London, 1959, p.396
122   Worth, Jean-Philippe, *A Century of Fashion*, Little Brown, Boston, 1928
122   Courtesy of Jane Ridley who had letters transcribed for her biography of King Edward VII.
124   Document online here: https://books.google.co.uk/books?id=XJJHvZplE1YC&dq=Mary+Bettans&source=gbs_navlinks_s
134   Cited here: https://trove.nla.gov.au/newspaper/article/18464203#pstart1017634
135   Staniland, Kay, *In Royal Fashion*, Museum of London Publications, London, 1997, p.13

9. Fits Like a Glove

139   Cited in Eldred, Ellis B., *Gloves and the Glove Trade*, Sir Isaac Pitman & Sons, London, 1921, p.53

Notes on Sources

142 Cited in Redwood, Mike, *Gloves and Glove-Making*, Shire Publications, London, 2016, p.38
142 Eldred, Ellis B., op. cit., p.73

10. Queens of Couture

150 Trubert-Tollu, Chantal, Tétart-Vittu, Françoise, Martin-Hattemberg, Jean-Marie and Olivieri, Fabrice, *The House of Worth 1858–1954: The Birth of Haute Couture*, Thames & Hudson, London, 2017, p.26
151 Hartnell, Norman, op. cit., p.15
151 Ibid., p.24
152 Ibid., p.30
152 Ibid., p.31
153 Ibid., p.33
153 Ibid.
154 https://hforhistory.co.uk/h-for-history-posts/2019/02/07/an-interview-with-betty-foster-the-background-to-jennifer-robsons-the-gown/
154 Ibid.
155 https://www.sfh.org.uk/news/my-experience-of-being-the-queens-dressmaker
156 McDowell, Colin, *A Hundred Years of Royal Style*, Muller, Blond & White, London, 1985, p.40
157 Oldfield, Bruce, *Rootless: An Autobiography*, Hutchinson, London, 2004, p.1
158 Ibid., p.20
158 Ibid.
158 Ibid., p.177
159 Ibid., p.178
159 Ibid., p.222
159 Ibid., p.227
159 Ibid., p.260
162 Kelly, Angela, op. cit., p.65

Notes on Sources

11. A Travelling Wardrobe

165 Mallet, Victor (ed), *Life with Queen Victoria: Letters from Court 1887–1901*, John Murray, London, 1968, pp.25–6

168 The design can be seen here, in the National Archives: https://beta.nationalarchives.gov.uk/explore-the-collection/stories/registered-design-for-expanding-travelling-basket/

169 Online journals here: http://www.queenvictoriasjournals.org/search/displayItem.do?FormatType=fulltextimgsrc&QueryType=articles&ResultsID=3443636762508&filterSequence=0&PageNumber=1&ItemNumber=1&ItemID=qvj09048&volumeType=PSBEA

170 Oliver Montagu's journal, Royal Photographic Collection, RPC 04/0004/1

170 Saturday, 22 August 1868, Queen Victoria's Journals online archive: http://www.queenvictoriasjournals.org/search/displayItem.do?FormatType=fulltextimgsrc&QueryType=articles&ResultsID=3443636762508&filterSequence=0&PageNumber=1&ItemNumber=7&ItemID=qvj12984&volumeType=PSBEA

170 Saturday, 12 September 1868, Queen Victoria's Journals online archive: http://www.queenvictoriasjournals.org/search/displayItem.do?FormatType=fulltextimgsrc&QueryType=articles&ResultsID=3443646204097&filterSequence=0&PageNumber=1&ItemNumber=8&ItemID=qvj13005&volumeType=PSBEA

171 Tuesday, 24 April 1888, Queen Victoria's Journals online archive: http://www.queenvictoriasjournals.org/search/displayItem.do?FormatType=fulltextimgsrc&QueryType=articles&ResultsID=3443654523567&filterSequence=0&PageNumber=1&ItemNumber=18&ItemID=qvj20162&volumeType=PSBEA

171 Frost, Sarah Annie, *The Art of Dressing Well*, Dick & Fitzgerald, New York, 1870, p.61

171 Stoney, B. and Weltzien, H., op. cit., p.50

171 Ibid., p.88

Notes on Sources

172 Saturday, 11 August 1858, Queen Victoria's Journals online archive: http://www.queenvictoriasjournals.org/search/displayItem.do?FormatType=fulltextimgsrc&QueryType=articles&ResultsID=3443827877010&filterSequence=0&PageNumber=1&ItemNumber=6&ItemID=qvjo8260&volumeType=PSBEA

173 Stoney, B. and Weltzien, H., op. cit., p.89

173 Kelly, Angela, op. cit., p.217

173 Ibid., p.209

175 The National Archives, London, England, UK, *War Office: Soldiers' Documents, First World War* W0363

177 Celebrating 100 Years, The Papworth Trust, https://www.flipbookpdf.net/web/site/bda0aec73f1cbebd1d8e76ba1c397fcdfff62e23FBP20426560.pdf.html#page/92

177 Kelly, Angela, op. cit., p.219

12. Sharp Suits

179 Cited in Blackman, Cally, 'Walking Amazons: The Development of the Riding Habit in England During the Eighteenth Century' in *Costume*, Vol.35, 2001, p.49

180 Thursday, 28 September 1837, Queen Victoria's Journals online archive: http://www.queenvictoriasjournals.org/search/displayItem.do?ItemNumber=1861&FormatType=fulltextimgsrc&QueryType=articles&ResultsID=3448820247810&filterSequence=0&PageNumber=2&ItemID=qvj01861&volumeType=ESHER

182 Cited in Unite-Jones, W., *The Button Industry*, Sir Isaac Pitman & Sons, London, 1924, p.53

182 Cited in ibid., p.56

184 North, Susan, 'John Redfern & Sons 1847–1892' in *Costume*, Vol.42, 2008, p.153

184 Ibid.

187 Vanderbilt Balsan, Consuelo, *The Glitter and the Gold*, George Mann, Maidstone, 1973, p.99

Notes on Sources

189 Cited in Kjellberg, A. and North, S., *Style and Splendour: The Wardrobe of Queen Maud of Norway*, V&A Publications, London, 2005, p.94

191 Cited in Walker, Richard, *The Savile Row Story*, Prion Books, London, 1988, p.86

192 Ibid., p.162

192 https://fashiontourslondon.co.uk/the-last-tailor-of-bespoke-riding-breeches/

13. Off-duty Tweed

195 Sky news interview, June 2022: https://www.youtube.com/watch?v=Uw9g1Q74t4s

196 Cited here: https://www.scottishtartans.co.uk/Act_of_Proscription_1746_-_The_Tartan_Ban_-_Fact_or_Myth.pdf

198 Kinloch-Anderson, Deirdre, *Tailored for Scotland*, Waverley Books, Glasgow, 2020, p.44

198 Ibid., p.63

200 Barty-King, Hugh, *Pringle of Scotland and the Hawick Knitwear Story*, JJG Publishing, Norfolk, 2006, p.110

203 Cited in Walker, Richard, op. cit., p.53

204 Howarth, Stephen, op. cit., p.55

204 Henry Poole & Co., 15 Savile Row, Livery Ledger 1863–1869, Folio 25

205 Howarth, Stephen, op. cit., p.42

206 Howarth, Stephen, op. cit., p.67

207 Cited in Weston, Siân, *The Changing Face of Burberry*, Bloomsbury Visual Arts, London, 2023, p.21

209 Kitson, Brian, *Burberry Days*, Austin Macauley, London, 2016

14. The Secrets of Stockings

211 https://ietarchivesblog.org/2022/05/12/a-right-royal-get-together/

213 Cited in Farrell, Jeremy, *Socks and Stockings*, Batsford, London, 1992, p.8

214 Palmer, Marilyn, *Framework Knitting*, Shire Publications, London, 1984, p.6

214 Cited in ibid., p.14

Notes on Sources

216 *The Milliner and Dressmaker*, May 1875, p.24
216 *The Young Ladies' Journal*, December 1890, p.346
217 *Greenock Telegraph and Clyde Shipping Gazette*, 27 February, 1901
222 https://www.walesonline.co.uk/business/business-news/mix-old-new-takes-hosiery-2167224

15. Silk and Structure

226 Barry, William, *The Corset and the Crinoline*, Ward, Lock & Tyler, London, 1868, p.195
226 Mactaggart, R. A., 'Half a Century of Corset Making: Mrs Turner's Recollections', in *Costume*, Vol.11, 1977, pp.123–32, p.126
228 Caplin, Roxey, *Health and Beauty or Woman and Her Clothing*, Kent & Co., London, 1856, p.114
230 Cited in Adburgham, Alison, *Shops and Shopping 1800–1914*, Barrie & Jenkins, London, 1989, p.133
233 Mactaggart, R. A., op. cit., p.132
234 Kenton, June, *Storm in a D Cup*, Briars House, London, 2017, p.27
234 Ibid., p.41
235 Ibid., p.2

16. What Lies Beneath

237 Allen, Nicholas, *The Queen's Knickers*, Hutchinson, London, 1993, p.1
238 Cited in Ridley, Jane, *Bertie – A Life of Edward VII*, Chatto & Windus, London, 2012, p.81
238 Ibid., p.85
239 Cited in Wynne, Deborah, '"The Despised Trade" in Textiles: H. G. Wells, William Paine, Charles Cavers and the Male Draper's Life, 1870–1914' in *Textile History*, Vol.46, Issue 1, 2016, pp.99–113, p.99
240 Wells, H. G., *Experiment in Autobiography*, J. P. Lippincott, Philadelphia, 1934, pp.89–90
250 Allen, Nicholas, op. cit., p.31

Notes on Sources

17. Hidden Women

253 RA/VIC/ADDJ/1591,1592
254 Cited in Battiscombe, Georgina, *Queen Alexandra*, Sphere Books, London, 1972, p.202
254 RPC/03/0069, Folio 4
255 https://helenrappaport.com/queen-victoria/the-curious-tale-of-queen-victorias-dresser/
256 Letter in the Royal Archive – RA/Z/20262
258 RA/QM/PRIV/CC058/162
258 Ibid.
261 MacLeod, John, 'The Remarkable Reign of QE3' in the *Scottish Daily Mail*, 15 September, 2018
261 Ibid.
261 Ibid.
262 English, Rebecca, 'The row that drove Queen to sleep in servants' quarters', *Scottish Daily Mail*, 2 February, 2019
262 Kelly, Angela, op. cit., p.22
263 Ibid.
263 Ibid., p.23
263 Ibid., p.27
264 Ibid., p.81
265 Cited in Stoney, Benita and Weltzien, Heinrich C. (eds), op. cit., p.64
265 Stoney, Benita and Weltzien, Heinrich C. (eds), op. cit., p.66

18. Public Grief

270 Muller, Helen, *Jet Jewellery and Ornaments*, Shire Publications, London, 1980, p.16
273 Speight, Alexanna, *The Lock of Hair*, self-published, London, 1871, p.83
273 Ibid., p.84
274 Ibid., p.87

Notes on Sources

276 Taylor, Lou, *Mourning Dress: A Costume and Social History*, George Allen & Unwin, London, 1983, p.211
277 Ibid., p.217
277 Ibid., p.219
278 Coleman, D. C., *Courtaulds: An Economic and Social History Volume 1*, Clarendon Press, London, 1969, p.241
278 Cited in Taylor, Lou, op. cit., p.197
279 Mallet, Victor (ed), op. cit., p.204
280 Cited here: https://www.theguardian.com/uk-news/2022/sep/19/royal-family-turns-out-in-flawless-fashion-for-the-queens-funeral

Epilogue: New Beginnings

284 Greville, Charles, *A Journal of the Reign of Queen Victoria from 1837 to 1852*, Longmans, Green & Co., London, 1885, p.107
286 Strong, Sir Roy, *Coronation: A History of Kingship and the British Monarchy*, HarperCollins, London, 2005, pp.372–4
287 *The Caledonian Mercury*, Monday, 13 June, 1831, p.2

Select Bibliography

Abrevaya Stein, Sarah, *Plumes: Ostrich Feathers, Jews and a Lost World of Global Commerce*, Yale University Press, New Haven, 2008

Adburgham, Alison, *Shops and Shopping 1800–1914*, Barrie & Jenkins, London, 1989

Amies, Hardy, *Hardy Amies: Still Here – An Autobiography*, Weidenfeld & Nicolson, London, 1984

Arch, Nigel and Marschner, Joanna, *Splendour at Court: Dressing for Royal Occasions since 1700*, Unwin Hyman Ltd, London, 1987

Barty-King, Hugh, *Pringle of Scotland and the Hawick Knitwear Story*, JJG Publishing, Norfolk, 2006

Campbell, U., *Robes of the Realm: 300 Years of Ceremonial Dress*, Michael O'Mara Books Ltd, London, 1989

Clabburn, Pamela, *The Norwich Shawl*, Norfolk Museums Service, Norfolk, 1995

Cox, Pamela and Hobley, Annabel, *Shopgirls*, Arrow Books, London, 2014

Farrell, Jeremy, *Socks and Stockings*, Batsford, London, 1992

Field, Leslie, *The Queen's Jewels*, Harry N. Abrams Inc., New York, 1987

Hartnell, Norman, *Silver and Gold*, Evans Brothers Ltd, London, 1955

Howarth, Stephen, *Henry Poole: Founders of Savile Row*, Bene Factum Publishing, Honiton, 2003

Jones, Stephen, *Hats – An Anthology*, V&A Publications, London, 2009

Kay-Williams, S., *An Unbroken Thread: Celebrating 150 Years of the Royal School of Needlework*, ACC Art Books, Woodbridge, 2022

Kelly, Angela, *The Other Side of the Coin*, HarperCollins, London, 2019

Kenton, June, *Storm in a D Cup*, Briars House, London, 2017

Kinloch-Anderson, Deirdre, *Tailored for Scotland*, Waverley Books, Glasgow, 2020

Select Bibliography

Kjellberg, A. and North, S., *Style and Splendour: The Wardrobe of Queen Maud of Norway*, V&A Publications, London, 2005, p.94

MacCarthy, Fiona, *Last Curtsey: The End of the Debutantes*, Faber & Faber, London, 2006

Matthews David, Alison, *Fashion Victims*, Bloomsbury, London, 2015

McDowell, Colin, *A Hundred Years of Royal Style*, Muller, Blond & White, London, 1985

McDowell, Colin, *Hats: Status, Style and Glamour*, Thames & Hudson, London, 1992

Menkes, Suzy, *The Royal Jewels*, Guild Publishing, London, 1985

Muller, Helen, *Jet Jewellery and Ornaments*, Shire Publications, London, 1980

Oldfield, Bruce, *Rootless: An Autobiography*, Hutchinson, London, 2004

Pick, Michael, *Rayne: Shoes for Stars*, AAC Editions, Woodbridge, 2015

Redwood, Mike, *Gloves and Glove-Making*, Shire Publications, London, 2016

Staniland, Kay, *In Royal Fashion*, Museum of London Publications, London, 1997

Stoney, Benita and Weltzien, Heinrich C. (eds), *My Mistress the Queen: The Letters of Frieda Arnold, Dresser to Queen Victoria*, Weidenfeld & Nicolson, London, 1994

Strong, Sir Roy, *Coronation: A History of Kingship and the British Monarchy*, HarperCollins, London, 2005

Taylor, Lou, *Mourning Dress: A Costume and Social History*, George Allen & Unwin, London, 1983

Thaarup, Aage, *Heads and Tales*, Cassel & Co., London, 1956

Walker, Catherine, *Catherine Walker: An Autobiography*, HarperCollins, London, 1998

Walker, Richard, *The Savile Row Story*, Prion Books, London, 1988

Westman, Annabel, *Fringe, Frog and Tassel*, Philip Wilson Publishers, London, 2019

Weston, Siân, *The Changing Face of Burberry*, Bloomsbury Visual Arts, London, 2023

Index

References in *italics* refer to images.

Abraham, Samuel, 41, 42
Abraham, Victor, 41, 42
Act of Proscription (1746), 196
Ada Lewis Women's Lodging House, London, 32
Addley Bourne, 229–30, 233, 236
Addley Bourne, Ann *née* Philpot, 228–30, 236
Albert, Prince of Saxe-Coburg and Gotha, 6–7, 107, 196, 197, 245, 268, 269, 276, 280
Alexander McQueen, 280, 288
Alexandra, Queen Consort, 15, 30, 76, 78, 82, 83–4, 89, 90, 170, 238
   coronation garments and regalia, 15, 27, 30–3, 65, 284
   corsets and, 228, 236
   dressers and, 253–4, 255–7, 262
   dressmakers and, 121–2, 123, 126–8, 136
   luggage and, 165, 168, 169
   rheumatic fever and scoliosis, 129–30, 136
   riding habit, 204
   shoes and stockings, 216
   tailoring and, 180, 182–3, 184, 186–7, 189, 193–4
   travelling from Denmark to London, 165, 169
   Welsh flannel and, 220
Alice, Princess of Battenberg, 70
Allan, Nicholas, 237, 250
Allen, Johnny, 192

Amies, Hardy, 42, 84–6, 88, 99, 101, 156, 160, 261
Anderson, William, 197, 210
Andrew, Thomas, 269
Andrews, Charles, 253
Andrews, Mary Ann, 253
Anello & Davide, 106, 118
Anne, Princess Royal, 68, 137
Anne, Queen of Great Britain, 2
anti-Semitism, 127, 158
Appleby, Mark, 71
Aquascutum, 206
Armes, Elizabeth *née* Fish, 75–6
Armes, William, 75–6, 88
Arnold, Frieda, 10–11, 171–3, 177, 178, 252, 253, 265
arsenic, 97–8
Art of Dressing Well, The (Frost), 171
Arthur, Prince, Duke of Connaught and Strathearn, 67
Ashmolean Museum, Oxford, 138–9
Asnières-sur-Seine, France, 167
Asscher, Joseph, 62
Atwood, Ada, 207–8, 209
Atwood, Annie, 207–8, 209
austerity policies, 71

Baalum, Emily, 238–9, 243, 244, 250
Balance, Arthur, 244
Balmoral Castle, 103, 195–6, 197, 253, 267

Index

Banner, Bernadette, 227
Barker, J. W., 270–72
Barrett Street Trade School, London, 38
Barry, William, 226, 227
Basingstoke, 206, 207, 208
Batteson, Rose, 22
Battle of Culloden (1746), 196
Battle of Mons (1914), 66
Battle of Passchendaele (1917), 176
Battle of the Somme (1916), 176
Beard, Eliza, 183
Beard, John, 13–14, 15
Beard, Maud, 85–6, 88
Beaton, Cecil, 42, 98
Beatrice, Princess of the United Kingdom, 163
Beaumont, George Howland, 244
Beazley, Caroline, 183
Beck, William, 199
bedding ceremonies, 237–8
Bedfordshire, 90, 94
Belgian border, 165, 169
Berkeley dress show, 160
Berlei Corset School, London, 234
Bernard Weatherill, 190–91, 192, 194
Bettans, Mary, 123–5, 126
Bettans, Samuel, 123–4, 125
Bingley, Charles, 205
Bingley, Godfrey, 91
Birkin, Ann, 215, 216–18, 217, 219, 223
Birmingham, 182
Black and White (magazine), 35
Blackfriars, London, 7–8
Blackpool, 132, 135
Blazeby, Amelia, 11, 50, 58
Blossier, Albert, 128
Blossier, Victoire *née* Morin, 127–8, 129
Board of Trade, 55, 207

Bobergh, Otto Gustav, 150
Bocking Mill, Braintree, 277, 278, *278*
Boer Wars, 62
Bond Street, London, 116, 117, 133, 135
Book of Illustrations (catalogue), 230
Book of the Feet, The (Hall), 110
Boulton, Miss, 31
Bourne, Benjamin, 229, 230
Bowen Richardson, Louise, 153, 163
Box, James Alexander, 175–6, 178
Braintree, Essex, 13–14, 15, 18, 277, 278
Branston, Mary Ann, 232
Branston, Sarah Elizabeth, 232
Bridge, John, 63
Britain
  etiquette, 279
  fashion, 149–65
  post-war, 46, 60, 67, 144–5, 154, 157, 208, 211, 234
British Empire, 61
British Pathé, 21, 99, 101, 104, 117, *117*
Brown, Cornelius, 55
Brummell, Beau, 179
Bruton Street, London, 3, 37, 152, 153–4
Bucephalus (dummy horse), 205, 206
Buckingham Palace, 2, 25, 45, 49, 68, 86, 106, 146, 153, 159, 234–5, 245, 253
  census, 242, 257
  Dresser's Floor, 103, 178, 263–4
  exhibition of the Queen's wardrobe, 40–41
  garments and regalia from Charles III coronation, 28, 287
  linen and, 242, 244
Burberry, 196, 207–10, 222
  fakery, 208
  trench coat (Tielocken), 207–8, 210
Burberry, Thomas, 206–7, 210
Burney, Fanny, 95
Burritt, Elihu, 247

Index

Busvine, John, 187–8
Busvine, William, 188–9

Caledonian Mercury, 287
Cambridgeshire Tuberculosis Colony, 174
Camilla, Queen Consort, 28, 285, 287
    coronation dress, 160, 287
    ivory *peau de soie*, 287
Campbell, Donald, 161
Campbell, Miss (Cammie), 85
Canter, Charles, 55
Caplin, Roxey, 228, 229, 233, 236
Capper, Walter, 238, 241
Carroll, Lewis, 97
Cartier, 60
Carver, Hilda, 18
cashmere knitwear, 199–200, 210
Catherine, Princess of Wales, 43, 88, 280, 288
Cavanagh, John, 156, 161
Cave, Benjamin, 167
Cave, Harriet Jane *née* Hackett, 167–9, 177
Central Saint Martins College of Art, London, 158
ceremonial robes, 4
    Dalmatica, 4
    Robe of Estate, 4, 5, 15, 17, 18, 37
    Robe Royal, 5
    Supertunica, 4, 286
    velvet robes of state, 285–6
Charles III, King of the United Kingdom, 28, 199, 209, 222
    Colobium Sindonis, 286
    coronation, 43, 283–4, 285–8
    coronation silk overshirt, 286
    crimson velvet robes of state, 285–6
    Imperial Mantle, 286–7
    purple velvet robes of state, 285–6
    Supertunica, 286

Charlotte, Princess Royal, 238
Charlotte, Queen Consort, 46, 237
Charnock family, 176
Chartres Cathedral, France, 4
Chelsea Design Company, 86–7
Cheriton, Ann *née* Poole, 52–4, 58
child labour, 92–3, 104, 124
Children's Employment Commission, 93
Churchyard, James, 76–8, 77, 88
Churchyard, Susannah, 76–7, 78
Clabburn Sons & Crisp, 76
Clapham, Emily, 123, 130–32, 132, 136
Clark, William, 113
Clarke, Jane, 127
Clarke, Louisa, 124
Clothworkers' Company, 137
coal-mining industry, 221
Collander, Helen, 197
Collett, Jess, 288
Complete English Tradesman, The (Defoe), 111
Cook, Fanny, 92
Cook, Sarah Jane, 91–2, 91, 93, 104
Copsey, Herbert Henry, 191
Corgi Socks, 221–3, 224
Cornelia James, 143–6, 148
Cornelius, William, 66–7
coronation velvet, 17
corsets, 225–36
    boning, 227
    corset-making industry, 226–32
    glove-fitting corset, 227–8
    royal corsets, 225, 227, 228–9, 230, 233, 234–6
    swanbill corset, 230
cost-of-living crisis, 283
cottage industry, 75, 111, 215
court dressmakers, 47–58
Courtauld, Samuel, 276

Index

Courtaulds, 276–9, 278
Courtaulds: An Economic and Social History, 278
couturiers, 149
Covid-19 pandemic, 29, 71, 103, 163
Cowes, Isle of Wight, 183, 184, 186
    regatta, 183
crape, 276–80
    black crape weavers, 268
    Courtaulds crape, 276–9, 278
Crown Jewels, 59–71
    Cambridge Lover's Knot tiara, 65
    Crown Jeweller, 64, 67–8, 71
    Elizabeth II engagement ring, 70, 71
    George III fringe tiara, 67–8
    Imperial Crown of India, 65
    Imperial State Crown, 4, 68, 69
    see also diamonds
Cruikshank, George, 239, 240
Cruikshank, Isaac, 237
Cubitt, Thomas, 245, 250
Culley, Alfred, 203
Cullinan, Thomas, 61
Cundy, Samuel, 206
Curzon, Mary, 284

Daly, Gwyneth, 232–3
David, Alison Matthews, 96–7
Davies, John, 219
Davies, Thomas, 220
Davies, William, 66–7
Debenham & Freebody, 58
Debenhams, 83
Debenham's Ladies' Club, 83
Debrett's, 279
debutantes, 45–7, 57–8
    deportment and the art of the curtsey, 57–8
    presentation gowns, 45–7, 58

Defoe, Daniel, 111
Delhi Durbar (1911), 65
Dent, Garwood, 203–4, 210
Dent, John, 139
Dents, 139–41, 143, *143*, 146, 147
Derby, Lady, 259
Desiree, Madame, 151, 152
diamonds, 60–61
    Cullinan diamond, 61–2
    cutting, 62
    diamond diadem, 63
    Koh-i-noor diamond, 60–61
Diana, Princess of Wales, 42, 65, 86, 87–8
    fittings at Kensington Palace, 159
    maternity blouse, 87
    tailored coats, 87–8
Dickens, Charles, 16–17, 61, 182, 239
Diderot, Denis, 140, 141, 226
Dieulafait & E. Bouclier, 78, *79*
Dior, Christian, 116
Dittweiler, Miss, 96
Dobbs, Agnes, 201
Dolby, Anastasia, 33
Doré, George, 15–17, 19, 27–8, *27*, 31
Douglas, Lewis, 223
Downing, Marie, 254–5
Dr Barnardo's Homes, 157
draper's shops, 206
drapery, 182, 219
Dress Diary of Mrs Anne Sykes, The, 148
dressers to the Queen, 251–65
    dressers' diaries, 258–9, 263–4
    principal dresser, 251–2
    'Relative to Household Appointments', 256
    second dressers, 252
    wardrobe maids, 252

316

Index

dressmaking for the Queen, 121–36
   corsage, 128–9, 130
   measurement system, 128
Drion-Regnier, Madame, 235–6
Drury, Roy, 177
Dudley, Martha, 123, 125, 126, 135
Duff Gordon, Lucile, 47–8, 149, 151–2
Duleep Singh, Maharaja of the Sikh Empire, 61
Duley, Edie, 38, 39, 42
Dust, Lucy Rudd, 51–2, 53, 58

E. Wolfe & Co., 65, 66–7
East End, London, 15–16, 19–20, 79
   workshops, 57
economic crash (2008), 71
Ede, Anne, 23, 27
Ede, Joseph, 23–4
Ede, Joseph (son), 24
Ede & Ravenscroft, 4, 14, 19, 20, 21–7, 26, 31, 286
Ede, Rosa, 28, 286
Edward III, King of England, 7
Edward VII, King of the United Kingdom, 30, 62, 89, 182
   coronation, 31, 284
   coronation mantle, 34–5
   fertility and, 238
   Kanné, Joseph Julius and, 169, 171
   scarlet wedding tunic, 204
   tartan and, 197
Edward VIII, King of the United Kingdom, 261
Egerton Burnett, 9
Elizabeth, the Queen Mother (Queen Consort to George VI), 3–4, 14, 67, 160, 176, 285
   corsets and, 235, 236
   death of, 267

   dressers and, 260, 260
   hats and, 98
   Pringle and, 200–201
   shoes and, 117
   wedding dress, 133
Elizabeth I, Queen of England and Ireland, 2
   coronation, 2
   coronation gloves, 138
Elizabeth II, Queen of United Kingdom, 2–5, 41, 60, 73, 81, 156, 157, 160, 178
   1957 white duchesse satin gown, 41
   Corgi Socks and, 222
   corsets and, 234–5
   death of, 71, 103, 209, 267, 279, 287
   dressers and, 259–64
   dressmakers and, 134
   engagement ring, 70, 71
   'Flowers of the Fields of France' gown, 40
   funeral of, 43, 279–80, 281
   George III fringe tiara and, 68
   Griffin, Richard and, 195
   hats and, 101–4
   honeymoon gloves, 145
   luggage and, 173–4, 176–7
   MacDonald, Margaret 'Bobo' and, 259–62, 260
   off-duty clothes, 196, 199, 200
   outerwear and, 73–4, 84–5, 88
   Platinum Jubilee, 162, 195
   postage stamps and, 63
   raincoats, 208
   riding clothes and livery, 191
   royal visit to Kayser Bondor, 211–12
   shoes and, 112, 117–19
   stockings and, 212, 223
   Supertunica, 286
   wedding, 68, 223, 261
   wedding dress, 2, 38, 153–4

Index

Elizabeth II, coronation of, 2–6, 38, 68, 261
   Colobium Sindonis, 5
   dress, 2–3, 37, 40, 153, 155
   gloves, 138
   Robe of Estate, 4, 5, 17, 18, 37
   shoes, 3–4
Ellis, Eldred, 142
'Elves and the Shoemaker, The' (fairytale), 105
Emary, John, 206
embroidery, 29–43
Emily, Princess of Great Britain (Amelia Sophia Eleonore), 179
Essam, Martha, 36
Essam, Ruby, 36–7, 42
Eugénie de Montijo, Empress of the French, 167, 264
Evening Standard, 259
Extraordinary Accounts, 240–41

Factories Act, 131, 152, 207
'factory gate' reels (Mitchell & Kenyon), 231
fascism, 233
fashion designers, 149–64
Fashion Museum, Bath, 187
feather industry, 54–8
   New York workshop, 57
   ostrich feather curlers, 55–7
   plumassiers, 54
Fechter, Charles, 204
Federation of Merchant Tailors, 191
Female Enemy Alien internment programme, 233
Femina (journal), 185
Ferragamo, Salvatore, 108, 116
Festival of Empire exhibition, 258
Field, Leslie, 60–61
Fifth Avenue, New York, 184
Filmer, Keturah, 114–16, 119

First of May, The (Winterhalter), 67
Fish, James, 75–6
Fisher family, 197
fit model, 2, 5–6
fitters, 48, 85–6, 205
Fleming, Catherine, 239, 249
fleur-de-lis, 4
Ford, Avis, 134–5, 135, 136
Forrer, Antoine, 275, 280
Foster, Betty, 153–4, 155
Foster, Elene, 134
Fowler, Miss, 86
Fox, Frederick, 101, 102, 103, 104
Fox, George, 63–4
Frederick, Prince of Württemberg, 238
Freedom of the City of London award, 241
French, Joe, 177
French dressmakers, 127
Frost, Sarah Annie, 171
Froud, Emma, 257
furniture trade, 78–9

gabardine, 206–7
Gadney, Frank, 22
Gage, Asha, 211
Ganderton, Lucinda, 245–6
Garrard & Co., 60, 64–5, 67
Gentry, Caroline, 277–8, 280
George II, King of Great Britain and Ireland, 23
George III, King of the United Kingdom, 23, 46, 63, 237
   coronation of, 23
   fringe tiara, 67
George IV, King of the United Kingdom, 63, 196–7, 286–7
George V, King of the United Kingdom, 121, 176, 191, 199, 285

Index

coronation regalia, 25
Robe of Estate, 15
George VI, King of the United Kingdom, 4, 133, 176, 199, 261, 285
   Colobium Sindonis, 286
   coronation regalia, 18, 37, 65
   death of, 267
   Supertunica, 286
Gervers Fellowship, 129
Gidal, Tim, 100
Gieve, Elizabeth, 123, 125, 126
Giltrap, Harriet, 255–7, 256
Globe-Trotter suitcases, 177
gloves, 137–48
   ceremonial, 138
   Elizabeth II's honeymoon gloves, 145
   fabric, 143
   glove cutters, 140–41
   glove making, 138–48, *140*, *143*
   Henry VIII's hawking glove, 139
   leather, 139–43
   workshops, 141
Gold, Sarah, 231
Gold State Coach, 2, 5
goldsmiths, 62–3
Goldsmiths & Silversmiths Company, 68
Goodenday, John, 211
Goodship, Harold, 68–70, *69*
Graham, Gerry, 200–201, 210
Great Depression, 208, 220
Great Exhibition (1851), 74–5, 168, 228, 269
   medal, 228, 236
Great Fire of London (1666), 8
Great Wardrobe, The, 7–8
Greville, Charles, 284
Griffin, Richard, 195
Gundry, Richard, 106, 118
Gundry, William, 107, 109, 111
Gundry & Son, 106, 107, *107*, 109–10

H. J. Cave, 167–9
H. & M. Rayne, 106, 112–13, 114–18, 119
Hackett, Samuel, 167
Hall, Joseph Sparkes, 106, 110–11, 118
Hampton Court, 30, 137
Hand & Lock, 42–3
hand-loom weavers, 15–16
Hand, Monsieur, 42
Handley-Seymour, Elizabeth *née* Fielding, 123, 132–5, 136
Hanhart, Margaretta, 276
Harding, Jean, 154–5
Hardman, William, 89
Harmsworth Encyclopaedia of Retail Trading, 20
Harrison, Eliza, 141–2
Harrison, Margaret, 141–2, 146, 147
Harrison, Thomas, 141
Harrods, 49, 199, 259
Hartnell, Norman, 84, 145, 149–56, 160, 163
   Colobium Sindonis, 5
   Elizabeth II's coronation gown and, 1–6, 153, 156
   Elizabeth II's wedding dress and, 153–4
   embellishment practices, 37, 38
   embroidery workshop, 39
   foundation of own couture establishment, 152–4
   path to fashion, 151–2
   royal commissions, 154–6
   sketches, *155*
Hartnell's, 38, 39, 43
Harvey, Anna, 159
Harvey, Henry, 112
Haslett, Caroline, 211
hats *see* millinery
Hattrick, Jane, 37–8, 39
'Haunted Lady or the Ghost in the Looking Glass, The' (Leech), 127

Index

haute couture, 150
Hawick, Scotland, 199–200, 201, 210
'Heady Stuff' (short film), 100–101
Health and Beauty (Caplin), 228, 229
Helena, Princess of the United Kingdom, 34
Henry VIII, King of England, 139
Henry Poole & Co., 196, 202–7, 209, 210
Heritage Crafts Association, 137–8
Highlands, Scotland, 196–7
   Highland dress, 197–8
Hill, Elizabeth, 111, 119
Hoath, Peggy, 262–3, 265
Hoffman, A. W., 97–8
Hogarth, William, 226
Holliday, Miss, 153, 154, 155, 163
Holt, Sarah, 109–10, 111, 119
Holyroodhouse, Edinburgh, 262
horse-riding, 202
hosiery, 199
House of Commons, 191, 194
House of Fraser, 177
House of Lords, 20
House of Lucile, 48, 50
House of Worth, 50, 122, 150–51
Household Words (magazine), 16, 182
Huguenots, 15–16, 42
Hull, 130, 132
   museum, 131
human hair jewellery, 272–6
   specialist hair workers, 268, 272–3, 275–6, 280
Hurley, Alec, 113
Hyderabad, India, 60

I. & R. Morley, 215, 216, 218
Illustrated London News, 230
Imperial State Crown, 4, 37, 68
In at the Deep End, 160
In Royal Fashion (Staniland), 135

Incorporated Society of London Fashion Designers, 156
India-rubber, 110
industrial change, 190
Industrial Revolution, 276
industrialisation, 80
internment, 144
Isaacson, Elise, *née* Jaeger, 127
Isle of Wight, 182–3

J. Busvine & Co., 180, 187–9, 194
jacquard fabrics, 287
James, Cornelia, 143–5, 147, 233
James Lawson, Genevieve, 144–7, 148
Jay's (London General Mourning Warehouse), 51–2
Jennens, 180
Jennens, Charles, 181
jet, 268–72, 276, 280
   'leading', 270
   Whitby jet, 269–72, 271
Jewelled Shoes (British Pathé film), 117, 117
Jewish people, 20, 41, 58, 144
jodhpurs, 202
Jones, Rhys, 221–22
Jones, Stephen, 90, 101, 280
Jones, Thomas, 219
Joseph Box shoe company, 106, 112, 118
Joseph Jennens & Co., 181
Judah, Cynthia, 116–17
Jurassic period, 268–9

Kanné, Joseph Julius, 169–71, 172, 173, 177
Kay-Williams, Susan, 35
Kayser Bondor stocking factory, 211–12
Kelly, Angela, 102–3, 118, 162, 163, 173–4, 177–8, 252, 262–4, 264, 265
Kelly's Directory, 113
Kensington Palace, 30, 87, 159

Index

Kenton, Harold, 234, 235
Kenton, June, 234–5
Kenya, 261
Kilgour (tailor), 192
Killerton House, Exeter, 81–3, 279
Kinloch Anderson, 196, 197–8, 200, 210
Kinloch-Anderson, Deirdre, 198
Kinloch, William, 198
Kitson, Brian, 209

labourer's smocks, 206
Ladies Field (journal), 189
ladies' sportswear, 199
Ladies' Work Society, 31, 32–3
Lady (magazine), 248
Lady's World (magazine), 51
Lambert, Madame, 236
Lambeth, London, 113–14
Lancaster, Ann, 218
Lawson, Andrew, 146
Lee, Lily, 17–19, *19*, 28
Lee, William, 213
Leech, John, 127
Leisure Hour (periodical), 182
Leopold I, King of Belgium, 253
Liber Regalis, 285
Liverpool, 188, 263
Lock of Hair, The (Speight), 272–5, *274*
Lock, Stanley, 42
London
   College of Fashion, 38
   Library, 2
   Marathon, 146
   Museum, 2
   Regiment, 66
   Zoological Gardens, 89
London Art Fashion Journal, 20
London City Trade Directories, 21

London County Council, 152
   bomb damage maps, 69
London Gazette, 158
London Palladium, 133
London Society (magazine), 58
London, Suzannah, 280
Lord Chamberlain's Department, 6–8, 64
Lord, Kitty, 113–14
Lord Steward's Department, 6–7
Loren, Sophia, 108
Louis IV, King of France, 105
Louis Vuitton, 166–7
Louise, Princess, Duchess of Argyll, 31
Lucas, Otto, 100–101
Lucerne, Switzerland, 170
Luftwaffe, 69
luggage, 166–78
   design, 166
   'Expanding Travelling Basket', 168
   lightweight suitcases, 177
   trunk making, 166, 176
Lumley, Robert, 105
Lunn, Walter, 64
Luton, Bedfordshire, 90, 93, 94
Lyons Corner Houses, 154, 155
Lyth, Joe, 270–72

MacCarthy, Fiona, 45, 49, 58
Macclesfield, Lady, 238
MacDonald, Margaret 'Bobo', 156, 252, 259–62, *260*, 265
Macintosh, Charles, 206
Mackay, Anne, 244
Mad Hatter (character), 97
Madame Clapham, 130–32, *132*
Madame Drion-Regnier, 225
Madame Elise, 126–7, 136
Madame Handley-Seymour, 133, *135*, 285
Madame Lambert, 225, 233

Index

Madame Marcyle, 225, 233
Madame Tussaud, 287
mail-order, 220, 230
Mallet, Marie, 165, 279
Mann, Cecil, 68
Mann, Horace, 179
Manning, R., 54
Mappin & Webb, 71
Marchant, Harry, 70–71
Marcyle, Madame, 236
Maréchal, Monsieur, 167
Margaret, Princess, Countess of Snowdon, 84, 117–18, 134, 176, 235
Maria Feodorovna, Empress of Russia, previously Princess Dagmar of Denmark, 122
Markham, Maureen, 38–41, 42
Marks & Spencer, 233
Marlborough House, London, 242, 244
Marriott, Louisa, 80, 88
Marryat, Charlotte, 36
Marshall & Snelgrove, 82, 83–4, 88, 130, 199
Mary II, Queen of England, 276
Mary of Teck, Queen Consort, 25, 48, 67, 86, 116, 211
   coronation regalia, 25, 284–5
   dressers and, 257–9, 263
   dressmakers and, 121, 123, 133
   sweetheart cushions and, 144
Masters, Violet, 157, 160
Matthew, Jean, 116–17, 117, 118, 119
Maud, Queen of Norway, 131, 189
Mayhew, Henry, 51
McDonald, Daniel, 197
McDowell, Colin, 89
McLaren, Stella, 102–3, 104
Meagher, Sarah Ann, 93
Meakin, John, 215, 218–19, 223
Meier, Christina, 276

Melbourne Cup (horse race), 145
Meldrum, James, 197
Menkes, Suzy, 60
mercury poisoning, 97
Messrs Rodger & Denyer, 239
metallic lace, 41
Metropolitan Museum of Art, New York, 129, 216
Mew, Charlotte, 183
military tunics, 203
Milliner and Dressmaker, 216
millinery, 73–4, 89–105
   animal pelts and, 97
   black mourning hats, 280
   chemicals and, 96–7
   milliners, 90, 94–5
   Parisien milliners, 96–7, 101
   Queen Victoria's mourning bonnet, 90
   royal millinery, 95, 101, 103
   straw, 90
   workrooms, 90, 100–101
   see also straw plait industry
Mirman, Simone, 104
Miss Gray (Fashion House), 84, 85–6
Mitchell and Kenyon, 231
Mobbs, Amelia, 55, 56, 57
Mobbs, Clara, 11, 55–7, 58
Mobbs, Ethel, 56, 57
Mobbs, James, 56
Mobbs, Matilda, 55, 56, 57
Mogul emperors, 60
Mole, Madame, 153
Monroe, Marilyn, 108
Montagu, Oliver, 170
Morin Blossier, 123, 127–30, 136, 284
Morin, Marie, 127–8, 129
Motcomb Street, London, 156, 157, 161, 163
moth infestation, 25–6

Index

Mountbatten, Louis, 1st Earl, 70
Mountcashell, Stephen Moore, 3rd Earl, 204–5
Mrs Addley Bourne (fashion retailer), 225
Mrs Halliburton's Troubles (Wood), 139
Mundy, Lily, 147–8
Museum of Jewish Heritage, New York, 41
Museum of London, 25, 113, 228

Napoleon III, Emperor of the French, 264
Narcissus, 276–7
Nasjonalmuseet, Oslo, 189
National Archives, 8, 240
Nazi regime, 144
New Mills factory, Braintree, 13, 14, 15
New York, 56, 106, 188, 227
Newton Abbot, Devon, 73
Newtown, Wales, 219–20
Nora Bradley Ltd, 49
Norfolk, Bernard Fitzalan-Howard, 16th Duke, 5
Norris, Sally, 147–8
Northampton, 111–12
Norwich, 74–6
   museums, 75
Norwich Mercury, 74, 76
Nottingham, 213, 216

Oatham, Delia, 80
Oatham, Edith, 88
off-duty clothing, 196
   equestrian wear, 202
   knitwear, 199–201
   riding habits, 180–81, 188, 189, 202–6
   tartan, 196–9
   tweed, 196
   waterproof clothing, 206–10
Office of Registrar of Designs, 168
Office of the Robes, 6, 7, 9–10, 254

Office of Woods and Forests, 7
O'Grady, James, 207
Old Vic, London, 113
Oldfield, Betty, 157
Oldfield, Bruce, 149, 157–60, 163, 287
Oliver Twist (Dickens), 61
Order of the Garter, 180
Osborne House, Isle of Wight, 183, 245, 253
outerwear, 73–88
   coats, 73–4, 84–5, 86–8
   dolman, 78
   passementerie, 78–82, 88
   shawls, 74–8
Oxford, 22
   Art College, 156

Palmer, John, 21–2
Papworth Hall, 174–5, 176
Papworth Industries, 174–7
Paris, France, 66, 128–9, 134, 150, 166–7
   World Exhibition (1867), 168
Parsons, Caroline, 95–6, 98
Parvin, Stewart, 149, 160–63, *164*
Pattle, Hugh, 177
Peller, Margit, 233, 234
Pendragon Travel Goods, 174, 176, *178*
Peninsular Wars, 202
Perryman, Mary Frances, 95–6, 98
Perryman & Parsons, 96
'petites mains' (little hands), 30, 87
Philip Antrobus (jewellery house), 70
Philip, Prince, Duke of Edinburgh, 5, 68, 70, 262, 267
Phillips, Mark, 68
Pictorial Encyclopedia of Trades and Industry (Diderot), 140, 141
Picture Post, 116
Plymouth House, London, 69

Index

Poiret, Paul, 133
Ponsonby, Henry, 254
Poole, Edith, 53
Poole, Eliza, 52
Poole, Emma *née* Walker, 205, 206
Poole, Henry, 20, 202–3, 204–6
Poole, James, 202–3
Post Office London Directory, 51, 78–9
postage stamps, 59
Potter, Carrie, 231
Potter, Lily, 231
Powell, Mary, 219
Pranger, Honorina, 125
Prentice, May, 262
Pringle, John, 199
Pringle (magazine), 202
Pringle of Scotland, 196, 199–200, 210
Pryce-Jones (mail-order company), 219–21, 221
Pryce-Jones, Pryce, 219–20, 223–4
public grief, 268–80
  black attire, 279–80
  death of monarchs, 267–8
  mementos of mourning, 268–72, 280
  Operation London Bridge, 267
  see also crape; human hair jewellery; jet
Punch, 58, 127
Punjab, 61

Queen (journal), 90, 184
Queen's Knickers, The (Allan), 237, 250

racism, 157
railways, 167, 201, 220
Ralph Lauren, 222
Ramsay, Allan, 23
Ranjit Singh, Maharaja of the Sikh Empire, 61
Rappaport, Helen, 255
Ravenscroft, Rosanna Ellen (Rosa), 24–6, 27

Rayne *see* H. & M. Rayne
Rayne, Edward, 106
Rayne, Henry Edward, 113, 115, 116
Rayne, Mary Ann *née* Clark, 113–14, 116, 119
Redfern, John, 180, 182–4, 186, 194
Redfern (couture), 50, 182–6, 185, 186, 194
Reeve, Jane, 238–9
Reeves, Betty, 84, 86
Regent Street, London, 51–2, 112, 114, 275
Report on the Employment of Women, 278
Reville & Rossiter, 284
Richard II, King of England, 285
Richmond, London, 96, 239, 245–6, 249–50
Rigby & Peller, 225, 233–5
Rigby, Bertha, 233, 234
RMS *Campania*, 188
RMS *Lusitania*, 188–9
robe makers, 21–8
Robinson, Jessie, 31, 32
Robson, Jennifer, 153
Roden, George, 192
Rolls, John, 183
Rose Yard, Norwich, 76–8
Rowlandson, Thomas, 46
Royal Albert Hall, London, 99
Royal Archive, 8, 218, 252, 256, 258
Royal Ascot, 98
royal bedlinen, 237–8, 241
Royal Collection, 101, 156, 160, 170, 180, 215, 216, 251, 276
Royal College of Art, 116
royal design, 150–64
Royal Field Artillery, 175
royal jewellers, 60
royal journeys, 165–6, 169–78
  packing, 171–3
  royal courier, 169–71, 173
  see also luggage

Index

royal linen, 237–50
   Chedgey box mangle, 247
   laundering, 239, 242, 245–50
   linen maids, 238, 242–4, 248, 250
   royal laundry basket labels, 246, 246
   royal steam laundry, 245–9
Royal Ontario Museum, Toronto, 129
Royal Protection Officer, 195
Royal School of Needlework, 32, 33–7, 284–5, 286
royal tomb effigies, 59
Royal Warrant of Appointment, 8–9
rubberised coats, 206
Rue de la Paix, Paris, 128, 129, 150
Rules and Manners of Good Society, 46
Rundell, Bridge & Rundell, 63
Rundell, Phillip, 63–4
Rush, Richard, 63

Salaman, Isaac, 55
Salaman, Myer, 55
Sandringham Estate, 253, 254
Savile Row, London, 20, 27, 42, 84, 181, 191, 192, 202, 203
sawdust hearts, 144
Schabner, Andrew, 22
School of Art Needlework, 33, 34, 35
'Scientific Corsetry', 233
Scotland, 196–7
Scott, Walter, 196
seamstresses, mistreatment of, 126–7, 131
Second Anglo–Sikh War (1849), 61
Seidon, Tessa, 234
Selfridges, 176
sewing machines, 226, 231
Seymour-Howell, Mrs, 149
Shah, Shuja, 61
shoes/shoemaking, 105–19, 109
   black court shoes, 118

buttonholing, 115
designers, 116–18
elastic boots, 110–11
Elizabeth II's bridal sandals, 118
evening slippers, 107
Louis IV's red heels, 105
machinery and, 111–12
royal women and, 105, 106
Victoria's bridal shoes, 107
wooden lasts, 108, 118
Shrimpton, Jean, 145
Shudall family, 22–3
Shudall, Martha, 23, 24, 27
Sibley, Ada Gertrude, 252, 257–8, 259, 260, 265
Sieveking, Dr, 238
silk
   velvet, 13, 17
   weaving, 14–16
Silver and Gold (Hartnell), 38, 151
Simons, Eleanor *née* Hancock, 238–9, 242–4
Sinclair, Bessie *née* Temple, 252, 253–4, 262, 265
Skerrett, Marianne, 251, 252, 253, 265
Sketches by Boz (Dickens), 239, 240
Smith, John, 112
Smith, Michael, 192–3
Smith, Rosina, 31, 32
socks, 221–22
Somerville, Philip, 102, 103
Sophie, Countess of Wessex, 280
South Africa, 61–2
South Wales, 212, 221
Southgate, Vera, 105
Sparkins, Horatio (character), 239, 240
Sparks, Elizabeth, 248, 249
Sparks, Mary Ann, 248, 249
Sparks, Sarah, 239, 248–9, 250
Speight, Alexanna *née* Harper, 272–5

Index

Speight, Alfred, 273, 275
Sphere (magazine), 37
Spitalfields, London, 15–17
St Edward's Crown, 5
St Mary's Church, Tewantin, 1
Staniland, Kay, 135
Steinegger, Ann, 276
Stewart Parvin couture, 161
stockings, 211–21, 223–4
    cheveners, 215–18
    manufacture, 211–21
    'Stocking Embroideress (HM)', 218
    stocking-frame machine, 213–14, *214*, 218
Stockmar, Baron, 6–7
straw plait industry, 90–93, *91*, 104
    markets, 93–4, *94*
    Mrs Scott's plait school, 93
    plait schools, 92–3
strikes, 190–91
Swan & Edgar, 53
swimwear, 234
Switzerland, 275
Sydney Morning Herald, 134, 135
Sykes, Ji Hae An, 26, *26*
Symington, William, 231
Symington's, 231–3, 236

tailoring, 179–94
    breeches, 191, 192
    buttons, 181–2
    convertible apron skirt, 188
    mail order, 184
    Queen Alexandra's waistcoats, 187
    riding habits, 180–81, 188, 189
    sharp tailoring, 179–94
    tailor strikes, 190–91
    tailor-made garments, 183–7
    Windsor uniform, 180–81, 182
Taubl, George, 70–71

tartan, 196–9
    Balmoral tartan, 197–9
    clan tartans, 196
    Royal Stewart pattern, 197
    traditional weaving, 197
Taylor, Lou, 276
Temple, Nettie, 252, 253–4
Tewantin, Queensland, 1, 283
Textile Conservation Centre, 137
Thaarup, Aage, 95, 98–100, *100*, 104, 233
Thackery, Miss, 89
theatrical costuming, 113
Thomas, Ian, 149, 155–7, 161, 163
Thompson, Peter, 181, 194
Thomson, John, 247
Thomson, William Sparks, 227–8
throne, cover for the, 41
Times, The, 31, 97–8, 126, 165, 258
Tower of London, 60, 62, 64
Trade's Hosiery Industry Working Party, 211
Transvaal people, 62
Treacy, Philip, 280
Trevor-Morgan, Rachel, 104
Trip Through Libertyland, A (film), 232
Trubert-Tollu, Chantal, 150
Trump, Margaret, 82–3, 88
Tryhorne, Teresa, 147–8
tuberculosis, 56, 174
Turnbull & Asser, 286
Turner, Brian, 80–81, 88
Turner, Mrs (corset maker), 226–7, 233
Tyler, James, 259

undergarments, 225–36, 237–50
    bras, 234–5
    crinolines, 230
    girdles, 234

Index

knickers, 237
  linen drapers and, 239–41
  see also corsets; royal linen
unionisation, 190
Unitt, Sarah Ann, 95, 125, 126

Vacani school of dance, 57
Vanderbilt, Consuelo, 187
Varrier-Jones, Pendrill, 174, 176
velvet robes, 15, 17–28
Vernon, 180, 189–90, 194
Vernon, Madame, 189–90, 194
Victoria & Albert Museum, 133–4, 156
Victoria, Princess of Saxe-Coburg-Saalfeld, 123
Victoria, Queen of the United Kingdom, 2, 6, 9, 10, 23, 24, 30, 33, 46, 64, 95, 98, 168, 184
  Arnold, Frieda and, 10–11, 171–3, 265
  coronation, 23–4, 41, 216, 284
  corsets and, 227, 228, 230
  cream satin wedding gown, 124
  death of, 25, 33, 61, 67, 284
  dressers and, 251, 252–3, 254–5, 263, 264–5
  dressmakers and, 123–4, 125–6, 135
  funeral pall, 33–4
  Golden Jubilee, 89–90
  Great Exhibition and, 74
  grief and, 268, 275, 276, 279, 280
  Kanné, Joseph Julius and, 169, 170–71
  Koh-i-noor diamond and, 60–61
  National Archives and, 240–41
  postage stamps, 59, 63
  Scotland and, 197
  shawls and, 74, 76
  shoes and, 106–7, 109, 110–11, 118
  stockings and, 212, 215, 216, 218–19, 223
  tartan and, 196, 197
  Welsh flannel and, 220
  widowhood gowns, 125
  Windsor uniform, 180–81, 182, 193
Vienna, Austria, 128, 144
Viennese College of Art, 144
Vivier, Roger, 3–4, 116
Vogue, 98, 117, 145, 159
Vuitton, Louis, 166–7, 168

W magazine, 26–7
W. H. Hallett & Sons, 146
Wade, Louisa, 34, 35
Waite, E., 204
Wakeford's (retailer), London, 49
Wale, Ethel, 142–3, 146, 147
'walkabout, the', 84, 86
Walker, Catherine, 86–8
Walker, Elizabeth, 205
Walkley, Mary Ann, 126
Waller, Charlie, 54
Walpole, Horace, 23, 179, 183, 193
Walters, Stephen, 287
Wanderer, The, (Burney), 95
Wandsworth, London, 69–70
  raids, 69
Warminster, Wiltshire, 147
Warner, Benjamin, 15
Warner family, 14–15, 17
Warner & Son, 13–14, 15, 18, 28, 31
Warner, William, 14
Warrant Holders Association, 8–9
Warron, James, 191
Watson family, 15
Watson, Sam, 15, 17, 19, 28
Weatherill, Bernard, 190–91
Weatherill, Bernard 'Jack', 191–2
'Wedding Night, The' (Cruikshank), 237–8
Weiss, Sophie, 253
Welby Gregory, Victoria (Lady Welby), 33

Index

Wells, H. G., 239–40
Welsh wool flannel, 219
Wendeline, George, 70
Wendeline, Lily, 70
Westman, Annabel, 78
Westminster Abbey, London, 2, 5, 18, 284, 285
Westminster City Council, 152
Whichelo, Nellie, 34–5, 36, 42
Whitby, Yorkshire, 268–71
White, Ellen, 208, 209
White, J. E., 93
William IV, King of the United Kingdom, 287
Williams, Harry, 255
Wimbledon Endowed Almshouses, 36, 37
Winchester School of Art, 137
Windsor Castle, 82, 103, 180, 244, 253
Winnipeg Free Press, 255
Winterbottom, Edwin, 93
Winterhalter, Franz Xaver, 67
Wolff, Ernest, 65
Wolff, Johann Jacob, 65
Wolkenfeld, Felix, 158–9
Wolkenfeld, Judith, 158–9
Wolverhampton Steam Laundry, 243
women, 9
   Chelsea Design Company and, 86–7
   Corgi Socks and, 222
   corsets and, 225–6, 231–4
   court dressmaking, 48–50
   dressers to the Queen, 251–65
   dressmakers to the Queen, 123, 124–36
   embroidery and, 31–41
   feather industry and, 54–7
   gloveresses, 141–8
   Great Depression and, 208
   horse-riding and, 202
   Jewish, 54
   in later life, 35–6
   pensions and, 35–7
   Redfern and, 184–5
   sharp tailoring and, 179–80, 193–4
   shoemaking and, 108
   shop work and, 109–10
   silk gauze dusting and, 97
   straw plaiting and, 91, 92, 104
   unequal pay and, 207
   working conditions of, 126–7, 131, 278
   working women's lodging houses, 32
   see also debutantes
Wood, Henry, 139
Woodfield Road, No. 29, Braintree, Essex, 13
Woods, Lisa, 222
wool, 199
Woolger, Grace, 183
Worcester, 138, 139, 141, 142, 147
working conditions, 126–7, 131, 190, 278
World Exhibition, London (1862), 168
World Exhibition, Paris (1867), 168
World War I (1914–18), 131–2, 144, 174, 188, 198
World War II (1939–45), 39, 69–71, 204, 208, 222
   Blitz, 204
   rationing, 83, 145, 212, 223
Worth, Charles Frederick, 121–2, 150
Worth, Jean-Philippe, 121
Worth, William, 150

Yeomen of the Guard, 64
York Castle Museum, 272
Young Ladies' Journal, 216
Youth Employment Office, 102
YouTube, 108, 227